Writing British Muslims

MANCHESTER
1824

Manchester University Press

Writing British Muslims

Religion, class and multiculturalism

REHANA AHMED

Manchester University Press

Published by Manchester University Press
Altrincham Street, Manchester M1 7JA
www.manchesteruniversitypress.co.uk

British Library Cataloguing-in-Publication Data
A catalogue record for this book is available from the British Library

Library of Congress Cataloging-in-Publication Data applied for

ISBN 978 1 5261 1677 2 *paperback*

This edition first published 2017

Typeset in Bembo by
Koinonia, Manchester
Printed and Bound in Great Britain by
TJ International Ltd, Padstow

For Sam
and for Keir

Contents

Acknowledgements

This book was completed with the help of an Arts and Humanities Research Council Fellowship (grant reference AH/1000577/1). I gratefully acknowledge the generous support of the AHRC. In addition, I owe thanks to many colleagues and friends who have supported me in a variety of ways throughout the writing of this book. First, I am grateful to Elleke Boehmer, under whose supervision the book began its life. Elleke was, and remains, an inspiring mentor, whose early input and advice continue to influence me and have, over the years, helped me to become a better reader of texts. More recently, Susheila Nasta has offered me enabling academic guidance. I am particularly grateful to her for reading and commenting on chapters of this book. Further, the opportunity to work on the AHRC-funded project 'Making Britain: South Asian Visions of Home and Abroad, 1870–1950', directed by Susheila, provided this contemporary study with an important historical context and informs much of the book's opening chapter. Lyn Innes and Steph Newell read the proposal for this book and provided me with useful feedback. Steph has been a tremendously important source of encouragement and advice to me, always generous with her time. Peter Morey and Amina Yaqin's positive interest in and support for my research have been invaluable. I have benefited hugely from the opportunity to collaborate with them, as well as with Claire Chambers, Anshuman Mondal and Stephen Morton who have also been very good friends to my work. In addition, I owe thanks to Rachel Carroll, Madeline Clements, Helen Davies, Ole Birk Laursen, Sumita Mukherjee, Ben Rogaly and Florian Stadtler for their collegiality and friendship, and to the wonderful staff and services at the British Library and the Institute of Race Relations.

Beyond academia, I am grateful for the excellent childcare my son has received from Margaret Shepherd, whose qualities are legion. My family and friends have been vital to me throughout the course of researching and writing this book but especially during the last two years of difficult life events. Thanks, especially, to Ayesha Ahmed, Nina de la Mer, Kate Evetts, Stefanie Gehrig Clark, Kate Morris, Alex Reece and Lisa Westbury. My parents, Haroon and Anne Ahmed, have never failed to support me. Moreover, this book is underpinned and inspired by the lessons they taught me about social justice and by the love of reading they cultivated in me from a very early age. My greatest debt of gratitude is to Sam Hayden, without whom this book could not have been written. Throughout the long duration of its writing, he has debated ideas with me, read drafts for me, and done more than his fair share of childcare. He has believed in me, sustained me and loved me unconditionally, through the best and worst of times. This book is dedicated to Sam, and to our son Keir Nizam, with all my love.

A short extract from Chapter 1 first appeared in my essay 'Networks of resistance: Krishna Menon and working-class South Asians in Britain', in Rehana Ahmed and Sumita Mukherjee (eds), *South Asian Resistances in Britain, 1858–1947* (London: Continuum, 2011), pp. 70–87. A version of part of Chapter 3 first appeared as 'Occluding race in selected short fiction by Hanif Kureishi', *Wasafiri*, 58 (24:2) (June 2009), 27–34. A version of Chapter 4 first appeared as 'A materialist reading of Monica Ali's *Brick Lane* and its reception', *Race & Class*, 52:2 (October 2010), 25–42. A version of part of Chapter 6 first appeared as 'Reason to believe? Two "British Muslim" memoirs', in Rehana Ahmed, Peter Morey and Amina Yaqin (eds), *Culture, Diaspora, and Modernity in Muslim Writing* (New York and Abingdon: Routledge, 2012), pp. 52–67 (Copyright © 2012 from *Culture, Diaspora, and Modernity in Muslim Writing* edited by Rehana Ahmed, Peter Morey and Amina Yaqin. Reproduced by permission of Taylor and Francis Group, LLC, a division of Informa plc). I gratefully acknowledge permission to reproduce this material.

Introduction

The haves the have nots
The haves but will not
The ones that call shots
The ones that get shot
That, is the only clash of civilisations I know.

(Avaes Mohammad, 'The clash'[1])

A SNAPSHOT OF TWENTY-FIRST-CENTURY MULTICULTURAL BRITAIN

In September 2013, a new strategy designed to facilitate 'integration' in the 'super-diverse' east London borough of Newham hit the headlines. Sir Robin Wales, the mayor of Newham, had cancelled public library subscriptions to foreign language newspapers, dramatically reduced translation services and abolished funding for community events focused on a single ethnic or religious group. These measures, he claimed, would work against the segregation in the borough, which he compared to that of apartheid South Africa, and reinforce 'British values' including 'trust', 'reciprocity', 'respect' and 'tolerance' as well as a sense of pride in being British.[2] This is not the first time Newham has occupied the limelight in debates on multiculturalism in Britain: plans by Tablighi Jamaat to build a large mosque – branded the 'mega-mosque' – next to the main 2012 Olympics site were met with considerable hostility and opposition not only from within the local community but also from political figures and media commentators. The story first appeared in the national press in November 2005, just a few months after London won their bid to host the 2012 Olympic Games in the borough and, less than twenty-four hours later, four British Muslims detonated bombs on the London Underground and a London bus, killing over fifty people and injuring some seven hundred others. Media constructions of the planned Abbey

Mills Mosque repeatedly emphasised the large scale of the mosque and its 'Islamicisation' of space; its threat to the national image that would be broadcast across the globe at the Olympic Games 2012; its 'foreignness' due to contributions to its funding from abroad; and alleged (and unsubstantiated) links between Tablighi Jamaat and terrorism, including the 7 July 2005 bombings.[3] An excerpt from a 2006 article in the *Telegraph* underlines the first two of these themes: 'When television viewers around the world see aerial views of the stadium during the opening ceremony in six years' time, the most prominent religious building in the camera shot will not be one of the city's iconic churches that have shaped the nation's history, such as St Paul's Cathedral or Westminster Abbey, but the mega-mosque.'[4] Predictably, the controversy was then exploited by far right groups such as the English Defence League (EDL) in order to spread Islamophobia.[5]

As Daniel Nilsson DeHanas and Zacharias P. Pieri point out, in the wake of the successful Olympic bid one might have expected a warm welcome for the mosque 'as a multicultural Olympic landmark'.[6] For images of London's cultural diversity were successfully deployed to sell the city to the International Olympic Committee. A group of children 'representing the cultural and ethnic mosaic of London's East End' accompanied Sebastian Coe to Singapore's elite Raffles Hotel on the morning of the final speeches and announcement of the winning city.[7] The multicultural character of Stratford, the part of Newham which would apparently undergo the most regeneration as a result of the Games, was cited repeatedly as 'evidence' of the 'legacy' benefits the Games would bring to 'ordinary' Londoners. Trevor Phillips, chair of the Commission for Racial Equality, declared London's victory 'a brilliant vindication of the gamble made by Sebastian Coe and Ken Livingstone to stress the city's successful ethnic and racial integration'.[8] The diversity emblematised by the Games was contrasted to the monoculturalism which, it was claimed, underpinned the horrific 7/7 terror attacks. The media emphasis on the fact that two of the bombs targeted parts of London with a significant Muslim population – Aldgate in Newham's neighbouring borough, Tower Hamlets, which has a large Bangladeshi population, and Edgware, which is home to a substantial community of Arabs – was suggestive of this message: the bombs were not just an attack on the UK or London, but on the diversity that London represents. Phillips, too, drew a link between the successful Olympic bid and the bombings via the issue of cultural diversity:

the great issue of our times is this: can the peoples of a multi-ethnic and multi-faith world share the planet in peace? Can we cross the lines of difference? ... Most people want the answer to be a resounding yes. But we saw last week in London the desperate acts of people determined to show that we cannot, and should not, live and let live. To these extremists, London's easy-going mix is a daily affront.[9]

Here, the multicultural character of London, and of the victims, functions as corroboration of 'our' inclusive, open and diverse culture, which is then counterposed to 'their' singular, homogenising bid to destroy 'our' way of life, obscuring the role played by the government's foreign policies and the presence of western troops in Muslim lands in motivating Islamist extremists.[10]

The discourse surrounding the proposed Abbey Mills Mosque and Newham's mayor's controversial 'naturalising' strategies echoes this dichotomised conceptualisation of diversity versus singularity which maps neatly onto one of integration versus separatism. While concerns about the isolationist tendencies of Tablighi Jamaat may have been justified, the spectre of the separatist, alien and threatening Muslim Other pitted against the modern and diverse Britain projected as the site of the Olympic Games serves to stigmatise Islam, or its presence in the public sphere, and mask the exclusions that shape the multiculture of the surrounding area. Similarly, Sir Robin Wales's assertion that he values diversity and supports people 'coming together' while opposing single ethnicity events obfuscates structural inequalities caused by deprivation and racism behind a veneer of inclusivity which is projected as 'British', and implies minority cultural practices are intrinsically separatist and ultimately illegitimate (tellingly, he consigns cultural heritage to the domain of memory: 'it's great for people to remember their heritage but the council shouldn't be paying for it'[11]). Wales's integrationist strategies are challenged by the 'ethnicity paradox' that Tariq Modood discusses and that informs his advocacy of 'equality through pluralism'. Citing the research of American sociologists Robert E. Park and W. I. Thomas, Modood argues that 'allowing more space to ethnic minority communities to do their own thing enables them to become a feature of the new society and creates a secure base from which participation in the institutions of the wider society follows'.[12] Justin Beaumont and Christopher Baker's analysis of British Muslim study circles corroborates this view; they found that while participating in a study circle reinforced religious identity, in fact the feelings of solidarity and resilience gained through belonging to the group encouraged 'a broader sense of confidence in participation that moves beyond a proactive care for the Muslim *ummah* into *more generic forms of citizenship*'.[13] Anshuman A. Mondal makes a similar point by reframing the establishment of Muslim communities in Britain ('the building of mosques, the arrival of *halal* butchers and Asian grocery stores') precisely as 'evidence of Muslim integration and commitment to Britain' rather than 'as signs of "separatism" and "segregation"'.[14] Indeed, as Ziauddin Sardar asks, comparing Jewish communities in north London and Chinatowns to Muslim 'ghettoes', why should 'Muslims aspiring to domestication of their identity, creating the infrastructure that supports the lived identity they wish to pass from generation to generation, as other minorities clearly do', be considered 'segregated communities and inherently "a problem"?'[15]

As Alana Lentin and Gavan Titley observe, citing David Edgar:

> The apparent death of left–right divisions has moved progressive thinkers to 'posit a raft of new fault lines – liberty versus authority, secularism versus religion, free speech versus censorship, universalism versus multiculturalism, feminism versus the family – all of which are cast in forms that put the progressive middle class on one side and significant sections of the poor on the other.'[16]

The displacement of hierarchies of class and race as well as religion by these fault lines, which locate Muslims and also the poor firmly on the wrong side, can be seen both in the discourse used by Wales and in the gap between the marketing of Newham as potential site of the 2012 Olympic Games and the material realities of many of its residents. Wales's withdrawal of translation services and foreign language newspapers will inevitably affect the most disadvantaged members of Newham's minority groups, including the poor, the newest arrivals and the elderly, who are least likely to have competence in English. Newham is the second most deprived borough in Britain, with 32.7 per cent of its residents in income-deprived families.[17] With a white population of just 16.7 per cent, it is also one of the most diverse boroughs in Britain. According to the 2001 census, a quarter of its population is Muslim, but it is likely that figure is higher now.[18] Muslims in Newham are especially socio-economically disadvantaged compared to other residents. A large proportion of Newham's residents are Pakistani or Bangladeshi, and poverty and deprivation are more marked in these ethnic groups than in other Muslim groups.[19] Bangladeshis are Britain's poorest minority group, and approximately seven out of ten British Bangladeshi and Pakistani children live in poverty.[20] If it is really the case, as Phillips maintains, that 'our capital offers the best real-world answer that humanity has to the challenge of ethnic and religious diversity', then it is clear that humanity's answer falls short of a basic standard of living for the majority of more than one ethnic group in one of the richest nations in the world.[21]

Crucial questions remain, too, about exactly who will benefit from the legacy of the Games, and how. As Neil Smith points out, regeneration – promised by the London Olympics committee to east Londoners – has, in the present period of global capitalist expansion, 'become the means of embedding the logics, threads and assumptions of capital accumulation more deeply than ever in the urban landscape'.[22] Regeneration is offered to city dwellers as a 'cure' for the city's ills, when in fact it can be a mechanism by which social inequalities (those very ills) are created and maintained.[23] The example of Margaret Thatcher's government's development of London's Docklands area in the 1980s illustrates this clearly. Far from 'trickling down' to its working-class residents, the creation of wealth in this pocket of east London benefited the corporations that were located there. Today, the wealthy inhabitants of Docklands are not its pre-development communities (black, brown or white) but the (predominantly white) City workers who could afford to move there after the area's gentrification. The diversity of this gentrified area works as a convenient screen for its stark inequalities.[24] There is a real danger that the development of Newham will follow a similar path and that the material needs of Coe's young escorts and their peers will get lost behind the glossy images of our multiethnic capital. Anne Power argues that so far the enormous amount of money injected into Newham for the Games has largely bypassed its disadvantaged inhabitants. While the feared inflation of house prices in the borough did not materialise and school performances have improved through investment, Newham's unemployment rose faster than average in London between 2005 and 2010 and a small minority of the construction jobs created by the Games went to its residents. The supply of subsidised social housing has declined, regeneration schemes have removed homes and failed to deliver on promises of compensatory benefits, and the supposedly affordable new homes to be converted from the Athletes' Village will remain out of the reach of the area's poorest residents, including the majority of its Muslims.[25]

MUSLIMS, MULTICULTURALISM AND CLASS
IN CONTEMPORARY BRITAIN

Writing British Muslims: Religion, Class and Multiculturalism seeks to intervene in debates surrounding multiculturalism and Islam in Britain by examining a selection of contemporary literary texts. Offering readings of a range of texts by British writers of South Asian Muslim heritage, including fiction by Salman Rushdie, Hanif Kureishi, Monica Ali and Nadeem Aslam and five British Muslim memoirs, it explores and illuminates the ways in which literature can add to our understanding of multicultural Britain and the position of South Asian Muslims within it. It takes its impetus from a number of concerns captured in the brief snapshot of multicultural Britain above: the frequent occlusion of material structures of power beneath images of an 'inclusive' diversity; the liberal discomfort with expressions and manifestations of religion, especially Islam, in the public sphere; the cultural racism that underpins dichotomising discourses of integration versus separatism, especially where Muslims are concerned; the criticism and attack that multiculturalism has withstood over the last three decades or so; and the importance of local space when considering multicultural controversies in Britain. Tariq Modood has written about the historical depth of a culturalist racism – one that 'builds on biological racism a further discourse that evokes cultural differences from an alleged British, civilized norm to vilify, marginalize, or demand cultural assimilation from groups who also suffer from biological racism'. Forms of cultural racism such as anti-Semitism and Islamophobia are in fact the oldest in Europe, Modood points out, while the contemporary version of culturalist racism can be traced at least to the New Commonwealth immigration to and settlement in Britain.[26] The centrality of cultural difference to racism has meant, moreover, that British Muslims in particular, the majority of whom are of Pakistani or Bangladeshi heritage, have been the target of verbal and physical attacks, as a group who tend to want to maintain and assert elements of their culture and religion which are not easily assimilable to a majoritarian British way of life.[27]

Several events over the last two and a half decades in particular have sharpened hostility towards Muslims in Britain. The *Satanic Verses* controversy of 1988–89 cast a long shadow over perceptions of Muslims and Islam in the decade that followed. The July 2001 riots in Bradford, Burnley and Oldham and the terror attacks of 11 September 2001 and 7

July 2005, as well as the 'war on terror' and the Muslim anger it provoked, boosted reductive and stigmatising images of Muslim male youth in particular and heightened Islamophobic feeling. A range of controversies and episodes have punctuated the years in between and since, in both Britain and other European countries, including the murder of white schoolboy Richard Everitt in 1994 by a group of Bangladeshi boys; the Madrid train bombings of 2004; the murder of Dutch filmmaker Theo Van Gogh by self-confessed Islamist Mohammed Bouyeri in the same year; the publication of cartoons depicting the Prophet Mohammed in Danish newspaper *Jyllands-Posten* in 2005; Labour Member of Parliament Jack Straw's construction of the niqab as a 'visible statement of separa-tion and of difference' which sparked anger among Muslims in 2006,[28] and *l'affaire du foulard* in France which erupted in 1989, 1994 and 2003. In Britain a series of 'honour killings', as well as grooming cases involving Pakistani men, have triggered heated debate and entrenched culturalist fears of a retrogressive and violent Muslim patriarchy. Muslims and Islam have come to figure increasingly as secular modernity's fundamentalist Other. As Peter Morey and Amina Yaqin observe:

> The headlines that scream out at us every day from front pages and tele-vision screens seem unanimous in the picture they paint of Muslims: unen-lightened outsiders who, while they may live and work in the West, still have an allegiance to values different from those recognized in Europe and North America. Whether the controversy is over veiling, cartoons of the Prophet Mohammed, conflicts in Afghanistan, Iraq, and Israel-Palestine, or protests about the knighthood given to Salman Rushdie, Muslims appear always as a problematic presence, troubling those values of individualism and freedom said to define Western nations.[29]

The raging and violent Islamic fifth columnist; his manipulated, gull-ible and sheep-like male prey; the oppressed, veiled woman; and the scheming but servile matriarch: these stereotypes circulate and saturate the media that we consume in large daily doses. It is not just far right Islamophobic groups such as the English Defence League, or right-wing journalists such as Melanie Phillips or Richard Littlejohn, who help to create and perpetuate these images, but also media commentators and politicians on the liberal left of the political spectrum. As Elizabeth Poole says of the left-of-centre *Guardian* in her study of media representations of British Muslims in the 1990s, 'its exclusive form of liberalism did not always extend to Muslims because its secular approach ... marginalizes religion to the private realm. Its liberal approach to human rights further rendered "Islamic" practices irrational and barbaric.'[30] Indeed, the so-called extremist Islamophobic discourse of the EDL is, as Lentin and Titley describe, 'a product of a decade of recited truths' circulating in politically mainstream discourse, 'an almost genealogical rehearsal of the suturing of liberal goals and rhetoric to an exclusionary, laundered culturalism'.[31]

Inextricable from these stereotyping constructions of Muslims is a sustained attack on British multiculturalism. For the British Muslim has become a cipher for the excesses of multiculturalism. Just as a critique of multiculturalist practices and policies can function as a means of marginalising and stigmatising Muslims, so the supposed cultural excesses of Muslims provide a useful vehicle for criticising multiculturalism. Lentin and Titley describe how the hijab, niqab and burqa have become

> nodal signifiers for significant lines of multicultural discontent, standing for the theocratic and patriarchal submission or oppression of women; as manifestations of parallel communities and weak integration; as an assault on the secular nature of public institutions and, in some instances, public space; and perhaps above all, as a relativist affront to the exceptional cultures of gender equality which have prospered in the West.[32]

The obsessive focus on Muslim veiling practices by political and media commentators over the last two or three decades can be traced to the powerful signifying function of this simple item of clothing; to its use as a means of discrediting multiculturalism and legitimising liberalism's exclusions, as well as of justifying the invasion of Afghanistan as a mission to rescue President Bush's poor, benighted 'women of cover'. Clearly evident here is the deployment of gender in criticisms of Muslims and multiculturalism. The image of the submissive female victim of retrogressive patriarchal practices bolsters stereotypes of the brutal, barbaric and irrational Islamic male, and vice versa, while attacks on multiculturalism are predicated on a gendered conceptualisation of minority Muslim communities as oppressive (to their women), self-segregating (partly in order to curtail their women's freedom) and alien (symbolised by their women's hijabs and niqabs). Thus in certain liberal discourses about British Muslims and multiculturalism, gender – specifically a myopic Eurocentric feminist concept of gender – can work as a smokescreen, corroborating the emancipatory animus of liberalism, which seeks to protect and liberate women from oppression, while obfuscating its partiality and exclusions, especially where communal religious identities and practices are concerned. The polarisation of gender equality and cultural equality that emerges from such discourses is highly problematic.[33]

Through its readings of a selection of novels, short stories and memoir, *Writing British Muslims* seeks to complicate and challenge such attacks on multiculturalism. Following the riots of 2001 and 9/11 in particular, significant leftist, including purportedly anti-racist, figures have declared the 'failure' of multiculturalism. Ostensibly this marked a shift from the celebration of Britain's cultural diversity that accompanied Tony Blair's election to government in 1997. As Morey and Yaqin argue via Andrew Pilkington, the 1999 publication of the Macpherson Report, written in response to the racist murder of black teenager Stephen Lawrence, bolstered the inclusive impetus of Blair's government; its declaration of Britain's police force as 'institutionally racist', which led to the 2000 Race Relations (Amendment) Act, pushed anti-racism firmly onto the national agenda.[34] Yet, how far Blair's government's apparent commitment to diversity and equality would have gone towards embracing real difference as a cultural good if the events of 2001 had not taken place remains highly debatable. In winter 2001, in the wake of the riots and the publication of the Cantle Report, which highlighted the South Asian Muslim rioters' supposed failure to integrate as a key cause, erstwhile anti-racist campaigner Kenan Malik accused multiculturalism of helping 'to segregate communities far more effectively than racism', while home secretary David Blunkett spoke of an 'excess of cultural diversity' and accused the Muslim rioters of 'self-styled' segregation.[35] David Goodhart's 2004 articles 'Discomfort of strangers' and 'Too diverse?' argued for the incompatibility of cultural diversity and national cohesion, and the following year Trevor Phillips accused Britain of 'sleepwalking to segregation'.[36]

A number of scholars have challenged these attacks on multiculturalism. Key among them is Tariq Modood whose pioneering scholarship, which draws on that of Charles Taylor and Bhikhu Parekh among others, is integral to this book. Crucially, Modood advocates a multiculturalism or 'politics of difference' that is not colour- or culture-blind but recognises and respects difference, accommodates collectivities or groups (including religious groups) as well as individuals, and breaches the public–private division that is essential to liberalism. He refutes arguments that the recognition of a collectivity is based on the erroneous notion of a natural essence and blankets over internal heterogeneity. Yet, he argues, group identities are no less real for this: 'The non-white groups that are the focus of multiculturalism have a visibility and are subject to forms of exclusion that continue to sustain group identity; above all, there can be passionate commitments to those identities in personal, institutional and political ways that belie that these identities are symbolic or cultural heirlooms.'[37] Further, he debunks the idea of the neutrality of the public sphere, arguing instead that the latter is inevitably shaped by the dominant group in society and so an insistence on the privatisation of minority identities is necessarily a marginalisation of those identities.[38] Equality can only be attained by practising 'equal respect' alongside 'equal dignity': whereas the latter is concerned with what people have in common, the former is concerned with the importance of difference for understanding and implementing equal relations and rights. The denial or invisibilisation of a group identity, Modood argues, is a form of oppression which not only makes 'equal respect' impossible but also threatens 'equal dignity' for minorities.[39] Further, Modood repudiates claims by hardline secularist liberals that religion, unlike race or sex, is chosen, and therefore that Muslims do not need the same legal protection as other minorities and religion cannot be part of equality as recognition: 'No one chooses to be or not to be born into a Muslim family', he writes, 'no one chooses to be born into a society where to look a Muslim or to be a Muslim creates suspicion, hostility, or failure to get the job you applied for'.[40]

Modood's elucidation of the limits of liberalism for an equal society is crucial to my readings of literary texts that follow. Equally important, however, is a recognition of the centrality of class to multicultural politics in Britain. In his discussion of the 2001 riots in Bradford, Burnley and Oldham, Modood comments on the government reports' and the media's attribution of blame to so-called Muslim schools which were represented 'as the source of the problem of divided cities, cultural backwardness, riots, lack of Britishness, and a breeding ground for militant Islam'. While some of the schools in question were over 90 per cent Muslim, they were not Muslim-run, Modood writes, but 'local, bottom-of-the-pile, comprehensive schools that had suffered from decades of underinvestment and "white flight" and were run by white teachers according to a secular national curriculum'.[41] The conflation of Muslim-run schools with secular run-down schools captures the prejudices of a liberal culturalism that transmutes the problems of poverty, racism and Islamophobia into a 'problem' of culture and cultural 'separatism'.[42] Sardar makes a similar point, arguing that 'The social, economic and environmental disadvantages that afflict Muslim communities around the country are not primarily Muslim issues; they are generic issues of blight, deprivation, neglect and decay.'[43] *Writing British Muslims* centralises class in its readings of multicultural texts and contexts. By doing so, it challenges the liberal dichotomies that stand in for and obfuscate structures of power and stigmatise Muslims and multiculturalism: 'liberty versus authority, secularism versus religion, free speech versus censorship, universalism versus multiculturalism, feminism versus the family'.[44] Here the work of Slavoj Žižek proves useful. For Žižek, the 'postmodern identity politics of particular (ethnic, sexual and so forth) lifestyles' has defused and obscured the need for 'politics proper'. While the latter aims for a restructuring of the 'entire social space', or a challenge to capitalist structures of power and oppression, the former simply enables each group to be accounted for and assigned its particular place within the existing (neoliberal capitalist) social order.[45] The opposition between a right-wing conservativism and a tolerant liberalism obfuscates the real material divisions that stratify the world: 'In this uniform spectrum, political differences are more and more reduced to merely cultural attitudes: multicultural/sexual (etc.) "openness" versus traditional/natural (etc.) "family values".'[46]

In this spectrum, moreover, any real difference, including cultural difference, is delegitimised, and potentially forced into extremist or fundamentalist forms. A 'tolerant liberal multiculturalism', for Žižek, merely pays lip-service to cultural difference; it is willing to experience 'the Other deprived of its Otherness' and shares with populist racism 'the need to keep others at a proper distance':[47] 'Liberal "tolerance" condones the folklorist Other deprived of its substance – like the multitude of "ethnic cuisines" in a contemporary megalopolis; however, any "real" Other is instantly denounced for its "fundamentalism" … the "real Other" is by definition "patriarchal", "violent", never the Other of ethereal wisdom and charming customs.'[48] While Modood could be criticised for his marginalisation of the role of class in creating social divisions and of a class-based politics,[49] Žižek's materialism leads him to a degree of colour- and culture-blindness. He justly challenges a liberal multiculturalism, yet there is little space in his analysis for an alternative approach to racial, cultural and religious minorities in the west so that cultural difference appears at times to be almost reducible to class. By diminishing 'ethnic' 'lifestyles' to little more than a means of screening material divisions, he denies the significance of cultural difference both as a root cause of prejudice and oppression on the part of majoritarian

European societies and as a valid source of group identity and social and political mobilisation. This book, conversely, aims to bring together a materialist, class-based analysis with a recognition of the role of cultural, including religious, difference in stratifying society and marginalising certain – especially Muslim – members of society. It explores the relationship between class and minority religious identity while advocating a positive recognition of cultural and religious difference in the public sphere as a means of working against its unevenness and challenging this stratification, marginalisation and stigmatisation. By combining a materialist approach with a recognition of the significance of religious faith, it sutures the political and the religious, the public and the private.

Žižek also makes the important point that the rejection or 'surpassing' of a specific ethnic (and, by extension, religious) identity category is shaped by class.[50] A dismissal of communal identities as inherently repressive and reactionary is therefore likely also to be an elitist dismissal of working-class subjectivities. Indeed, if group support, pride and mobilisation are important means of combatting oppression, then it is probable that working-class Muslims are especially inclined to form groups and identify more strongly as Muslims.[51] Madeleine Bunting's allusion to the work of American community activist Saul Alinsky is suggestive of this link between religion and class. Drawing his evidence from working among impoverished communities in 1930s depression Chicago, Alinsky traced a clear link between religious commitment and poverty: 'What Alinsky had spotted', Bunting writes, 'was that in poor communities, the strongest institutions with the deepest roots were faith-based; they provided vital resources to poor communities – a measure of dignity and a sense of meaning in lives scarred by poverty.' Bunting transposes this into contemporary Britain to point to the elitism of the hardline secularism which saw figures such as Richard Dawkins support the emblazoning of slogans declaring the non-existence of God on London buses. Highlighting the contrast between some of the working-class (and quite possibly Afro-Caribbean) passengers reading Bibles or prayer books and the privileged members of the liberal intelligentsia who would approve of the slogans, Bunting powerfully captures the imbrication of class and the religious/secular dichotomy.[52]

Bunting's sketch shines a spotlight on a further concern of *Writing British Muslims*: the significance of space when considering Muslims in multicultural Britain. A slogan on a bright red London bus, which weaves itself through the city noisily, dominates metropolitan space. It is a slogan of the powerful, of those who lay claim to that space, and in turn it shapes the space it occupies. By contrast, the disempowered, who lack ownership of space (the non-white, non-secular passengers travelling home to Robin Wales's Newham), must find alternative means of infiltrating the domain of the powerful and carving their place in the world. Michel de Certeau's theorisation of space captures the materiality of this unevenness. He compares the 'strategies' of powerful subjects to the 'tactics' of those who lack power. Whereas the strategy 'assumes a place that can be circumscribed as *proper* (*propre*)' and has a panoptical power, the tactic lacks a place of its own and a 'view of the whole', and must 'insinuat[e] itself into the other's place, fragmentarily', seizing opportunities 'on the wing' and 'mak[ing] use of the cracks that particular conjunctions open in the surveillance of the proprietary powers'.[53] David Harvey and Henri Lefebvre have also demonstrated the significance of space to capitalist structures of power. As Harvey says, 'The whole history of territorial organization, colonialism and imperialism, of uneven geographical development, of urban and rural contradictions, as well as of geopolitical conflict testifies to the importance of such struggles within the history of capitalism'.[54] It is through space that capitalist structures of power are realised – or, as Lefebvre maintains, 'Social relations ... have no real existence save in and through space'.[55] Space, therefore, is not just a site of class struggle; it is shaped or constituted by that struggle and is an object of that struggle.

Lefebvre describes how the bourgeoisie and the workers struggled *for* space as well as in space in nineteenth-century Paris.[56] Similarly, in contemporary Britain, Muslims' struggle to lay claim to Britain and Britishness is a struggle for space. For it is by embedding their religious culture in social space – whether in the form of building a mosque or a school, or wearing the hijab in a public place – that this process takes shape. Consequently, space is central to anxieties and debates about Muslims and multiculturalism in Britain, as is highlighted in the sketch of Newham. Resistance to the building of mosques and complaints about Muslim 'ghettoes' are grounded in fears of the 'Islamicisation' of space,[57] while controversies surrounding the Muslim headscarf are in fact about whether or not (and to what extent) this item of clothing should be allowed to infiltrate public space. The issues of 'integration' and 'segregation' are constantly and contentiously discussed, especially since the 2001 race riots and Ted Cantle's description of the Asian and white youths involved leading 'parallel lives'.[58] The binary of integration versus segregation is predicated on an abstraction and fragmentation of space which obscures the social relations that shape it. In this configuration, the so-called segregation of certain Muslim majority parts of Bradford or the East End, for example, is abstracted from its context so that it becomes a function of the space as such and the culture that fills it, rather than of the social and racial divisions produced by capitalism that are materialised in space.[59] As Lefebvre tells us, space must be considered as 'a (social) product' and therefore as relational and dialectical.[60] Once socio-spatial divisions within culturally diverse areas such as Tower Hamlets are exposed, and once the social relations that connect the impoverished Bangladeshi communities of east London to their privileged City-worker neighbours are revealed, the diversity of some parts of Britain and the 'ghettoes' of other parts can no longer be polarised – and the liberal binary that pits pluralism and freedom against singularity and constraint cedes to a focus on social inequalities.

Indeed, it is partly through a materialist engagement with space that this book seeks to reframe literary controversies involving Britain's Muslim minority. Focusing on the 1988–89 *Satanic Verses* controversy and the dispute surrounding Monica Ali's 2003 novel *Brick Lane* and its filming in 2006, as well as on protests by Muslims against H. G. Wells's *A Short History of the World* in 1930s Britain, *Writing British Muslims* grounds these outbreaks of religious minority offence in their local material conditions. By highlighting the unequal access to spatial, economic and cultural capital that shaped them, it complicates normative representations of such disputes in terms of creative freedom and religious censure and censorship. The *Satanic Verses* controversy has come to symbolise the supposedly antagonist relationship between creative freedom and religious (especially Islamic) authoritarianism, a binary which has been strengthened by subsequent disputes involving religious minorities in Europe including the *Brick Lane* dispute, the 2004 protests against the staging of Gurpreet Kaur Bhatti's play *Behzti* at the Birmingham Repertory Theatre, the 2005 Danish cartoons affair, and the controversy surrounding Sherry Jones's romantic fictionalisation of the life of the Prophet Mohammed's most favoured wife Aisha, *The Jewel of Medina*, in 2008. Arthur Bradley and Andrew Tate describe the secularist sacralisation of the novel on the part of New Atheists such as Richard Dawkins, Sam Harris, Christopher Hitchens and Daniel Dennett, especially since the 9/11 attacks, and the concomitant threading of New Atheist thought through the work of novelists Ian McEwan, Philip Pullman and Martin Amis as well as Rushdie:[61] 'To McEwan and his contemporaries, the contemporary novel represents a new front in the ideological war against religion, religious fundamentalism and, after 9/11, religious terror.'[62] In this construction, Islam in particular is portrayed as 'irrational, immoral and ... violent', whereas a 'neo-romantic celebration of the aesthetic imagination' is sacralised, along with 'evolutionary biology' and 'scientific enlightenment'.[63] Thus, in a post-9/11 context, when New Atheist thought permeates the view of dominant members of the intelligentsia, the antagonistic opposition between creativity and Islam that was mapped out during the Rushdie affair is entrenched. While for the liberal secularist critic and proponent of free expression the explosion of taboos is vital to an expansion of freedom, a hardline adoption of this position which fails to take into account the material specificities of a Muslim (or any religious) response to a creative work, including the demography of the respondents, will result in the stigmatisation and potentially a curtailment of the freedom of a religious minority.

In an insightful discussion of freedom of speech debates in the context of the Netherlands, Judith Butler describes the Dutch state's role in determining 'whose freedom of expression will be protected and whose will not' and the way in which the notion of freedom of speech has been instrumentalised by the state as a means of stigmatising its non-white Muslim minority. If the state 'casts its own Muslim population as a threat to the value of freedom', she writes, 'then it protects one claim of freedom only through the intensification of unfreedom'.[64] While the specificities of the Dutch context and the particular incidents Butler discusses (the implementation of the Dutch Civic Integration Examination in particular) do not apply directly to the British context, nevertheless the point she makes remains relevant: British Muslims get cast as outsiders and interlopers through discourses surrounding free speech controversies; the delegitimisation of their speech in response to the publication of works that they find offensive is precisely a form of 'unfreedom', even where it is not enacted by the state. In relation to the Danish cartoons affair, Talal Asad makes a similar point: secular criticism 'doesn't merely liberate ideas from taboos ... it also reinforces the existing distinction between the paradigmatically human and candidates for inclusion in true humanity who do not as yet own their bodies, emotions, and thoughts'. In other words, 'it reinforces ... the ideological status of European Muslims as not fully human because they are not yet morally autonomous and politically disciplined'.[65] Here, with his repetition of the word 'yet', Asad also evokes the temporalising approach which characterises normative representations of Muslims, configuring them as lagging behind their secular European counterparts rather than as coeval others, with their own distinct, heterogeneous trajectories.[66] As well as a materialist approach to specific controversies, then, undoing the dichotomy of creative freedom versus religious censure and censorship requires breaking down a rigid binary between religion and secularism and thereby dislocating religion from a blanket identification with authoritarianism, intolerance and censorship in opposition to secularism's freedom of thought and speech, tolerance, rationalism and progressiveness. In particular, it requires disturbing the normativity of secularism so that its limits and exclusions can be exposed and explored.[67] In his more recent work, Jürgen Habermas has recognised and legitimised the active presence of religion in the public sphere, and sought to map out a 'post-secular' conception of society which views religion as a positive force for the religious and non-religious alike.[68] It is this idea of the 'post-secular', where there is self-reflexivity on the part of the secular and the religious as well as the potential for crossover, commonality and convergence between the two, which seems most fruitful for working towards a more equal and just multicultural Britain.[69]

THE SCOPE OF THE BOOK

Writing British Muslims explores the literary text as a site of struggle between competing and unequal discourses, and as an object of struggle in disputes between the intelligentsia and some British Muslims. In view of the humanistic, bourgeois heritage of the novel, and in the light of the New Atheist understanding of the novel as emblematising 'free speech', 'individuality' and 'rationality' in opposition to an intolerant, oppressive Islam, it examines the extent to which contemporary fiction authored by writers of South Asian Muslim heritage pushes beyond liberal secularist parameters in its representation of British Muslims and multiculturalism. In his *A Theory of Literary Production*, Pierre Macherey maintains that literary discourse is a 'contestation of language' rather than a 'representation of reality'. But while it distorts rather than reflects, fiction is much more than a deceptive illusion: 'Fiction is not truer than illusion … But it can set illusion in motion by penetrating its insufficiency, by transforming our relationship to ideology … Fiction deceives us in so far as it is feigned; but this is not a primary act of deception, because it is aimed at one even more profound, exposing it, helping to release us from it.'[70] Through its 'gaps and contradictions', through the 'juxtaposition and conflict of [its] several meanings', a work of fiction displays its own ideologies. It is in this sense that the work of fiction contains within it 'an implicit critique of its ideological content'.[71] It is in this sense, too, that the literary actively engages the social world (by exposing social contradictions that are normatively obscured by ideology) and that it has the potential to transform the reader's relationship to ideology. In particular, Macherey's emphasis on the importance of textual silences informs this book. My readings of the selected texts focus on what they do not – and cannot – say, their curious gaps, elisions and omissions, which in turn reveal what they *can* say about Muslims and multiculturalism in Britain, and the limits of this speech, thus shedding light on the ideological pressures operating in the social context.[72]

By combining detailed readings of texts with a sustained engagement with their social context, this book demonstrates the significant contribution that literature can make to our understanding of multicultural Britain and the place of Muslim citizens within it. Morey and Yaqin comment on the 'sheer ubiquity of images of Muslims and the insistent repetition of certain reductive tropes'. As they point out, 'the stereotyping of Muslims takes place in repeated acts of representation by politicians, the press and media, and even those claiming to speak on their behalf'.[73] Hence, it is in the domain of representation, as well as in the social and political domains, that critical intervention is necessary, as Morey and Yaqin's *Framing Muslims* so powerfully demonstrates through a highly insightful analysis of a range of non-literary cultural forms including film, television, radio and other media. While literary representations are not as pervasive as media images, their complexity and depth mean that they have a particular capacity to shed light on the tensions and conflicting ideological pressures which shape multicultural Britain and public understanding of Muslims and multiculturalism, thus taking us beyond the straw-target stereotypes circulated by the English Defence League and their ilk onto more complex terrain. Following Fredric Jameson's analysis of the 'strategies of containment' by which narrative contains or displaces the 'unresolvable social contradictions' of capitalism, I explore the ways in which my chosen texts manage the contradictions of multicultural Britain.[74]

Further, in recent years, representations of Muslims have become increasingly prominent within the domain of literature, reflecting a mainstream British readership's spurious desire to 'know' the Muslim Other in the context of events such as 9/11 and 7/7. The reception of

Monica Ali's *Brick Lane*, which I discuss in Chapter 4, and the proliferation of British Muslim memoirs since 9/11 and 7/7, examined in Chapter
6, are highly suggestive of such an anthropological interest in – and
consumption of images of – British Muslims. Works by acclaimed British
literary figures such as Sebastian Faulks and John Lanchester as well as
Martin Amis have featured Muslim characters (*A Week in December*, 2009;
Capital, 2012; *The Second Plane*, 2008), while renowned writers including
Amis and McEwan have publicly aired their (often ignorant) views about
Islam.[75] Muslim writers, including Kamila Shamsie and Mohsin Hamid,
have also assumed, or been assigned, the role of public intellectual in the
wake of 9/11, commenting on 'Muslim issues' in the broadsheet press. In
addition, Pakistani fiction, in particular, has featured in the media and
on literary prize shortlists.[76] In 2006 the Muslim Writers Awards were
established in Britain; a 2010 edition of the prestigious literary magazine *Granta* featured new Pakistani writing; and in 2013 *Granta*'s list of
Britain's twenty most promising young writers, published once a decade,
featured Muslim writers Kamila Shamsie (Pakistani), Tahmima Anam
(Bangladeshi) and Nadifa Mohamed (Somali), as well as British Indian
writer Sunjeev Sahota whose debut novel features a young Muslim man
who is drawn towards an act of terror. These literary texts enter the
public domain with considerable rhetorical power, demanding exploration and scrutiny.[77]

Writing British Muslims devotes chapters to particular texts by Salman
Rushdie, Hanif Kureishi, Monica Ali and Nadeem Aslam, and a chapter
to the memoirs of Ed Husain, Sarfraz Manzoor, Yasmin Hai, Zaiba Malik
and Shelina Zahra Janmahomed. All of the authors have origins in India,
Pakistan or Bangladesh, although Janmahomed's family emigrated from
the Indian subcontinent to East Africa and then to Britain. The decision
to narrow my focus to *South Asian* Muslim British texts (authored by
South Asian Muslim Britons and depicting South Asian Muslim communities and cultures in Britain) stems from my interest in the historical and
social: the South Asian Muslim community has a specific history and
demography and has faced a particular set of conditions and challenges
that differ from those of Muslims originating from parts of Africa and the
Arab world. My overriding interest in class, especially, requires a focused
engagement with the South Asian Muslim diaspora which has consistently
occupied a position at or near the bottom of Britain's social scale. This
has necessitated the omission of some fascinating and insightful recent
British Muslim fiction, in particular Sudanese writer Leila Aboulela's

Minaret (2005) and British Syrian Robin Yassin-Kassab's *The Road from Damascus* (2008) – both of which I consider in the Conclusion – as well as British Zanzibarian Abdulrazak Gurnah's *By the Sea* (2001). There are also some illuminating literary representations of Muslims in Britain by non-Muslim writers which are beyond the scope of this book, including Zadie Smith's comic depiction of the Bangladeshi Iqbal family in her best-selling *White Teeth* (2000), Faulks's two-dimensional sketch of an Islamist in *A Week in December*, and Sahota's brilliant portrayal of a radicalised young British Pakistani in *Ours are the Streets* (2011). Other British Asian writers of Muslim heritage have literary concerns that diverge from the key preoccupations of this book and so do not feature in it: for example, Aamer Hussein's beautifully crafted depictions of cosmopolitan London, Pakistan and elsewhere.

A range of scholarly works addressing black and Asian British writing emerged in the early 2000s. Many of these – including Susheila Nasta's *Home Truths: Fictions of the South Asian Diaspora in Britain* (2002) and James Procter's *Dwelling Places: Postwar Black British Writing* (2003) – explore the work of some of the writers considered here, yet they do not focus on religion as an integral part of cultural identity and difference. More recently, Ruvani Ranasinha's *South Asians in Britain: Culture in Translation* (2007) touches on Islam in its discussion of work by Kureishi, as does Sara Upstone's *British Asian Fiction: Twenty-First Century Voices* (2010) in its examination of works by Kureishi, Aslam and Ali, while Dave Gunning's *Race and Antiracism in Black British and British Asian Literature* (2010) includes a group of chapters on 'Islam and antiracist politics' as well as substantial engagement with the politics of multiculturalism in an insightful study of the cultural impact of race and anti-racism in Britain. Geoffrey Nash's *Writing Muslim Identity: The Construction of Identity* (2010) offers an over-view of the representation of Muslims and Islam, by both Muslim and non-Muslim authors, in a wide range of written forms; and Peter Morey, Amina Yaqin and my edited volume of essays, *Culture, Diaspora, and Modernity in Muslim Writing* (2012), also takes in a broad sweep of authors, nations and diasporas, including studies of Muslim writing from North America and the Arab diaspora, and by white secular writers. In her *British Muslim Fictions: Interviews with Contemporary Writers* (2012), Claire Chambers offers illuminating interviews with a wide spectrum of Muslim writers tracing their heritage to South Asia, Africa and the Arab world, accompanied by deft analysis and contextualisation.[78] With its focus on the literary production of the Muslim South Asian diaspora in Britain,

its preoccupations with the role of class in shaping Muslim identities and
cultures and the politics of multiculturalism, and its historicised approach
to contemporary debates and controversies, *Writing British Muslims* seeks
to complement these works but also to push the field of diasporic British
fiction further beyond the parameters of a secular liberalism to a materialist, post-secular engagement with multicultural Britain.

The content and structure of the book is shaped by an interest in the
historical as an integral part of its commitment to the material. Hence,
the book follows a chronological trajectory and opens with a chapter that
explores the presence and practices of South Asian Muslims in Britain from
the early twentieth century to the 1980s. It thereby crucially historicises
the ideological narratives and counter-narratives that surround British
Muslims today and contextualises the readings of contemporary fiction
that follow. Countering the conventional view that South Asian Muslims
only migrated to Britain after the Second World War, it focuses on the
activities of the predominantly working-class South Asian Muslims
who worshipped in east London in the 1930s and 1940s, as well as their
more elite counterparts at the Shah Jahan Mosque, Woking, and shows
how South Asian Muslims in Britain have been forming collectivities
and communities, and mobilising for the right to practise their faith in
the public sphere, for at least a century. In particular it considers two
controversies involving the Jamiat-ul-Muslimin, a group affiliated to
the East London Mosque: a protest by members of the Jamiat against
H. G. Wells's *A Short History of the World* for its representation of the
Prophet Mohammed and the Quran, which they considered to be offensive; and a struggle for control of the East London Mosque between the
Jamiat and the contrastingly elite trustees of the mosque. Each example
yields significant insights into recent controversies centring on British
Muslims and multiculturalism. The chapter also reads the H. G. Wells
dispute against a contemporaneous Indian freedom of expression dispute
– that triggered by the publication of the controversial Urdu language
collection of short stories *Angare* in 1932. By doing so, it highlights the
complexity of literary controversies and the important roles that class
and place, as well as other contextual factors, can play in them. A consideration of the secular literary and political culture enacted by elite South
Asian Muslim figures in Britain towards the end of empire – including
Angare contributor Sajjad Zaheer's novella *A Night in London* (*Landan Ki
Ek Raat*, 1938), to my knowledge the only fictional attempt to map the
South Asian experience of London from that period – casts light on the

diverse forms and meanings of resistance in late imperial Britain, and the different ways in which religion, class, gender, race and place can interact to form a narrative of resistance. Finally, a brief exploration of the secular forms of anti-racist activism that dominated after the Second World War, considered in the light of the preceding historical narrative, seeks to challenge the thesis – propounded by Kenan Malik among others – that the rise of religious public identities and mobilisation from the 1980s was the unfortunate offspring of multicultural policies imposed from above.

Chapter 2 begins by providing a crucial context to the Britain-based controversy surrounding the publication of Salman Rushdie's 1988 novel *The Satanic Verses*, establishing the importance of a dialectical understanding of race, class and religious affiliation and grounding the protests in their material conditions. It reads the novel alongside and against the dispute that it generated: an engagement with the social context illuminates the presence of ideological contradictions within the novel which in turn shed light on the complexities and contradictions of multicultural politics in 1980s Britain. While Rushdie himself delegitimised the protest by attributing it to a retrogressive monoculturalism and fear of the hybridisation that the novel valorises, the chapter shows that the antagonisms generated by the Rushdie affair arose in large part from the exclusions of a secular liberal anti-racist politics. Focusing primarily on Rushdie's representations of the fictional immigrant area 'Brickhall' in London, the chapter argues that the oppositional anti-racism that underpins the representation of the largely Muslim community's struggle against the racism of Thatcher's Britain is in tension with the endorsement of secular individualism against religious communalism that pervades the novel. The chapter reveals the strategies by which the novel attempts to manage and resolve this tension which is embedded within it and which emerged in the form of protests and book-burnings soon after its publication. Selected work by Hanif Kureishi forms the focus of Chapter 3. As well as examining Kureishi's explicit representations of British Muslims in *The Black Album* (1995), the short story and screenplay versions of 'My Son the Fanatic' (1997) and selected essays, the chapter also explores texts that touch upon Islam elliptically and, it is argued, at times uneasily (*Intimacy*, 1998; *My Ear at his Heart: Reading my Father*, 2004; *Something to Tell You*, 2008; and a range of short stories). The chapter tracks the way in which this writer and cultural spokesperson, well known for his powerful opposition to the sanctioned racism of Thatcherism, has responded to the shift to a neoliberal multiculturalism, and explores the position of Muslims and a

Muslim identity within the multiethnic cityscapes peopled by mixed-race subjects that Kureishi creates. It argues that Kureishi's work has helped to shape British multiculturalism both by legitimising a new, culturally diverse Britishness and, crucially, by articulating limits to this legitimacy. His valorisation of a secularist liberal individualism against religious collectivism leads to the emergence of a series of reductive binaries, at odds with the deconstructive thrust of his work, and problematically delegitimises subaltern minority – in particular Muslim – formations.

In contrast to the middle-class multicultural worlds encountered in Kureishi's oeuvre, Monica Ali's best-selling novel *Brick Lane* (2003) is situated in an 'enclaved' working-class British Muslim community.[79] The chapter argues that this minority community is largely abstracted from its context in majority Britain so that the problems of the community (the oppression of women, drug addiction, religious extremism, rioting) are rooted in its (religious) culture and isolated from the exclusions of majority Britain. Hence, the trajectory from constraint to freedom that the protagonist Nazneen follows is shaped primarily by patriarchal structures within the community and their evasion or subversion, and there is little sense of the pressures that are exerted on the community's men from outside this space. The chapter explores the reception of the novel by the literary establishment and the contrasting response of members of the Bangladeshi community, and argues that the social contradictions that are repressed in *Brick Lane* emerge at the point of its reception by the British Muslims who inhabit the area surrounding Brick Lane and protested against the novel and its filming. Its aim is not to advocate literary censorship but rather to expose the racially and culturally (including religiously) coded nature of the principle of freedom of expression, and to offer a more nuanced account of the protest as a struggle *for* recognition and self-representation and *against* the structures of inequality which obstruct its protagonists' path to these rights. While not itself the subject of a controversy, despite its venture onto the scabrous terrain of 'honour crime', Nadeem Aslam's 2004 novel *Maps for Lost Lovers*, the focus of Chapter 5, thematises and explores the politics of minority offence and the binary of individual freedom versus cultural censure and censorship that has framed responses to controversies surrounding artistic representations of Islam and Muslims. In tracing the presence and complication of this binary in *Maps for Lost Lovers*, the chapter explores how far the novel, which emerged at a particularly fraught moment in British multicultural politics, gets beyond the gendered culturalist discourses that have underpinned pronouncements on the 'failure' of multiculturalism from both left and right. It argues that despite contextualising the oppressors' behaviour within their own disempowerment in Britain, the novel appears to present just two alternative positions: either individual withdrawal and dissent from community, culture and faith, or complicity with the community's oppressive practices whose victims are primarily its women and children. The potential for a positive communitarianism formed around a shared religious culture is constantly deflected or stymied, often through a focus on the abuse of women, so that a thoroughgoing multiculturalism predicated on a 'politics of recognition' (including the public recognition of religion)[80] and a commitment to gender equality are held in tension.

The final chapter of the book considers a selection of the autobiographical memoirs by young British Muslims that proliferated in the wake of 9/11 and 7/7: Ed Husain's *The Islamist* (2007), Sarfraz Manzoor's *Greetings from Bury Park: Race, Religion and Rock 'n' Roll* (2007), Yasmin Hai's *The Making of Mr Hai's Daughter: Becoming British* (2008), Shelina Zahra Janmahomed's *Love in a Headscarf* (2009) and Zaiba Malik's *We are a Muslim, Please* (2010). It considers the varying ways in which these narratives are shaped by and inform discourses surrounding British Muslims, and how they negotiate the weighty burden of representation that they carry as the reading public seeks 'insider' knowledge of the 'authentic' Muslim Other. Each memoir charts the author's personal history in the context of wider social and cultural issues relating to Islam and multiculturalism. Each considers the role of religious faith and culture in the life of a young British Muslim; the rise in 'Islamic fundamentalism' among British Muslim youth; the place of politics in religion; the competing demands of secular modernity, *mahalla* and mosque; and the complex relationship between individual, family, community and nation. The chapter investigates the ways they negotiate these issues in their articulation of British Muslim selfhoods, and explores how far they intervene in Muslim–majority relations and mediate intercultural understanding in post-9/11 Britain.

NOTES

1 © Avaes Mohammad. Reproduced with kind permission of the author.

2 Catrin Nye, *Naturalising Newham*, BBC Radio Asian Network (broadcast 19 September 2013). For the term 'super-diverse', see Kaveri Harriss, 'Muslims in the London borough of Newham', background paper for COMPAS (University of Oxford, n.d.), www.compas.ox.ac.uk/fileadmin/files/Publications/Research_Resources/Urban/Newham_Background_Paper_0506b.pdf, 2 (last accessed 6 November 2014). This paper also offers a helpful overview of Newham.

3 Daniel Nilsson DeHanas and Zacharias P. Pieri, 'Olympic proportions: the expanding scalar politics of the London "Olympics mega-mosque" controversy', *Sociology*, 45:5 (2011), 798–814, 806. DeHanas and Pieri dispute the links between Tablighi Jamaat and terrorism while commenting on the group's inward-looking character and suggesting its isolationism (804–5, 809).

4 Philip Johnston, 'The shadow cast by a mega-mosque', *Telegraph* (25 September 2006), www.telegraph.co.uk/comment/personal-view/3632591/The-shadow-cast-by-a-mega-mosque.html (last accessed 6 November 2014).

5 The council finally rejected plans to build the mosque in December 2012.

6 DeHanas and Pieri, 'Olympic proportions', 801.

7 Jason Cowley, 'London 2012: smaller, greater, braver', *Observer* (10 July 2005), www.theguardian.com/uk/2005/jul/10/olympics2012.olympicgames3 (last accessed 6 November 2014).

8 Trevor Phillips, 'Let's show the world its future', *Observer* (10 July 2005), www.theguardian.com/uk/2005/jul/10/olympics2012.olympicgames (last accessed 6 November 2014).

9 *Ibid.*

10 Seamus Milne, 'It is an insult to the dead to deny the link with Iraq', *Guardian* (14 July 2005), www.theguardian.com/politics/2005/jul/14/july7.uk (last accessed 6 November 2014).

11 Quoted in Nye, *Naturalising Newham*.

12 Tariq Modood, *Multicultural Politics: Racism, Ethnicity and Muslims in Britain* (Edinburgh: Edinburgh University Press, 2005), pp. 109–10.

13 Christopher Baker and Justin Beaumont, 'Postcolonialism and religion: new spaces of "belonging and becoming" in the postsecular city', in Justin Beaumont and Christopher Baker (eds), *Postsecular Cities: Space, Theory and Practice* (London: Continuum, 2011), pp. 33–49, pp. 42–5 (emphasis mine).

14 Anshuman A. Mondal, *Young British Muslim Voices* (Oxford and Westport, CT: Greenwood, 2008), p. 96.

15 Ziauddin Sardar, 'Spaces of hope: interventions', in Richard Phillips (ed.), *Muslim Spaces of Hope: Geographies of Possibility in Britain and the West* (London: Zed Books, 2009), pp. 13–36, p. 14.

16 Alana Lentin and Gavan Titley, *The Crises of Multiculturalism: Racism in a*

Neoliberal Age (London: Zed Books, 2011), p. 28; David Edgar, 'In the new revolution, progressives fight against, not with, the poor', *Guardian* (24 August 2009), www.theguardian.com/commentisfree/2009/aug/24/revolution-1989-1979 (last accessed 6 November 2014).

17 Paul Gallagher, 'Deprived Newham watches bemused as council ponders move from £110m building after just three years', *Independent* (24 September 2013), www.independent.co.uk/news/uk/politics/deprived-newham-watches-bemused-as-council-ponders-move-from-110m-building-after-just-three-years-8836972.html (last accessed 6 November 2014).

18 Nye, *Naturalising Newham*; Harriss, 'Muslims', 3.

19 Harriss, 'Muslims', 7.

20 Madeleine Bunting, 'This is about real victims', *Guardian* (11 December 2004), www.theguardian.com/world/2004/dec/11/race.religion (last accessed 6 November 2014).

21 Phillips, 'Let's show the world'.

22 Henri Lefebvre, *The Urban Revolution*, trans. Robert Bononno (Minneapolis and London: University of Minnesota Press, 2003), p. xxi.

23 Doreen Massey, *Docklands: A Microcosm of Broader Social and Economic Trends* (London: Docklands Forum, 1991).

24 Peter Kalliney, 'Globalization, postcoloniality, and the problem of literary studies in *The Satanic Verses*', *Modern Fiction Studies*, 48:1 (2002), 50–82, 62–3.

25 Anne Power, 'The Olympic investment in East London has barely scratched the surface of the area's needs', London School of Economics and Political Science, British Politics and Policy blog entry (15 August 2012), http://blogs.lse.ac.uk/politicsandpolicy/olympics-newham-investment-power/ (last accessed 6 November 2014).

26 Modood, *Multicultural Politics*, p. 28.

27 *Ibid.*, p. 40.

28 Jack Straw, '"I felt uneasy talking to someone I couldn't see"', *Guardian* (6 October 2006), www.theguardian.com/commentisfree/2006/oct/06/politics.uk (last accessed 6 November 2014).

29 Peter Morey and Amina Yaqin, *Framing Muslims: Stereotyping and Representation after 9/11* (Cambridge, MA: Harvard University Press, 2011), p. 1.

30 Elizabeth Poole, *Reporting Islam: Media Representations of British Muslims* (London and New York: I. B. Tauris, 2002), p. 248.

31 Lentin and Titley, *Crises of Multiculturalism*, p. 37.

32 *Ibid.*, pp. 85–6.

33 For a clear précis of the exclusions of liberalism, see Bhikhu Parekh, *The Future of Multi-Ethnic Britain: The Parekh Report* (London: Profile, 2000), pp. 46–7, and *Rethinking Multiculturalism: Cultural Diversity and Political Theory* (Basingstoke: Palgrave Macmillan, 2nd edn, 2006 [2000]), pp. 109–13, 338–9.

34 Morey and Yaqin, *Framing Muslims*, pp. 49–50; Andrew Pilkington, 'From institutional racism to community cohesion: the changing nature of racial

discourse in Britain', *Sociological Research Online*, 13:3 (2008), www.socreson-line.org.uk/13/3/6.html, 1.1–1.3 (last accessed 6 November 2014).

35 Tariq Modood, *Multiculturalism: A Civic Idea* (Cambridge: Polity, 2007), pp. 10–11; Tahir Abbas, 'British South Asian Muslims: before and after September 11', in Tahir Abbas (ed.), *Muslim Britain: Communities under Pressure* (London and New York: Zed Books, 2005), pp. 3–27, pp. 12, 4.

36 David Goodhardt, 'Discomfort of strangers', *Guardian* (24 February 2004), www.theguardian.com/politics/2004/feb/24/race.eu (last accessed 6 November 2014), and 'Too diverse?', *Prospect* (20 February 2004), www.prospectmagazine.co.uk/magazine/too-diverse-david-goodhart-multiculturalism-britain-immigration-globalisation/#.Une9XotFDcs (last accessed 6 November 2014); Trevor Phillips, 'After 7/7: sleepwalking to segregation', speech given at the Manchester Council for Community Relations (22 September 2005).

37 Modood, *Multiculturalism*, p. 106.

38 *Ibid.*, p. 54.

39 *Ibid.*, pp. 51–3.

40 *Ibid.*, pp. 70, 71.

41 Modood, *Multicultural Politics*, p. 202.

42 Similarly, the schools at the centre of the allegations of religious extremism in Birmingham in 2014 (Operation Trojan Horse) were not Islamic schools but secular state schools in deprived areas with a high proportion of Muslim pupils. Allegations of the imposition of fundamentalist, intolerant interpretations of Islam on pupils and the curriculum were disturbing. Yet, media, government and Ofsted responses to and representations of the controversy reveal a number of worrying misconceptions, including a highly problematic association of religious conservatism with terrorism, as well as with 'self-segregation' and ghettoisation; and a muscular assertion of so-called 'British values' as a solution to the perceived problems. The segregation of communities in Birmingham must be grounded in poverty and white flight rather than identified with Islam, and enabling Muslim pupils from deprived backgrounds to integrate their faith into their school life (granting them religious freedom rather than imposing so-called British values on them) might well have contributed to the strikingly high standards that were evident at Park View (rated 'Outstanding' by Ofsted until its sudden downgrading during the furore), as well as at some of the other stigmatised schools that are located in deprived areas of the city. See Seamus Milne, 'Michael Gove's toxic assault is based on naked discrimination', *Guardian* (11 June 2014), www.theguardian.com/commentisfree/2014/jun/11/michael-gove-assault-on-schools-naked-discrimination (last accessed 6 November 2014); Gus John, '"Trojan horses" and policing "extremism" in schools' (7 June 2014), www.gusjohn.com/2014/06/trojan-horses-and-policing-extremism-in-schools (last accessed 6 November 2014).

43 Sardar, 'Spaces of hope', p. 18.

44 Lentin and Titley, *Crises of Multiculturalism*, p. 28.

45 Slavoj Žižek, 'A leftist plea for Eurocentrism', in *The Universal Exception: Selected Writings*, vol. 2 (London and New York: Continuum, 2006), p. 203.

46 Slavoj Žižek, 'Why we all love to hate Haider', in *The Universal Exception*, p. 34.

47 Slavoj Žižek, 'Liberal multiculturalism masks an old barbarism with a human face', *Guardian* (3 October 2010), www.theguardian.com/commentis-free/2010/oct/03/immigration-policy-roma-rightwing-europe (last accessed 6 November 2014).

48 Slavoj Žižek, 'Multiculturalism, or, the cultural logic of multinational capitalism', in *The Universal Exception*, p. 162.

49 See Sarah Glynn, 'Liberalizing Islam: creating Brits of the Islamic persuasion', in Phillips (ed.), *Muslim Spaces of Hope*, pp. 179–97, p. 184.

50 Žižek, 'Multiculturalism', pp. 174–5.

51 Modood argues that Muslims 'draw strength from the sources of their group pride', or from their Muslimness (*Multicultural Politics*, pp. 107, 122).

52 Madeleine Bunting, 'Religions have the power to bring a passion for social justice to politics', *Guardian* (12 January 2009), www.theguardian.com/commentisfree/2009/jan/12/madeleine-bunting-religion-social-justice (last accessed 6 November 2014).

53 Michel de Certeau, *The Practice of Everyday Life*, trans. Steven Randell (Berkeley and Los Angeles: University of California Press, 1984), pp. xix, 36–7.

54 David Harvey, *The Condition of Postmodernity* (Oxford: Blackwell, 1990), p. 237, cited in Stuart Elden, *Understanding Henri Lefebvre: Theory and the Possible* (London and New York: Continuum, 2004), p. 181.

55 Henri Lefebvre, *The Production of Space*, trans. Donald Nicholson-Smith (Oxford: Blackwell 1991), p. 404.

56 Henri Lefebvre, *Key Writings*, ed. Stuart Elden, Elizabeth Lebas and Eleonore Kofman (London and New York: Continuum, 2003), p. 154.

57 Kenan Malik, *From Fatwa to Jihad: The Rushdie Affair and its Legacy* (London: Atlantic Books, 2009), p. 47.

58 Ted Cantle, 'The Cantle report – community cohesion: a report of the Independent Review Team', Home Office (December 2001), http://resources.cohesioninstitute.org.uk/Publications/Documents/Document/Download-DocumentsFile.aspx?recordId=96&file=PDFversion (last accessed 6 November 2014).

59 Doreen Massey, *Space, Place and Gender* (Cambridge: Polity, 1994), pp. 19–20.

60 Lefebvre, *Production of Space*, p. 27.

61 Arthur Bradley and Andrew Tate, 'Introduction', in *The New Atheist Novel: Fiction, Philosophy and Polemic after 9/11* (London: Continuum, 2010).

62 *Ibid.*, p. 11.

63 *Ibid.*

64 Judith Butler, 'The sensibility of critique: response to Asad and Mahmood', in Talal Asad, Wendy Brown, Judith Butler and Saba Mahmood, *Is Critique*

Secular? Blasphemy, Injury and Free Speech (Berkeley, CA: Townsend Center for the Humanities, 2009), pp. 101–36, pp. 126–34.

65 Talal Asad, 'Free speech, blasphemy, and secular criticism', in Asad *et al.*, *Is Critique Secular?*, pp. 20–63, pp. 55–6.

66 Doreen Massey, *For Space* (London: Sage, 2005): see especially pp. 68–70.

67 For works that endeavour to do this, in different ways, see, for example, Terry Eagleton, *Reason, Faith, and Revolution: Reflections on the God Debate* (New Haven and London: Yale University Press, 2009); Asad, 'Free speech'; Saba Mahmood, 'Religious reason and secular affect: an incommensurable divide?', in Asad *et al.*, *Is Critique Secular?*, pp. 64–100; Charles Taylor, 'Why we need a radical redefinition of secularism', in Judith Butler, Jürgen Habermas, Charles Taylor and Cornel West, *The Power of Religion in the Public Sphere*, ed. Eduardo Mendieta and Jonathan Vanantwerpen (New York: Columbia University Press, 2011), pp. 34–59; Timothy Fitzgerald, *Religion and Politics in International Relations: The Modern Myth* (London and New York: Continuum, 2011).

68 See Jürgen Habermas, 'Equal treatment of cultures and the limits of post-modern liberalism', *Journal of Political Philosophy*, 13:1 (2005), 1–28; 'Religion in the public sphere', *European Journal of Philosophy*, 14:1 (2006), 1–25; 'Notes on a post-secular society', Signandsight.com (18 June 2008), 1–23.

69 Anshuman A. Mondal's new book, *Islam and Controversy: The Politics of Free Speech after Rushdie* (Basingstoke: Palgrave Macmillan, 2014), is a highly important exploration of the moral questions raised by a range of Muslim-related freedom of speech controversies, and, like this book, offers a critique of the liberal arguments for freedom of speech. Unfortunately, it was published when this book was already in production, so too late for inclusion in its discussion of these issues.

70 Pierre Macherey, *A Theory of Literary Production*, trans. Geoffrey Wall (New York and London: Routledge, 1996 [1978; French original 1966]), p. 64.

71 *Ibid.*, pp. 84, 100.

72 *Ibid.*, pp. 86, 94.

73 Morey and Yaqin, *Framing Muslims*, p. 2.

74 Fredric Jameson, *The Political Unconscious: Narrative as a Socially Symbolic Act* (London: Routledge, 1981), pp. 56, 79.

75 See Ginny Dougary, 'Martin Amis interviewed by Ginny Dougary', *Times Magazine* (9 September 2006); Ian McEwan, 'Martin Amis is not a racist', *Guardian* (21 November 2007), www.theguardian.com/world/2007/nov/21/religion.race; Stuart Jeffries, '"Everybody needs to get thicker skins"', *Guardian* (11 July 2008), www.theguardian.com/books/2008/jul/11/salman-rushdie.bookerprize (both accessed 6 November 2014).

76 Saeed Shah, 'As their country descends into chaos, Pakistani writers are winning acclaim', *Guardian* (17 February 2009), p. 23. In the British context, Muslim authors who have been shortlisted for the Man Booker Prize since

2000 include Monica Ali (2003), Hisham Matar (2006) and Mohsin Hamid (2007); see Rehana Ahmed, Peter Morey and Amina Yaqin, 'Introduction', in Rehana Ahmed, Peter Morey and Amina Yaqin (eds), *Culture, Diaspora, and Modernity in Muslim Writing* (Abingdon and New York: Routledge, 2012), pp. 1–17, pp. 1–2.

77 In addition, a host of cinematic and televisual representations of British Muslims has emerged in recent years: Ayub Khan-Din and Damien O'Donnell's *East is East* (1999), Ayub Khan-Din and Andy DeEmmony's *West is West* (2010), Simon Beaufoy and Kenny Glenaan's *Yasmin* (2004), Peter Kosminsky's *Britz* (2007), Chris Morris's *Four Lions* (2010) and the sitcom *Citizen Khan* (Adil Ray and Chris Wood, 2013–), as well as sketches by comedian Shazia Mirza.

78 Susheila Nasta, *Home Truths: Fictions of the South Asian Diaspora in Britain* (Basingstoke: Palgrave Macmillan, 2002); James Procter, *Dwelling Places: Postwar Black British Writing* (Manchester: Manchester University Press, 2003); Ruvani Ranasinha, *South Asians in Britain: Culture in Translation* (Oxford: Oxford University Press, 2007); Sara Upstone, *British Asian Fiction: Twenty-First Century Voices* (Manchester: Manchester University Press, 2010); Dave Gunning, *Race and Antiracism in Black British and British Asian Literature* (Liverpool: Liverpool University Press, 2010); Geoffrey Nash, *Writing Muslim Identity: The Construction of Identity* (London and New York: Continuum, 2010); Ahmed *et al.* (eds), *Culture, Diaspora, and Modernity*; Claire Chambers, *British Muslim Fictions: Interviews with Contemporary Writers* (Basingstoke: Palgrave Macmillan, 2012).

79 Pnina Werbner, *Imagined Diasporas among Manchester Muslims: The Public Performance of Pakistani Transnational Identity Politics* (Oxford: James Currey, 2002).

80 Tariq Modood, 'Muslims, religious equality and secularism', in Geoffrey Brahm Levey and Tariq Modood (eds), *Secularism, Religion and Multicultural Citizenship* (Cambridge: Cambridge University Press, 2009), pp. 164–85, p. 168

I

Muslim culture, class and controversy in twentieth-century Britain

At the setting of the sun three men prostrated themselves towards Mecca, placing their foreheads on the ground. Surmounting the dome above their heads a gilded crescent cut the sky of a London suburb.

... The cry of the muadhdhin calls the faithful to prayer, five times a day in the oasis of the Sahara and by the mountains of Kashmir, in the cities of Egypt, Persia and Turkey.

The same call, strange as the crying of a gull herd [*sic*] miles inland, goes up from the steps of the mosque at Woking ... thirteen centuries after the death of Muhammad, the religion which once cleft the world like a scimitar, has a small foothold in England. (*Islamic Review*, 1934[1])

HISTORICISING BRITISH MUSLIM SPACE

In a 1931 *Spectator* article, a British woman expresses the commonplace aversion of the time to interracial marriages: 'When I see a veiled woman, it is as if she shouted at me "My menfolk are barbarians".' The allusion to veiling suggests she has Muslims in mind, and that her primary objection is to unions between 'barbaric' Muslim men and the white women who supposedly become their victims.[2] The resonance of this remark with contemporary stereotypes underlines the long history of gendered constructions of Muslims and points to the importance of considering history when exploring controversies surrounding British Muslims in the present day. A. Sivanandan opens his powerful study of racism in Britain from the 1950s to the 1980s by highlighting three acts of anti-colonial resistance on British soil: Udham Singh's 1940 assassination of Sir Michael O'Dwyer for the part he played in the massacre of unarmed Indians at Jallianwala Bagh, Amritsar, in 1919; the fifth Pan-African Congress's pledge to fight for an end to imperialism in Manchester in

1945; and the hold-up in 1975 of restaurant staff and customers by three West Indian men who demanded money to finance the liberation struggle in Africa. While the 'pattern' of black British struggle 'was set on the loom of British racism', this struggle was 'woven' from the 'strands' of anti-colonial resistance Sivanandan identifies.[3] Similarly, the more recent and better known struggles of South Asian Muslims in Britain – for the right to wear the hijab and niqab in schools and workplaces and to access halal meat and prayer facilities, as well as against Salman Rushdie's *The Satanic Verses* – can be traced to the strands of resistance that are visible within historical accounts of an earlier period of Muslim migration to and settlement in Britain. Further, these early strands can cast light on our analysis of the contemporary period and of contemporary cultural representations by and of South Asian Muslims in Britain.[4] This chapter will focus on particular moments of Muslim space-claiming, controversy and cultural resistance in early twentieth-century Britain. It will close by offering a brief sketch of Muslim agency through the period of heightened racial tension that followed the Second World War, and up until the beginning of the *Satanic Verses* controversy of 1988–89. In doing so, it seeks to historicise and thereby add complexity and nuance to understandings of tensions involving Muslims in contemporary multicultural Britain that form a context to the readings of literary texts that follow.

In his ground-breaking study of Muslims in Britain from 1800 to the present, '*The Infidel Within*', Humayun Ansari charts an increase in anti-Islamic prejudice in Britain in the early nineteenth century, with the erosion of the Ottoman Empire and Britain's heightened sense of superiority as it extended its rule over Muslim lands. By the mid- to late nineteenth century, pseudo-scientific theories of race, as well as missionary activity in India in particular, had consolidated this prejudice, and Muslims were perceived as inferior beings, in need of 'civilising' and 'saving'. The image of the 'Turkish tyrant' during the decline of the Ottoman Sultanate hardened stereotypes of fanatical, despotic, depraved and irrational Muslims which circulated in literature, travel writing and the visual arts.[5] The increase in anti-British agitation on the part of the Indian community in Britain, which led to their surveillance by the Indian Political Intelligence,[6] compounded negative images, as did Ottoman involvement on the side of the Germans in the First World War.[7] In the early twentieth century, the treatment of Muslims in Britain shifted with fluctuations in the economy. During the First World War, Britain needed men from the colonies to work on ships and in shipyards and munitions factories, but, with the economic stagnation and then depression that followed in the 1920s and 1930s, they began to be perceived as a threat to indigenous Britons and their livelihoods.[8] The 1919 race riots centred around the perception that these non-white citizens were stealing employment opportunities and housing as well as women from their white British counterparts, and racially discriminatory legislation, including the 1919 Alien Restriction (Amendment) Bill, the 1920 Aliens Order, the 1925 Special Restrictions Order and the 1935 British Shipping (Assistance) Act, was put in place.[9] The materialisation of racism in legislation entrenched grassroots prejudice, and working-class Muslims suffered from this as well as poverty.

In his study, Ansari emphasises the intersection of class with race and religion in the experience of Muslims in Britain.[10] While elite visitors to Britain experienced less prejudice, the lascars who arrived in port cities in increasing numbers suffered tremendous hardship and discrimination.[11] Further, Muslim responses to hostility and their interactions with British society more generally were shaped by class and cultural background, as well as by the social and economic conditions in Britain at the time.[12] In the early twentieth century working-class Muslims in Britain tended to lead fairly autonomous lives, maintaining a degree of separation between their communities and the white majority. Ansari puts forward numerous reasons for this, including the gathering of Muslims in certain areas of employment, particularly shipping, and racist housing policies.[13] Of course, some of these pioneer Muslim settlers wished to remain within 'Muslim' areas through fear of humiliation and attack, especially from the working classes whom they perceived as more prejudiced than their educated compatriots.[14] Yet, there were also more positive reasons for so-called segregation. It enabled Muslims to 'establish communities with a distinctive identity in which they could take some pride' and facilitated the continued practice of their faith and the retention and intergenerational transmission of Muslim values.[15] Further, autonomous living enabled Muslims to mobilise for their rights and against discrimination – either as Muslims or in more broad-based identity groups centring on class, employment or their status as colonial subjects. As hostility towards Muslims gathered force, Muslims in Britain became increasingly resolute to identify, gather and organise collectively.[16] Along with their participation and activism in secular political and social organisations, including the Indian Workers' Association, the Colonial Seamen's Association and Swaraj House, Muslims' establishment of communities as well as mosques and associated societies can be considered as a claiming of space in Britain and, therefore, as a form of cultural resistance.[17] Indeed, Ansari describes the powerful function of mosques both as sites of community- and identity-building, resistance against discrimination and empower- ment through the 'assertion of cultural rights', and as the focus of racial anxieties in their aesthetic and social disruption of British space and the threat they posed 'to Britain's heritage and to "the British way of life"'.[18]

The description of Eid at the Shah Jahan Mosque, Woking, from a 1934 article in the *Islamic Review*, reproduced as an epigraph to this chapter, captures the way in which Islam had begun to shape British space in small but significant ways in the early twentieth century. While Muslims had been creating sacred spaces in ordinary houses since the nineteenth century,[19] the Shah Jahan was the first purpose-built mosque in Britain. Established in 1897 by the former registrar of the University of Punjab, Gottlieb Leitner, it became significant in the establishment of a Muslim presence in Britain in 1913 only when Indian lawyer Khwaja Kamaluddin assumed responsibility for it.[20] It served as an important hub for Muslims in early twentieth-century Britain, attracting worshippers, mainly from elite backgrounds, from across Britain and across the globe, and remains active today. In 1944 the Islamic Cultural Centre, which was eventually to become the London Central Mosque, was opened in Regent's Park.[21] Elsewhere in Britain, Muslim convert William H. Quilliam founded the Liverpool Mosque and Institute in 1891; Cardiff's Peel Street mosque, consisting of three terraced houses, opened in 1945; and in South Shields Muslim burials were being practised from 1919.[22] Societies, some of them associated with particular mosques, also began to emerge, with the inauguration of the London branch of the Anjuman-i-Islam as early as 1886. The beginnings of the East London Mosque can be traced to November 1910 when a fund for a mosque in London was inaugurated. In 1926 a deed of trust was executed, and the London Mosque Fund formally founded, with Sir Ernest Hotson as Honorary Secretary and distinguished Muslims, including Sir Hassan Suhrawardy, Syed Ameer Ali and Feroz Khan Noon, among its trustees.[23] Initially, prayers were held at various venues in west London but poor attendance and the reali- sation that the majority of Muslims in London lived in its East End led to the relocation of worship to the King's Hall on Commercial Road in 1935, and then to the purchase and conversion of three houses on the same street. The East London Mosque was inaugurated at a ceremony on 1 August 1941 by the Egyptian Ambassador Hasan Nachat Pasha, and remains a significant place of worship today.[24] The East London Mosque and its affiliated organisation, the Jamiat-ul-Muslimin, form the focus of the next section, which explores two early twentieth-century controversies involving some of their working-class members.[25]

EAST ENDERS GO WEST

Today, London's East End is well known for its cultural diversity and immediately identified with Britain's Bangladeshi Muslim minority. Brick Lane and the surrounding streets are known as Banglatown in recognition of the community who have shaped the area and the struggles they have undergone to make it their home, and street signs sport Bengali script alongside conventional Latin script. The Brick Lane Jamme Masjid, on the corner of Brick Lane and Fournier Street, encapsulates the history of immigration to the area. Founded in 1976, it replaced a disused synagogue after the Jewish community had moved in large numbers to the north London suburbs. Before this, the building had been used as a Methodist chapel which had in turn replaced a Huguenot church. Yet, less known is the mapping of the area by South Asians, the majority of them Muslim,[26] in the decades preceding Indian independence and the more substantial migration to Britain from the Indian subcontinent. On Commercial Road, near the site of the East London Mosque, was the Shah Jolal, the café of Ayub Ali, a Sylheti migrant who travelled to Britain as a lascar and settled in London in 1920. Ali also provided refuge for Indians at his lodging house on Sandy Row and later became president of the UK Muslim League.[27] The Shah Jolal was the location of the inauguration in 1943 of the East End branch of V. K. Krishna Menon's India League, attended by Indian seamen and factory workers, the majority of whom were Muslim; recorded names of participants include Shah Abdul Majid Qureshi, another former lascar who jumped ship at Tilbury Docks in 1936, as well as Surat Ali (secretary of the Colonial Seamen's Association and the Hindustani Social Club in the East End), Ismail Ali, Abdul Hamid, and Said Amir Shah (a key figure in the Jamiat-ul-Muslimin).[28] Meetings of the East End India League were also held at the Grand Palais on the same street; close by, on Christian Street, was the office of Shah Abdul Majid Qureshi's Indian Seamen's Welfare League; the local employment exchange where many Indian Muslims were registered was situated on Settles Street; and on nearby Old Montague Street was the shop of Said Amir Shah, as well as Krishna Menon's East End social centre where Tahsil

Miah worked as representative for the Indian Seamen's Union, encouraging lascars to strike against pay and conditions.[29] In 1945 Akbar Ali Khan and his organisation, Hindustani Mazdur Majlis, organised screenings of Indian films in Brick Lane which were attended by some five hundred South Asians, many of whom would have been Muslim.[30]

The majority of these are secular Indian social welfare and/or political organisations whose leaders, activists and participants were, however, predominantly Muslim and working class. Further, some of their protagonists re-emerge in archival material relating to the East London Mosque or the Jamiat-ul-Muslimin, suggesting that these early migrants formed collectivities and mobilised in Britain around their religious identities as well as a broader Indian identity and their class identities – and that these identities were not mutually exclusive but intersected and overlapped. Founded in 1934 and initially located at Canton Street, off East India Dock Road, the Jamiat-ul-Muslimin itself spanned the religious and the social in its purpose and function. Many of the aims that it lists in its original manifesto of 1935 are concerned with enabling the practice of Islam in Britain through the creation of communal spaces and fora for worship and education. They include, for example, 'to raise funds for a Mosque in the East End of London', to open 'a school for the training and education of Muslims' and to 'arrange meetings and organise functions with a view to propagate and serve the cause of Islam'. Yet these aims are combined with a focus on the social welfare of Muslims in Britain. The organisation sought 'to look after and provide for the education of orphans and other poor Muslim children', and to arrange 'the burials of poor, and destitute Muslims, and generally [do] all to help and alleviate the misery and want of the poor and needy'.[31] Indeed, it was successful in providing burials for poor Muslims in Britain; the 1941 pamphlet documents an Indigent Muslims' Burial Fund located at the mosque,[32] while Taslim Ali is recorded in Shah Abdul Majid Qureshi's oral narrative as Britain's first Muslim undertaker in the 1940s.[33] During the Second World War, the Jamiat campaigned successfully for the provision of 'Kosher margarine'; for access to rationed foods such as butter, rice and sugar and for the right to slaughter a sheep on the occasions of Eid-al-Adha and Milad-un-Nabi; and for its members to use the council's baths before Eid prayers.[34] By 1942, a Birmingham branch of the Jamiat-ul-Muslimin was being planned,[35] and a Glasgow Jamiat was in existence by 1944.[36]

Evident in the aims and activities of the Jamiat is an early mobilisation for minority religious rights on the part of Britain's Muslim community, one that resonates with the mobilisation to make halal meat available in schools in Bradford in the mid-1980s or for state-funded Islamic schools in the 2000s.[37] These contemporary campaigns have been met with considerable hostility by majority British culture – not only the overtly nationalist Thatcherite culture of the 1980s, but also the secularist liberal culture that became more prevalent during Tony Blair's term in government. This mobilisation for Muslim minority rights in east London in the 1930s and 1940s, and the intersection and overlapping of faith, culture and class evident in the aims of the Jamiat, problematise an understanding of Islam in Britain as discrete from the political, as a private, individual expression of faith. Here I allude to the liberal consignment of religion to the private domain which is dominant in contemporary discourses surrounding British Muslims, and the consequent refusal to recognise the rights of religious minority groups, including (and in particular) the rights of Muslims as a minority group, in addition to individual rights. Against this, Tariq Modood reiterates the need to recognise that 'the public sphere is not morally neutral, that the public order is not culturally, religiously, or ethnically blind' and therefore that the 'public/ private distinction may … act to buttress the privileged position of the historically integrated folk cultures at the expense of the historically subordinated or newly migrated folk'.[38] To confine Islam to the private domain, therefore, is to reinforce existing inequalities and to obscure these inequalities beneath a veil of 'neutrality'. To elucidate these points, I offer a brief exploration of two controversies in imperial Britain, drawn from the India Office archives, where the intersection of class, faith and minority status is evident, thereby breaking down the boundary between religion and the political, between private and public.

In August 1938 members of the Jamiat-ul-Muslimin gathered at one of their regular meetings in King's Hall on Commercial Road, east London. Here they 'ceremoniously committed to the flames' a copy of H. G. Wells's 1922 popular world history book, *A Short History of the World*, because of references to the Prophet Mohammed and the Quran which they considered offensive.[39] According to the *Guardian* of 13 August 1938, not only had Wells described Mohammed as 'a man compounded of … considerable vanity, greed, cunning and self-deception', but his book claimed that the Quran was 'certainly unworthy of its alleged divine authority'.[40] Rumours surrounding the Wells protests circulated widely: the press claimed that protesters planned to march on Wells's house, and to burn effigies of him in front of a London mosque in Putney.[41] These proved unfounded. In fact, the Jamiat organised a petition, signed by 136 local Muslims – 'merchants, pedlars, clerks, sailors, and others'.[42] The signatures are preceded by a short piece of text addressed to the High Commissioner which condemns Wells's assertions for their falsity and malice and the offence that they had caused Muslims across the world. It further demands a withdrawal of Wells's allegations and an apology from the writer. While some of the signatures that follow are written in English, a proportion of these appear to be penned by the same hand and have crosses next to them, suggesting the signatories are illiterate, and others are written in Arabic script.

The petition was delivered by members of the Jamiat-ul-Muslimin to India House, Aldwych, which accommodated the Indian High Commission, at the end of a protest march from their homes in the East End to Bank and then through Fleet Street and Canon Street to London's West End.[43] Marching west, into the heart of the metropolis, to assert their rights as Muslims and plead their cause with government officials, the protesters would have passed St Paul's Cathedral, the Royal Courts of Justice and several newspaper offices – British symbols of faith, justice and freedom of speech. As they marched, they shouted slogans such as 'Down with ignorant Wells!' and 'Allah is great!'.[44] The clear resonance of this protest with the British protest against Salman Rushdie's novel *The Satanic Verses* a half-century later unsettles perceptions that the Rushdie affair was the first of a series of challenges to creative freedom in Britain. Indeed, further parallels with the Rushdie affair can be found. It was a Mr Rau, correspondent for several 'ultra-communist and anti-British papers in India', who had spread news of the inflammatory passages in Wells's book in India, sparking protests in Calcutta, and then among the Indian Muslim community in east London.[45] Later, the protests spread to East Africa and then to Sindh province where the government ordered the detention of all copies of the book under Section 26 of the Indian Post Office Act, 1898.[46] Fifty years on, Indian journalist Madhu Jain is said to have initiated the dispute surrounding Rushdie's novel with an article published in *India Today* under the headline 'An unequivocal attack on religious fundamentalism', which was then exploited by Indian parliamentarian Syed Shahabuddin. It was only after this that the controversy reached Britain, before extending across the globe.[47]

At the end of the protest march, a deputation of six members of the Jamiat was received by Feroz Khan Noon who agreed to intervene on their behalf. As a fellow Muslim, Khan Noon expressed sympathy with the protesters' grievances. Yet he warned them that their chances were slim, advising them that 'in England only obscene or blasphemous books could be proscribed and blasphemy was only against the Christian religion'. Indeed, prior to the march, Khan Noon had warned Mohamed Baksh that, even when people do criticise the 'Christian religion and Jesus Christ' in England, 'nobody takes any notice of these things', further advising him that 'the best thing they could do was to keep quiet and live peacefully in the east end. After all, they were a very small minority and it would do them no good to try and be mischievous in this country, no matter how genuine their grievances were.'[48] The Secretary of State for India, Lord Zetland, responded to Khan Noon's intervention by agreeing to communicate the case to the publishers and expressing 'regret ... that offence should have been given to members of the deputation and those whom they represent, on a matter concerning their Faith', while asserting that he lacked the power to have the passage in question modified because of the freedom of expression permitted in England.[49] Unsurprisingly, both publishers, William Heinemann and Penguin Books, refused to remove the offensive passages from the text.[50]

The Secretary of State's relatively sympathetic response should be considered in the context of a volatile political situation in India at the tail-end of empire and the consequent need to tread carefully where Indian cultural sensitivities were concerned. Official responses to other South Asian Muslim protests against cultural works in both Britain and India in this period suggest a degree of fear at the prospect of exacerbating tensions by causing offence, rather than a genuine respect for religious sensitivities. In 1935 Aftab-ud-Din Ahmed, the Imam of the Shah Jahan Mosque at Woking, wrote a letter to the India Office on behalf of Muslims in Britain protesting against the depiction of Muslims in the highly successful Cary Grant film *Lives of a Bengal Lancer*. In his letter Ahmed singles out two episodes in the film: the force-feeding of pig's meat to an Afghan spy by the British who are attempting to extract a confession from him; and a scene which suggests that Muslims make a show of prayer while their minds are in fact filled with mundane affairs. In fact, these offensive scenes had already been removed for the Indian market, and in this instance the India Office felt compelled to cut them for the British market also.[51] In 1935, 1941 and 1948 the India Office, as well as UK High Commissioners in India and Pakistan, warned the publishers of the magazines *Every Woman's Magazine*, *Parade* and the *Mirror* of the need to avoid pictorial representations of the Prophet

Mohammed and informed them of the proscription of copies of issues containing such representations in India and, after Partition, Pakistan.[52] While the *Mirror*'s editor objected with the assertion that the magazine's 'audience is the student who, if he can read the English text of the magazine, will be of sufficient intelligence not to consider as objectionable a picture taken from a Mohammedan manuscript, especially when seen in the context of the article', the editor of *Parade* responded with more sensitivity, reassuring the India Office that 'we shall in future be careful wherever possible to avoid pictorial representation of the Prophet, and will endeavour to exclude from our columns anything likely to give offence on religious grounds'.[53]

These last objections may have been focused on offence in the context of the Indian subcontinent, but they nevertheless resonate with the 2005 protests across Europe against the publications of cartoons depicting the Prophet Mohammed in the Danish newspaper *Jyllands-Posten*, just as the 1938 Wells protest resonates with the *Satanic Verses* controversy, raising important questions about freedom of expression and offence which have gained prominence in public discourse in recent years. Indeed, a consideration of the Wells protest casts light on and enables a rethinking of contemporary disputes surrounding creative freedom and minority offence. First, the class status and local identity of Wells's dissenters as working-class Muslim East Enders are of consequence – as they were for the British protesters against Rushdie's novel fifty years later. As Madeleine Bunting shows in her discussion of community activist Saul Alinsky in 1930s Chicago, faith-based organisations played a highly significant role in providing dignity and meaning to the city's impoverished communities.[54] If this imbrication of faith and class is applied to a poor immigrant community in 1930s Britain, the Jamiat-ul-Muslimin's protest against Wells's book must be considered as a social as well as a religious act. Its construction as a form of cultural and social space-claiming by an oppressed minority religious group breaks down the boundary between the private-religious and the public-political.[55] Second, despite their subordinate status as working-class Muslim Indians in Britain and their lack of access to a public forum, the protesters found an alternative means to make their voices heard and have their cultural and religious sensibilities recognised in the public sphere, beyond the parameters of their own community. Thus, their cultural assertiveness counters representations of working-class South Asians in Britain as passive and docile which were especially dominant in the decades before the Rushdie affair, as I show below. Third, their protest underlines the significance of faith to a minority group in 1930s Britain. By doing so, it debunks reductive conceptions of British Muslims as unproblematically 'British Asian', or as having comfortably secular identities, in the pre-Rushdie affair era.[56] In other words, an event such as this destabilises the notion that the engagement of state multiculturalism with this minority as a religious group – its acknowledgement of religion as a primary component of minority identity – forged 'British Muslim' identities, thereby leading to cultural separatism and ghettoisation. I am alluding here to criticisms of state multiculturalism in the wake of 9/11 and the 2001 race riots in Bradford, Burnley and Oldham when cultural commentators from the left of the political spectrum began to expound the supposed failure of multiculturalism, focusing overwhelmingly on Muslims.[57] Fourth, the relatively sympathetic response to the Jamiat's protest on the part of British officials – notwithstanding their fear of provoking Indians in the context of a volatile political climate – suggests the hardening of a secularist liberal discourse in the contemporary period, and underlines the exclusions of this discourse where Muslims are concerned.

In 1943 the Jamiat-ul-Muslimin clashed with the elite executive committee members and trustees of the East London Mosque. These included Sir Hassan Suhrawardy, Muslim adviser to the Secretary of State for India, as well as former officials of British India, such as Sir Frederick Sykes and Sir Ernest Hotson.[58] The trustees had handed over the management of the affairs of the mosque to the Jamiat at its inauguration. In autumn 1943, however, Suhrawardy, on behalf of the trustees, terminated their role because the Jamiat had failed to adhere to the trustees' demand that no political activities be held at the mosque which should confine its activities strictly within the religious domain.[59] The documentation alleges that the Jamiat then attempted to gain total control of the mosque, and their refusal to accept the trustees' intervention led to their dismissal from the premises and subsequent meeting of protest at Conway Hall in Red Lion Square. The latter was attended by four hundred people, mainly Punjabi and Bengali Muslims, many of whom would have transgressed socio-spatial boundaries to make their way from east London to its centre, asserting their 'right to the city', if fleetingly.[60] While there was no disorder, there was, according to the report, an 'atmosphere of suppressed excitement', with 'the passions of those present' at risk of becoming inflamed.[61] This construction of the protesters as both passive and volatile recurs in representations of working-class South Asians in Britain in surveillance reports. The seamen and pedlars who formed the East End branch of the India League were dismissed as 'illiterate and far more concerned with their own comfort than with politics' – unless, of course, an 'isolated individual [is] worked up to a state of excitement by wild talk' and sought to emulate Udham Singh.[62] Similarly, the rank-and-file members of the Indian Workers' Association are said to 'dimly comprehend' the organisation's aims but nevertheless 'may be worked up to temporary excitement by inflammatory speeches'.[63] The contradictory construction of Indian subjects highlights the government's unease with these subjects; their depoliticisation and emasculation can be read as a strategy to deny the validity of their oppositional position and the threat that it poses to colonialism. This kind of representational strategy is revealingly suggestive of contemporary constructions of working-class British Muslim protesters as hotheaded, irrational and susceptible to the machinations of their imams or better educated leaders.[64]

The protest was led by Said Amir Shah, a key figure in the East End South Asian community, and particularly involved in the pro-Congress Committee of Indian Congressmen, headed by Subhas Chandra Bose's nephew, Amiya Nath Bose.[65] Shah was also an associate of V. K. Krishna Menon, the driving force behind the anti-colonial India League.[66] Some of Menon's fellow elite, non-Muslim anti-colonial activists were also at Conway Hall, including K. S. Shelvankar, Dr C. B. Vakil, I. G. P. Singh, A. N. Bose and Tarapada Basu, well-known representatives of various political organisations such as the Communist Party of Great Britain, Swaraj House and the India League.[67] Divesting the working-class dissenters of agency in a familiar gesture, the report claims that 'the Jamiat have for some time been making themselves difficult *having got into the hands of* Congress minded Moslems'. It goes on to state that the 'non-Muslim extremists' who attended the protest were not present 'out of any kindly interest in the welfare of the East London Mosque', the implication being that their motivation was purely an opportunistic bid to secure more support for their organisations.[68] Similarly, Shah's involvement in the protest and the Jamiat more generally is rather scathingly attributed to his ambition to become 'uncrowned king of the Muslim Community in Britain' while any 'religious motives' on his part are dismissed.[69]

While the report seems to occlude the possibility of a combined religious interest in the mosque and political interest in agitating against colonial rule, its description of the speech Shah made at the protest meeting inadvertently ties these interests together in a revealing manner. We are told that Shah implied in his speech

> that the India Office ran the affairs of the Mosque through its representatives, the Trustees. [Shah] did not consider the Muslim trustees as good Muslims, declaring that they put the interests of the British Government before their duty to Islam. He mentioned the name of Sir Hassan Suhrawardy whom he alleged never came to the Mosque merely to pray – there was always a sinister motive for his casual visits. Then there was Sayeedulla, the secretary of the Executive Committee, who rarely put in an appearance at the Friday prayer meetings. These were the type of Muslims on the London Mosque Fund whom the Jamiat wished to have replaced by conscientious and trustworthy Muslims.[70]

Especially when read through the lens of contemporary hegemonic constructions of British Muslims, these assertions by Shah, coupled with his colleague Sahibdad Khan's objections to the presence of non-Muslims on the board of trustees, might position him and his organisation as separatist, exclusionary and zealous. Indeed, a police report describes the leading members of the Jamiat as 'bigoted Muslims who, on a religious issue, would not hesitate to subordinate all their other interests to the cause of Islam'.[71] However, Shah's suspicion of the pro-government, elite trustees underscores the very different political interests of the Jamiat and its members (implicitly working class and anti-colonial). It links their desire to practise their faith autonomously to a rejection of colonialism and thereby locates their protest within a political framework. The members of the Jamiat can then be reconfigured as autonomous agents of resistance objecting to the paternalistic involvement of the officials rather than as zealous separatists. While this protest was not primarily a religious one, a religious identity and organisation became the means of mobilising for working-class agency and anti-colonial aims for the Jamiat's members. This again underlines the significant crossover between the religious, social and political spheres for working-class Muslims in imperial Britain, which foreshadows a similar interdependence of these spheres in contemporary controversies. To highlight this interdependence is also to contest the ideologically reductive Othering of political Muslims (in contradistinction to political Islam) in twenty-first-century Britain.

This is not to say that the members of the Jamiat-ul-Muslimin or other working-class protagonists of the anti-colonial mobilisation that took place in early twentieth-century Britain – whose voices we have limited access to and are always mediated – would necessarily have perceived their concerns and practices as I am interpreting them here. The wording of the Jamiat-ul-Muslimin's petition against Wells's book does not suggest that they considered their protest in political as well as religious terms. In the contemporary period, those Muslims who have campaigned for the right to wear the veil in public places or for halal meat to be available to their children, or against creative works that they perceive as offensive, may not represent these concerns in terms of minority rights or class consciousness. Dipesh Chakrabarty describes the gap that can separate the set of explanatory principles that a historian employs from the corresponding set that working-class protagonists themselves use, and argues for the productiveness of this dissonance: 'subaltern pasts ... act as a supplement to the historian's pasts ... they enable history, the discipline, to be what it is and yet at the same time help to show what its limits are'. Chakrabarty is referring to the 1855 Santal rebellion against the British, specifically the gap between the Santals' own understanding of God as the main force behind their rebellion and the Marxist historian's attribution of political agency to them. Adapting his theory, the potential dissonance between the way the protagonists of these struggles might have represented themselves and my reading of them can be seen to expose the irreducible nature of these 'minority histories', the impossibility of reducing their diversity and multiplicity to a singular or universal narrative of 'Muslim resistance', as well as the limitations of any historical excavation of subaltern lives.[72] Thus, my aim is not to speak for them but rather to unearth working-class agency from the fragmented and mediated accounts available within the archive in order to break down the stereotypes that can often work to freeze dissenting subaltern figures into the excitable pawns of India Office surveillance reports or of contemporary media representations of Muslim protests in Britain.

TEXTUAL RESISTANCES: *ANGARE, A NIGHT IN LONDON*
AND THE *ISLAMIC REVIEW*

Almost contemporaneous with the British Muslim protests against H. G. Wells's *A Short History of the World* were those in British India against the 1932 Urdu-language anthology of short stories *Angare*, written and compiled by four Indian Muslims: Ahmed Ali, Sajjad Zaheer, Rashid Jahan and Mahmuduzzafar.[73] Despite the location beyond Britain of the better known *Angare* controversy, it warrants a brief consideration here because of what it suggests about the complexity of literary disputes and the important roles that class and place can play in them. Further, while the controversy took place in India, two of its protagonists, Ali and Zaheer, spent time in Britain in the 1930s, and it was in London in 1935 that Zaheer co-founded the Progressive Writers' Association, partly in response to the *Angare* dispute. Zaheer and Ali were perhaps the most prominent Muslim Indian figures who contributed to Bloomsbury's literary culture in the first half of the twentieth century, while Zaheer's novella *A Night in London* (*Landan Ki Ek Raat*, 1938) is, to my knowledge, the only fictional attempt to map the South Asian experience of London from that period.[74] A brief exploration of this secular literary and political culture enacted by privileged South Asian Muslim figures, alongside the deeply religious elite culture surrounding the Shah Jahan Mosque, Woking, casts light on the diverse forms and meanings of resistance in late imperial Britain, and the different ways in which religion, class, gender, race and place can interact to form a narrative of resistance.

Angare has been described as 'a declaration of war by the youth of the middle class against the prevailing social, political and religious institutions'. The collection of ten short stories targeted 'enslavement to social and religious practices ... the disgraceful acquiescence [to] foreign rule ... the inequalities in Indian society ... [and] the enclosed and oppressive world of Muslim women enslaved to their husbands' demands and outworn religious and social dogmas'.[75] Its publication was met by outrage in British India. The Central Standing Committee of the All India Conference, Lucknow, declared the book 'filthy', claimed that it had 'wounded the feelings of the entire Muslim community', and urged the Government of the United Provinces to proscribe it. Articles in the Urdu press condemned the book for its assault on Islam, and fatwas were issued by maulvis against the book and its authors. On 15 March 1933, the book was banned by the UP Government under section 295A of the Indian Penal Code, and all but five copies were destroyed.[76] The authors responded by issuing a statement entitled 'In defence of *Angare*: shall we submit to gagging?' which was published in the Allahabad *Leader*. In it they defended 'the right of free criticism and free expression' and announced their intention to form a 'League of Progressive Authors'.[77] One of them, Sajjad Zaheer, went on to do just this, alongside fellow Indian writer and activist Mulk Raj Anand, in the Nanking Chinese restaurant in London's Bloomsbury in November 1934.[78] In their manifesto, the Progressive Writers' Association articulated their belief that Indian literature should engage with 'the basic problems of our existence to-day – the problems of hunger and poverty, social backwardness and political subjection', and resolved 'to fight cultural reaction; and, in this way, to further the cause of Indian freedom and social regeneration' as well as to 'fight for the right of free expression of thought and opinion'.[79] Encouraged by the leftist British writer Ralph Fox, and influenced by European literary culture including the International Congress of Writers for the Defence of Culture held in Paris in 1935, the group held regular meetings in London until Zaheer left London for Paris and then India, where he helped to launch the All-India Progressive Writers' Association in April 1936.[80] After Zaheer's departure from London, however, the aims of the PWA continued to be pursued there, arguably, through the vehicle of the relatively short-lived literary-political magazine *Indian Writing* (1940–42) which Ahmed Ali co-edited.[81]

While the protagonists of the protest against Wells's book were effectively mobilising for a limit to freedom of expression, these elite South Asian Muslims in Britain were intent on pushing at the boundaries of what could be said or written in order to challenge political and religious authoritarianism and repression. In terms of the dichotomy between free speech and offence, they were on opposite sides of the fence. Yet both the Jamiat's protest and the literary and political activism of Zaheer and Ali can be seen as acts of resistance undertaken by Muslims against a powerful authority from a position of subordination. This illustrates Susheila Nasta's point about the multifarious nature of the very concept of resistance whose varied forms 'can be complicit and oppositional at the same time'.[82] While the Jamiat's protest could be seen as oppositional in so far as it involved a group of disempowered and disenfranchised subjects mobilising against the literary and political establishment, it could be also be seen as complicit with censorship; if *Angare* is most obviously oppositional against both the colonial and religious authorities, it could, as Aziz Ahmad maintains, be adjudged 'an unprincipled attack on religion' that fails to respect other people's views and, in this sense, as complicit with a hardline form of secularism.[83]

In her astute reading of the *Angare* controversy in relation to contemporary controversies involving Muslims in Europe and the governance of Muslims more generally, Maleiha Malik explores the complexity of navigating between the conflicting demands of protecting freedom for individual Muslims (including minorities, such as women, within the Muslim community) on the one hand, and recognising representative Muslim organisations on the other hand.[84] As she says, 'granting legitimacy to some Muslim representative groups as political representatives of Muslims can potentially detract from the agency and political autonomy of individual Muslims'.[85] Malik refers here both to the *Angare* controversy which saw an oppressive alliance between the colonial authority and the ulama, and to the contemporary endorsement of certain Muslim organisations on the part of the last Labour government. In the contemporary context, however, an attempt to bypass organisations in order to focus on individual Muslims (such as Hazel Blears's of 2008) risks 'limiting Muslims to a non-political and private role', an outcome which would suit politicians' discomfort with Muslims occupying the public sphere.[86] The *Angare* dispute, as Malik illustrates, attests to the need for scepticism towards community representatives, especially in order to protect marginalised members of communities. Yet, a focus on individual Muslims, or minorities within Muslim communities (e.g., women), can conversely serve as a means of delegitimising communal Muslim protest, as was the case with the *Satanic Verses* and *Brick Lane* disputes. The Wells dispute underlines the need for a reclaiming of the concept of individual freedom from its valorisation as a transcendental good against which minority religious protest can be reductively stigmatised as regressive and censorious. Read together, the *Angare* and Wells controversies emphasise the need to attend to the fact that there are different kinds of oppression, both external (racism and Islamophobia, as well as class) and internal (patriarchy within a community), and that Muslim subjects use different strategies and form different alliances to challenge each; or, put differently, the need to attend to social and spatial hierarchies – the class, racial and religious position of those who protest within the space that they occupy – when considering controversies involving free speech.[87]

Angare, the PWA and *Indian Writing* were influenced by European Enlightenment notions of freedom of expression that were attained or at least nurtured by their authors' or members' residence in London.[88] Indeed, the formation of the PWA and *Indian Writing* were arguably enabled by their location in Britain where anti-colonial views and criticism of Indian society could be articulated with relative safety. In this sense the PWA and *Indian Writing* were British creations, and yet they were focused almost uniquely on India. Zaheer wrote in his 'Reminiscences' of the realisation by the PWA of the need to relocate to India in order to put into practice the organisation's aims, and of the 'orphanlike' nature of the literature they were writing in Britain;[89] while the stories of *Indian Writing*, many of them penned by Muslim South Asians resident in Britain, do not touch upon the Muslim or South Asian experience of Britain.[90] Thus, as the only known fictional representation of Britain by a Muslim in early twentieth-century Britain, Zaheer's novella is significant. Yet, in *A Night in London*, which follows the lives of a group of Indian students in London over an evening and night to the following morning, the city remains diffuse and abstracted. Like the author and his fellow South Asian writers and students in imperial Britain, Zaheer's characters for the most part skirt above the surface of the city and its hierarchies of power, brushing against them only during a racist incident in a London pub where two characters, Azam and Rao, are subjected to abuse from a drunk with a 'tomato-red face'. Indeed, in the pub scene in particular, Britain becomes almost 'exoticised', a touristic spectacle of the British working classes for the elite Indian reader to consume.[91]

Zaheer's somewhat stock characters range from the lazy but likeable doctoral student Naim to the Marxist Punjabi Ahsan and the conservative 'mimic man' Arif. There is only one Indian woman, Karima, among them and, significantly, she is the character who comes the closest to a stereotype. Judgemental of Sheila – a sympathetically drawn English woman – for her 'bold' eye contact with men, her 'tight-fitting clothes', her consumption of cigarettes and alcohol and her lack of honour and modesty, Karima emerges as a prudish and intolerant character, caught between tradition and modernity in a 'conflict of cultures' redolent of contemporary stereotypes of British Muslim women (48–50, 54–7). When asked to dance by Ahsan, Karima is 'suddenly reminded of how shameless a thing dancing is and felt angry with Indian – especially Muslim – men who had forgotten their customs to such an extent in this foreign land that they didn't even have the least bit of shame in entertaining the thought of an Indian Muslim girl dancing' (64). Here, Karima's religion is fleetingly identified as a source of her apparent retreat into 'tradition' – yet, as Ahsan remarks, she does not observe purdah, wears a Hindu sari, and is comfortable mixing with men (65). Her judgemental attitude and conservatism are more a product of jealousy and confusion than of a retrogressive religious orthodoxy, and her denouncement of European licentiousness is challenged by Ahsan not with a criticism of religious orthodoxy, but with a rejection of 'blind imitation of anything', whether Muslim, Indian or European. Further, while for the most part Ahsan is the political compass of the novella, his high ground is undermined by Karima's revelation that he shunned her while dining out with a white woman (65–7). Thus, her cultural conservatism and intolerance are momentarily reframed as legitimate grievances while Ahsan's comparative liberalism falls off its pedestal. Ultimately, the dichotomy that emerges in the novella is not one of an enlightened secularism versus religious repression, but rather one of a leftist, anti-colonial critique and activism versus an apathy, orthodoxy or oppressive practice that is not tied to a particular culture or religion.

In his foreword to *A Night in London*, Zaheer writes of his reluctance to have the novella published, having spent the two and a half years since writing it involved in India's revolutionary movement of workers and peasants (v). This rejection of the text that follows brings to mind the dichotomy between a valorisation of the literary aesthetic and the individual creative artist on the one hand and, on the other, a commitment to the political and collective action that caused a rupture between Zaheer and Ahmed Ali as well as within the PWA more generally.[92] Superficially, this might recall the fetishisation of art that emerges in discourses surrounding contemporary literary controversies and is counterposed to collective religious dogma.[93] Yet, the historical example complicates the contemporary binary because, while Zaheer and the more politicised wing of the PWA saw literature as a means of challenging religious dogma, they also understood it as profoundly political and materialist rather than treating it as a transcendental good. Of course, the urgency of a Marxist politics would have been palpable while Zaheer was conceptualising *A Night in London*: fascism was gathering force across Europe, and locally, in the East End of London, the battle for Cable Street saw activists mobilise against Oswald Mosley's British Union of Fascists. But, while the 1933 book-burnings in Nazi Germany were to become a signifier of fascism, as well as of censorship, exclusion, irrationalism and a retrogressive destruction of culture more generally, not far from Cable Street the Jamiat-ul-Muslimin's book-burning signifies differently if read as a form of class and minority cultural protest, and as not necessarily incompatible with the PWA's secular mobilisation against oppression. In this sense, the Jamiat's protest, when read alongside the *Angare* controversy and the objectives of the PWA, problematises the opposition between a secular Marxism and religion as well as bridges the division between secularism and religion more generally, and points to the importance of combining socialism or materialism with a recognition of religious culture when considering contemporary free speech controversies and multicultural politics.

While the concerns of the South Asian Muslim writers resident in early twentieth-century Britain were largely secular, privileged South Asians were among the worshippers at the Shah Jahan Mosque at Woking whose organ, the *Islamic Review*, offers some clues about their concerns as Muslims in Britain. Primary among these was a desire to challenge negative stereotypes surrounding Islam and Muslims. The inaugural issue of the journal, published in 1913 in the context of the demise of the Ottoman Empire and Britain's antagonistic stance towards Turkey, sets out the pressing need to correct misrepresentations of Muslims: 'Muslims are the greatest sufferers of all other communities through misrepresentation in Europe. With all this deluge of literature which is daily pouring from the Press in this cosmopolitan town, an average Londoner is more ignorant of the Islamic world than many Englishmen are of the Arctic Zone.'[94] In the following month's issue, Khwaja Kamaluddin, the Indian founder of the Woking Muslim Mission and editor of the *Islamic Review*, recounts the damaging misrepresentations of Islam he encountered during the first six months of his stay in Britain, listing distortions of 'polygamy, slavery, Jiziah, and Jehad', as well as of Islam's treatment of women and 'fanaticism', as key to these.[95] Indeed, the *Islamic Review* explicitly states the Mission's aim to begin by challenging the 'misconceptions regarding Islam' before it can go on to present the 'beauties of Islam to the Western public'. In 1934 it regarded its primary purpose not as conversion but as 'removing the spots which have been put, and the discolouring which has been given, to Islam by the Christian missionaries for propaganda purposes', and it regularly featured a section entitled 'What they think of us' comprising extracts from newspaper and magazine articles about Muslims and the Islamic world.[96] Yet, alongside this commitment to challenging misconceptions about Islam was a general desire to present the mosque as practising a modern brand of Islam that was compatible with British life and appealed to the British people. To this end, it tended to emphasise the similarities between Islam and Christianity, and declared halal meat non-obligatory and purdah impractical in the British environment.[97]

There are several articles throughout the periodical's lifespan defending Islam's treatment of women. In 1913 a critical response to Member of Parliament John Rees's *Daily Mail* article warning of the perils of Muslim–white marriages outlined the advantages of 'Mohammedan law' for the English woman and disputed Rees's claims about polygamous practices and the seclusion of women. Some thirty-seven years later, in similar vein, the Imam of the Woking Mosque challenged negative press coverage of the marriage of Farouq Farmer, a Muslim convert, and Ruby Susan Sheppard at the mosque, claiming, contrary to the newspapers' assertions, that Islamic law regards woman as the equal of man and that polygamy is only practised under certain regulated conditions. Indeed, perceptions of polygamy and purdah are recurrent topics, suggesting a pressing need to counter western stereotypes.[98] In a 1934 article, Maulvi Abul Hasant decries the western understanding of purdah as 'the very negation of liberty of the other sex' and goes on to detail the benefits that Muslim women enjoy and the important roles they have played historically in scholarship, daily life and war; while in 1958 a lengthy article on the attitude of the Quran towards veiling contends with Orientalist perceptions of 'harems and houris ... voluptuous sultans and sordid seraglios' and argues for the importance of purdah regulations for safeguarding the 'purity' of women.[99] As well as maintaining the equality of the sexes in Islam, the *Islamic Review* emphasises the religion's commitment to social and racial equality. Descriptions and photographs of the mosque's celebrations of Eid underline the multifarious nature of the worshippers, brought together across division of class, race and nationality, and articles draw attention to the links between Islam and socialism as well as to Islam's anti-racism.[100]

While the journal declares itself non-political, as well as non-sectarian,[101] it also clarifies the intrinsic link between Islam and politics in so far as Islam informs the whole of life and cannot therefore be consigned to a purely spiritual realm.[102] Indeed, in their aim to bring together and support Muslims and the practice of their faith in Britain – by enabling Islamic burials of soldiers at Brookwood, hosting Eid, or founding the Muslim Society of Great Britain[103] – as well as their challenge to stereotyping representations of Muslims, the Mission and its organ can be said to have enacted a social and political function. Yet, despite this, the mosque and its Mission were largely detached from the working-class communities of Muslims that inhabited the port cities and industrial centres in the first half of the twentieth century, with many of the journal's contributors based in India or others parts of the Islamic world rather than in Britain.[104] Ultimately, the Mission's leading figures belonged mainly to the professional upper middle class and inhabited the fringes of the British imperial establishment rather than wished to challenge it.[105] Hence, they navigated a difficult course between this position and their commitment to combatting prejudices and to embedding Islam in British space.

ANTI-RACISM AND BRITISH MUSLIMS AFTER THE SECOND WORLD WAR

In the years following the Second World War and the decolonisation of the Indian subcontinent, Britain's South Asian Muslim population grew considerably and changed in its composition. The announcement in 1961 of the Commonwealth Immigrants Bill of the following year triggered a large migratory flow from Pakistan in particular, while the building of the Mangla Dam in Mirpur in 1960 and its displacement of one hundred thousand people served as a key 'push' factor, propelling those who were already considering migration to Britain into action.[106] In the 1950s most South Asian Muslim immigrants were young men sharing houses with their compatriots and working shifts in factories, before they were joined by wives, children and elderly parents in the following decades. Religious observance tended not to be a priority for these male sojourners, and drinking alcohol and extra-marital sex were commonplace. Their priority was to earn money for their families who in turn prayed on their behalf.[107] According to Ansari, it was the arrival of their families that led Muslim immigrants to begin to think of themselves as settlers rather than sojourners, and that compelled them to turn their attention increasingly to the practice of Islam and adherence to their native cultural codes in Britain: 'they wanted to pass on their Islamic traditions to their children and grandchildren. The rapid creation of religious and cultural institutions, facilitated by the development of Muslim residential zones where they felt secure and could apply some social control over their communities, reflected this shift in their strategies for living in Britain.'[108] Abdullah Hussein's 2000 novel *Emigré Journeys* captures this shift, charting the life of the Punjabi protagonist Amir who, after years of single living with fellow Pakistani illegal immigrants in a run-down house in Birmingham where they enjoy regular visits by sex workers, is reunited with his wife and two children and attempts to build a home for them.[109] The terrible strictures Amir imposes on his family are deftly contextualised in the insecurity and hardship he suffered in his early years in Britain and his fears for his children in the racist climate of the 1980s and early 1990s.

The increasing significance of religious culture for South Asian Muslims can also be traced to their growing confidence in Britain. Early attempts to absorb and adapt to British cultural values and to gain social approval ceded to a more assertive determination to preserve and practise Muslim cultural traditions and codes for living, and they began to campaign more vociferously for access to halal meat, prayer facilities,

Islamic education and Islamic burials, as well as the right to wear the hijab in schools and the workplace.[110] Further, the tendency to cluster in particular urban areas – a product of chain migration, 'white flight', social deprivation, and a desire for mutual support as well as of 'reactive pride' in the face of racism and linguistic and cultural barriers – helped to reinforce Muslim communities.[111] While in the 1960s and 1970s Muslim organisations remained relatively detached from the state, which defined minority communities racially or ethnically, they were important mechanisms for creating the conditions to practise Islam in Britain and transmit it to successive generations.[112] The proliferation of mosques during these two decades, which served as community centres as well as places of worship, underlines the determination of Muslim communities to embed their religious life within British space.[113]

As Muslims were establishing these communities, racism in Britain was becoming increasingly prevalent, legitimised and violent.[114] Sivanandan traces the development of racism in Britain in the post-war decades, from the Notting Hill riots of 1958 and the Commonwealth Immigration Act of 1962 through the formation and rise of the National Front in the late 1960s and 1970s and the racist murders that ensued, to the Southall riots of 1979 and the New Cross massacre of 1981. As Sivanandan details, black and Asian Britons responded in the form of strikes and defence and campaigning committees and organisations, as well as riots. He describes this minority protest as forming a 'mosaic of unities', suggesting its composition of a number of different ethnicities and communities which nevertheless came together in their shared experience of racism and in the face of state and police brutality to form 'a black unity and a black struggle'.[115] While some issues, such as working conditions and wages, cut across ethnic and religious divisions, others, including the right to wear the turban or to pray in the workplace, were clearly the primary preserve of a particular minority group.[116] And, while some organisations brought together a range of minority groups (for example, the Campaign against Racial Discrimination, formed in the mid-1960s), others, such as the Pakistani Workers' Association (1961), had an ethnically defined membership.[117] Yet, discrete organisations would support one another, so that West Indians mobilised on behalf of issues that affected Asians predominantly, and vice versa.[118] This, together with crossover between membership of religious organisations such as the Jamiat-ul-Muslimin, for example, and secular organisations such as the Pakistan Caterers' Association or the Pakistan Welfare Association, suggests a fluidity of affiliation and identification on the part of minorities including British Muslims.[119]

The magazines published by anti-racist organisations during this period reflect this fluidity and modulate Kenan Malik's thesis that the move towards multiculturalist policies in the late 1970s and early 1980s caused division between communities which were, prior to this, not only unified but better integrated.[120] Certainly, these magazines focus primarily on racist attacks, immigration and housing policies and police harassment, and the need to challenge these in unity rather than as fragmented groups. For example, in a bulletin of the July 11th Action Committee, the United Black Youth League, twelve of whose members were arrested for making explosive devices but later acquitted on the grounds that they were acting in self-defence (the 'Bradford Twelve'), claims that 'black people can no longer afford the luxury of division' and calls for a 'single wall of resistance' formed by all minority ethnic groups.[121] Several publications of the time object to the segregated council housing scheme in Tower Hamlets, which saw Bangladeshis and whites consigned to different estates, as divisive and reminiscent of 'apartheid South Africa',[122] while the *Asian Voice in Hackney* protests against the council's attempts to divide the community into 'Asians' and 'Muslims'.[123] Nevertheless, there were several Muslim organisations present in Britain during this period. A 1981 newsletter of the Steering Committee of Asian Organisations records Newham North Islamic Association, Canning Town Muslim Welfare Association, Ilford Islamic Centre, Anjuman-i-Islam East Ham and Pakistan Muslim Association Barking among its members.[124] A 1987 newsletter of the National Association of Muslim Youth UK criticises a government-funded youth activity project in Croydon for neglecting the specific needs of Muslims by subsuming them within the reductive category of 'Asian'.[125] Moreover, the very fact that several Muslim organisations were affiliated to the Steering Committee of Asian Organisations, whose aims were to campaign against racism and build unity across Asian and other anti-racist organisations, deconstructs the reductive division between a more inclusive 'black' or 'Asian' identity and a 'Muslim' identity, as do comments in several articles in *Paikaar*, organ of the Pakistani Workers' Association. In an article in its inaugural issue, the magazine states the importance of 'Black unity' at the same time as asserting the organisation's conviction that 'Black people must unite firstly on the basis of their own particular experience, on the basis of their own culture and history'.[126] Articles that follow in the next few years criticise the state's policy of allocating funding to narrowly defined religious or ethnic minority groups, arguing both that it is divisive and that it is a way of policing and scrutinising communities, and representing it as a means of circumventing the real issue of combatting racism. However, the criticism is not incompatible with an emphasis on the importance of the maintenance and assertion of cultural and national differences and the recognition of 'religious and cultural rights'.[127] Not surprisingly, an extensive article on the *Satanic Verses* controversy expresses sympathy with the protesters, refutes accusations of Muslim 'separatism' and does not question their identification as Muslims in this particular context, yet simultaneously calls for 'black unity' in the face of the deep-seated racism in British society that the controversy highlighted.[128]

Malik is right that black and Asian immigrants 'recognized that at the heart of the fight for political equality was a commonality of values, hopes and aspirations between blacks and whites'. Yet his claim that the 'Islamization' of Bradford was a product of the 'power, influence and money that accrued to religious leaders in the 1980s as a result of Bradford City Council's multicultural policies', and that people began to identify themselves in terms of their ethnicity or religion as a product of the state's affirmation of ethnicity and religion, erases a history of Pakistani and Muslim self-organisation, divests minorities of agency and will, and denies the possibility of multiple and shifting context-based affiliations for minorities.[129] Citing Anandi Ramamurth, historian of the Asian Youth Movement, Malik recognises that the formation of this Bradford-based organisation in 1977 was 'an expression of the failure of "white" left organizations in Britain to effectively address the issues that affected Asian communities'.[130] Yet he cannot recognise the limitations of the colour-based anti-racist movements that preceded the institutionalisation of multicultural policies in Britain. Tariq Modood describes how both 'colour-blind humanism' and 'colour-conscious antiracisms' created a 'schizophrenic contradiction in many Asians'.[131] In the context of colour anti-racisms,

> there was no language in which to debate cultural difference and the extent to which Asian cultural differences were increasingly being racialized, no language in which to give expression to ethnicity while seeking, at the same time, to oppose racist stereotyping and public expressions of contempt, as well as right-wing culturalist constructions of identity; there was no form to express loyalty to one's own minority community within a public discourse of equality and civic integration.[132]

The need for a 'pluralist antiracism' that recognises cultural and religious difference was pressing in the 1980s, and remains so, not just to meet 'discourse with counter-discourse' in the context of a dominant cultural racism, but also to attain a true racial equality which, as Modood maintains, cannot be brought about by treating everybody as if they were the same – 'for that will usually mean treating everybody by the norms and convenience of the majority'.[133] Malik criticises the Greater London Council for its recognition and support of diverse minority groups because, for him, this changed the meaning of equality 'from possessing the same rights as everyone else, to possessing different rights appropriate to different communities'.[134] But, hamstrung by a myopic liberalism, Malik fails to recognise that a blindness to difference can only entrench the privileges of the majority. Unsurprisingly, Malik roots the British Muslim protests against *The Satanic Verses* in multiculturalist policies. The next chapter will begin by grounding the dispute conversely in social factors, building on and adding to the contextualising historical narrative offered here.

NOTES

1 Ian Coster, 'Islam calls the faithful in England', *Islamic Review*, 22 (1934), 227–33, 227–8. The *Islamic Review* is held at the British Library, St Pancras (hereafter BL).

2 Kenneth Little, *Negroes in Britain: A Study of Racial Relations in English Society* (London: Routledge & Kegan Paul, 2nd edn, 1972), p. 260, cited in Humayun Ansari, *'The Infidel Within': Muslims in Britain since 1800* (London: Hurst, 2004), p. 95.

3 A. Sivanandan, *A Different Hunger: Writings on Black Resistance* (London: Pluto, 1982), p. 3.

4 For a discussion of the connections between early twentieth-century and contemporary anti-racist mobilisation, see Rehana Ahmed and Sumita Mukherjee, 'Introduction', in Rehana Ahmed and Sumita Mukherjee (eds), *South Asian Resistances in Britain, 1858–1947* (London: Continuum, 2011), pp. xi–xxxi.

5 Ansari, *'The Infidel Within'*, pp. 59–68, 80–2.

6 The Indian Political Intelligence was formed in 1909 in response to an increase in Indian nationalist activities throughout Europe. It closed in 1947 (see Kate O'Malley, *Ireland, India and Empire: Indo-Irish Radical Connections, 1919–64* (Manchester: Manchester University Press, 2008), pp. 5–8).

7 Ansari, *'The Infidel Within'*, p. 10.

8 *Ibid.*, pp. 40–4, 96–7.

9 For an analysis of the 1919 race riots, see Jacqueline Jenkinson, *Black 1919: Riots, Racism and Resistance in Imperial Britain* (Liverpool: Liverpool University Press, 2009); for an analysis of the South Asian struggle for equal rights in late imperial Britain, see Rehana Ahmed, 'Equality of citizenship', in Ruvani Ranasinha, with Rehana Ahmed, Sumita Mukherjee and Florian Stadtler (eds), *South Asians and the Shaping of Britain, 1870–1950: A Sourcebook* (Manchester: Manchester University Press, 2012), pp. 21–79; for more information on immigration legislation see 'Making Britain: discover how South Asians shaped the nation, 1870–1950', www.open.ac.uk/researchprojects/makingbritain/ (last accessed 6 November 2014).

10 Ansari, *'The Infidel Within'*, pp. 55, 59–69, 99, 105.

11 Rozina Visram, *Asians in Britain: 400 Years of History* (London: Pluto, 2002), pp. 16–33 (ch. 8).

12 Ansari, *'The Infidel Within'*, p. 99.

13 *Ibid.*, pp. 105–7.

14 *Ibid.*, pp. 107–8.

15 *Ibid.*, pp. 100, 107–9.

16 Syed Ameer Ali founded the London branch of the All-India Muslim League in 1908 in the context of widespread antagonism towards Islam, while demands for a discrete communal space in the capital gathered force in the 1930s amid proposals for the partitioning of Palestine (see Humayun Ansari (ed. and intro.), *The Making of the East London Mosque, 1910–1951: Minutes of the London Mosque Fund and East London Mosque Trust Ltd* (Cambridge: Cambridge University Press, 2011), pp. 8–9, 12–13, 15).

17 Visram, *Asians*, pp. 269–73, 219, 272. For more information on these organisations, see 'Making Britain'.

18 Ansari, *East London Mosque*, p. 2.

19 *Ibid.*, p. 4.

20 Ansari, *'The Infidel Within'*, p. 126; see also 'Making Britain'.

21 Ansari, *'The Infidel Within'*, p. 134.

22 *Ibid.*, pp. 121–6; Shahed Salem, 'A history of mosques in Britain', *Architects Journal* (19 April 2012), www.architectsjournal.co.uk/a-history-of-mosques-in-britain/862962.article (last accessed 6 November 2014).

23 For more information on the Anjuman-i-Islam, Feroz Khan Noon and Syed Ameer Ali, see 'Making Britain'.

24 BL, India Office Collections: India Office Records (hereafter IOR), L/PJ/12/468, especially extract from New Scotland Yard report no. 199, 'Inauguration of the East London Mosque and Islamic Cultural Centre', 6 August 1941. For a history of the mosque, see Ansari, *East London Mosque*, pp. 1–35.

25 For information about the organisation's membership, see Ansari, *East London Mosque*, pp. 18–19. Its first president, I. I. Kazi, was a barrister, while some of its key members were tradesmen. The bulk of the membership, however, would have been pedlars and seamen originally from farming families in

Punjab and Bengal.

26 Ansari, 'The Infidel Within', pp. 35, 50–1.

27 Caroline Adams (ed.), *Across Seven Seas and Thirteen Rivers: Life Stories of Pioneer Settlers in Britain* (London: Eastside, 2nd edn, 1994 [1987]), pp. 41–3.

28 BL, IOR, L/PJ/12/455, 'India League: reports on members and activities', 6 January 1943 to 27 July 1944. For information on Shah Abdul Majid Qureshi, see Adams, *Across Seven Seas*, pp. 141–78; for more on Surat Ali, see Visram, *Asians*, pp. 239–53; for more on Said Amir Shah, see BL, IOR, L/PJ/12/468, Indian Political Intelligence note on Jamiat, 30 October 1943, and memo on Shah, 1 November 1943.

29 BL, IOR, L/PJ/12/455, 'India League: reports on members and activities', 6 January 1943 to 27 July 1944; L/PJ/12/630, extract from New Scotland Yard report no. 248, 'Indian Seamen's Union', 23 June 1943; *ibid.*, extract from New Scotland Yard report no. 156, 'Communist and anti British propaganda amongst East End Indians', 13 December 1939; L/PJ/12/468, memo on Said Amir Shah, 30 October 1943; L/PJ/12/630, misc. no. 12, 'V. K. Menon and the India League', 7 November 1939.

30 BL, IOR, L/PJ/12/646, 'Indian activities in the United Kingdom', 4 March 1945.

31 BL, IOR, L/PJ/12/614, report by Special Branch of Metropolitan Police, 17 August 1938.

32 BL, IOR, L/PJ/12/468, pamphlet of the East London Mosque and Islamic Cultural Centre, opening ceremony, 1 August 1941. This had been set up in 1927 by trustees of the London Mosque Fund (Ansari, *East London Mosque*, p. 23).

33 Adams, *Across Seven Seas*, pp. 53, 87, 160–1.

34 Ansari, *East London Mosque*, p. 34.

35 BL, IOR, L/PJ/12/646, 'Indian notes', 15 December 1942.

36 BL, IOR, L/PJ/12/646, 'Indian activities in the United Kingdom', 25 September 1944.

37 On the halal meat controversy in 1983 in Bradford, see Ansari, 'The Infidel Within', pp. 354–5; on Islamic schools, see Richard Stone (chair), *Islamophobia: Issues, Challenges and Actions. A Report by the Commission on British Muslims and Islamophobia* (Stoke-on-Trent: Trentham Books, 2004), pp. 47–53, including Box 25.

38 Tariq Modood, *Multicultural Politics: Racism, Ethnicity and Muslims in Britain* (Edinburgh: Edinburgh University Press, 2005), pp. 133–4.

39 'Mr Wells and Mohammed', *Guardian* (13 August 1938), p. 10. The book was Wells's attempt to write a popular and concise form of world history for the general reader. The discussion of the H. G. Wells controversy reproduces parts of and develops a short article I co-authored with Florian Stadtler: 'Muslims protest against H. G. Wells book in 1930s Britain', *Huffington Post* (19 September 2012), www.huffingtonpost.co.uk/rehana-ahmed/muslims-protest-against-h_b_1895942.html (last accessed 6 November 2014). It also

reproduces parts of and develops a conference paper I co-authored with Florian Stadtler, 'East Enders go west: the Jamiat-ul-Muslimin's protest against H. G. Wells's *A Short History of the World*', which was presented at the 'Muslims Making Britain' workshop, SOAS, University of London, July 2009. I am very grateful to Florian for his input and for locating and sharing the documentation of the controversy in the India Office Records, British Library. I am also grateful to Florian for the title of this section of the chapter, 'East Enders go west'.

40   'Mr Wells and Mohammed'. The offending passages can be found in Chapter 43, 'Muhammad and Islam' (*A Short History of the World* (London: Penguin, 1936), p. 137). Wells attributes to Mohammed a 'shifty character', describing him as 'the mind and imagination of primitive Islam' and contrasting him unfavourably with Abu Bekr, whom he describes as Islam's 'conscience and its will' (*ibid.*). Despite the disparaging remarks, however, Wells attests that Islam was still a religion from which much power and inspiration might be derived.

41   'Mr Wells and Mohammed'; BL, IOR, L/PJ/12/614, report by Special Branch of Metropolitan Police, 17 August 1938.

42   '"Down with Wells!" Moslem protest against his book', *Guardian* (19 August 1938), p. 7.

43   BL, IOR, L/PJ/12/614, leaflet for march of protest, 16 August 1938.

44   '"Down with Wells!"'

45   'Mr Wells and Mohammed'; BL, IOR, L/PJ/12/614, note by Feroz Khan Noon, 16 August 1938.

46   BL, IOR, L/PJ/12/614, letter from Government House, Nairobi, Kenya, to Secretary of State for the Colonies, enclosing letter from president of the Anjuman Himayat Islam (East Africa), 29 August 1938; *ibid.*, letter from Home Dept (Special), Sind Secretarial, Karachi, to Home Dept, New Delhi, 15 March 1939. See also further correspondence from Colonial Office, Foreign Office, India Office, and Kismu and Eldoret branches of the Anjuman Himayat Islam, *ibid.*

47   Salman Rushdie, *Joseph Anton* (London: Jonathan Cape, 2012), pp. 112–25.

48   BL, IOR, L/PJ/12/614, memo on deputation, 18 August 1938; *ibid.*, note by Feroz Khan Noon, 16 August 1938.

49   BL, IOR, L/PJ/12/614, letter from Secretary of State to Noon, 24 August 1938.

50   BL, IOR, L/PJ/12/614, letters from Heinemann (9 September 1938) and Penguin (12 September 1938).

51   BL, IOR, L/PJ/7/831, letter from Aftab-ud-Din, Imam, the Shah Jahan mosque, Surrey, 7 May 1935. For a brief discussion of this case, see Prem Chowdhry, *Colonial India and the Making of Empire Cinema* (Manchester: Manchester University Press, 2000), pp. 23–4, 82, 87.

52   BL, IOR, L/I/1/599, correspondence between India Office and Government

of India, December 1935; correspondence between India Office and editor of
Parade, 19–20 February 1941; Raymond Lerouge, 'He put Islam on the map',
Parade, 3:12 (September 1940), 65; correspondence between the Government,
the UK High Commissions in India and Pakistan, and D. de M. Guilfoyle,
Publishing Unit, Central Office of Information, 13–27 May 1948.

53 BL, IOR, L/I/1/599, letter from Guilfoyle to R. I. Hall (Downing Street), 25
May 1948; letter to India Office from editor of *Parade*, 20 February 1941.

54 Madeleine Bunting, 'Religions have the power to bring a passion for social
justice to politics', *Guardian* (12 January 2009), www.guardian.co.uk/
commentisfree/2009/jan/12/madeleine-bunting-religion-social-justice (last
accessed 6 November 2014).

55 *Ibid.*

56 I am very grateful to Maleiha Malik for her comments in response to my
co-authored *Huffington Post* article which helped me to clarify my thinking
on this point.

57 See Introduction, p. 9 nn. 35 and 36.

58 BL, IOR, L/PJ/12/468, 'East London Mosque', 7 October 1943.

59 Ansari, *East London Mosque*, p. 30.

60 Henri Lefebvre, *Writings on Cities*, trans. and ed. Eleonore Kofman and Elizabeth Lebas (Oxford: Blackwell, 1996), ch. 14.

61 BL, IOR, L/PJ/12/468, 'The Jamiat-ul-Muslimin in Great Britain', 30
October 1943; *ibid.*, 'East London Mosque', 14 October 1943.

62 BL, IOR, L/PJ/12/646, 'Indian activities in the United Kingdom', 22 January
1944; *ibid.*, 'Indian Workers' Union', 3 March 1943.

63 BL, IOR, L/PJ/12/645, 'The Indian Workers' Union', 17 December 1942.
Archival evidence underlines the political agency of working-class South
Asians, revealing their refusal of conscription in the Second World War, their
trafficking in black market goods as an anti-colonial gesture, and their strikes
against the conditions of seamen on British ships (*ibid.*, 'The Indian Workers'
Association', 14 April 1942; *ibid.*, 'Indian activities in the United Kingdom',
8 March 1944; *ibid.*, 'The Hindustani Majlis', 1 May 1944; L/PJ/12/658,
'Conscription of Indians resident in Great Britain', 16 February 1944). For a
discussion of working-class South Asian resistances in imperial Britain, see
Rehana Ahmed, 'Networks of resistance: Krishna Menon and working-class
South Asians in Britain', in Rehana Ahmed and Sumita Mukherjee (eds), *South
Asian Resistances in Britain, 1858–1947* (London: Continuum, 2011), pp. 70–87.

64 Anthony Burgess, 'Islam's gangster tactics', *Independent* (16 February 1989).

65 Significantly, Sir Hassan Suhrawardy, who played a key role in the dispute,
was a supporter of the Pakistan National Movement as well as an adviser to
the India Office (Ansari, *East London Mosque*, p. 29). Counter-allegations on
the part of British government officials suggested that the Committee of
Indian Congressmen declared an allegiance to the Indian National Congress
in order to conceal its true support for the pro-Axis Subhas Chandra Bose

(see BL, IOR, L/PJ/12/646, 'Indian note', 15 December 1942; *ibid.*, 'Indian organisations in the United Kingdom', 27 May 1943).

66 BL, IOR, L/PJ/12/468, 'The Jamiat-ul-Muslimin in Great Britain', 30 October 1943.

67 BL, IOR, L/PJ/12/468, 'East London Mosque', 14 October 1943.

68 BL, IOR, L/PJ/12/468, 'East London Mosque', 7 October 1943 (emphasis mine); *ibid.*, 'East London Mosque', 14 October 1943.

69 BL, IOR, L/PJ/12/468, 'The Jamiat-ul-Muslimin in Great Britain', 30 October 1943.

70 BL, IOR, L/PJ/12/468, 'East London Mosque', 7 October 1943; *ibid.*, 'East London Mosque', 14 October 1943.

71 BL, IOR, L/PJ/12/468, extract from Metropolitan Police report, 14 October 1943.

72 Dipesh Chakrabarty, *Provincializing Europe: Postcolonial Thought and Historical Difference* (Princeton and Oxford: Princeton University Press, 2000), pp. 97–113, p. 112.

73 For a discussion of the *Angare* controversy, see Carlo Coppola, 'The All-India Progressive Writers' Association: the European phase', in Carlo Coppola (ed.), *Marxist Influences and South Asian Literature*, vol. 1 (East Lansing: Asian Studies Center, Michigan State University, 1974), pp. 1–34, pp. 1–3; Priyamvada Gopal, *Literary Radicalism in India: Gender, Nation and the Transition to Independence* (Abingdon and New York: Routledge, 2005), ch. 1; Shabana Mahmud, '*Angare* and the founding of the Progressive Writers' Association', *Modern Asian Studies*, 30:2 (1996), 447–67.

74 Sajjad Zaheer, *A Night in London*, trans. Bilal Hashmi (Noida: HarperCollins India, 2011 [1938]). M. K. Gandhi and Jawaharlal Nehru published accounts of student life in imperial Britain, but these are autobiographical rather than novelistic (M. K. Gandhi, *An Autobiography: The Story of my Experiments with Truth* (London: Penguin, 2001 [1927, 1929]); Jawaharlal Nehru, *An Autobiography: Jawaharlal Nehru* (Delhi: Penguin India, 2004 [1936]).

75 Mahmud, '*Angare*', 447.

76 *Ibid.*, 448–50.

77 *Ibid.*, 450–1.

78 Carlo Coppola, 'About the author and his work', in Zaheer, *A Night in London*, n.p.

79 The manifesto was signed by Mulk Raj Anand, Dr K. S. Bhat, Dr J. C. Ghose, Dr S. Sinha, M. D. Taseer, S. S. Zaheer ('Manifesto of the Indian Progressive Writers' Association, London', *Left Review*, 2:5 (February 1936), 240).

80 Coppola, 'The All-India Progressive Writers' Association'.

81 For a discussion of *Indian Writing*, see Rehana Ahmed, 'South Asians writing resistance in wartime London: *Indian Writing* (1940–42)', *Wasafiri*, 27:2 (June 2012), 17–24.

82 Susheila Nasta, 'Negotiating a "new world order": Mulk Raj Anand as public

intellectual at the heart of empire (1924–1945)', in Ahmed and Mukherjee (eds), *South Asian Resistances in Britain, 1858–1947*, pp. 140–60, p. 154.

83 Maleiha Malik, '*Angare*, the "burning embers" of Muslim political resistance: colonial and post-colonial regulation of Islam in Britain', in Marcel Maussen, Veit Bader and Annelies Moors (eds), *Colonial and Post-Colonial Governance of Islam: Continuities and Ruptures* (Amsterdam: IMISCOE Research, Amsterdam University Press, 2011), pp. 199–210, p. 200; Coppola, 'The All-India Progressive Writers' Association', pp. 2–3.

84 Malik, '*Angare*', p. 204.

85 *Ibid.*, p. 205.

86 *Ibid.*, p. 206.

87 My argument here draws partly on an earlier, longer and unpublished draft of Malik's article (copy on file with author).

88 Malik, '*Angare*', p. 208; Coppola, 'The All-India Progressive Writers' Association', pp. 11, 16–17, 20.

89 Sajjad Zaheer, 'Reminiscences', in Sudhi Pradhan (ed.), *Marxist Cultural Movement in India: Chronicles and Documents (1936–47)* (Calcutta: National Book Agency, 1979), pp. 33–47, pp. 39–40.

90 Ahmed, 'Writing resistance'.

91 Zaheer, *Night in London*, pp. 25–8. All subsequent citations are given within the body of the chapter and are to this edition of the text.

92 See Ahmed Ali, 'The Progressive Writers' Movement and creative writers in Urdu', in Coppola, *Marxist Influences and South Asian Literature*, vol. 1, pp. 35–41, p. 36; Ahmed, 'Writing resistance', pp. 21–2.

93 Arthur Bradley and Andrew Tate, *The New Atheist Novel: Fiction, Philosophy and Polemic after 9/11* (London: Continuum, 2010), pp. 10–15.

94 'Foreword', *Islamic Review*, 1:1 (1913), 3.

95 Khwaja Kamaluddin, 'The editor the "Muslim India & Islamic Review" (London), to the members of the All-India Muslim League (Lucknow)', *Islamic Review*, 1:2 (1913), 65–6.

96 Syed Muhammad Siddiq, 'Islam in England', *Islamic Review*, 22:1 (1934), 18, 22; for example, volume 10 (1922).

97 Ansari, '*The Infidel Within*', p. 132.

98 'White wives of brown men: outcasts in the harem', *Islamic Review*, 1:6 (1913), 229–32; S. M. 'Abdullah (Imam), letter reproduced in 'A glance at the world of Islam', *Islamic Review*, 38:6 (1950), 49–50.

99 Abul Hasanat, 'The Islamic purdah or seclusion of women', *Islamic Review*, 22:7 (1934), 237–46; Rahim Bakhsh, 'The attitude of the Qur'an towards the customary veil in Muslim society: in early Muslim society women attended public meetings', *Islamic Review*, 46:7 (1958), 6–8.

100 'Chief distinguishing features of Muslim festivals', *Islamic Review*, 19:3/4 (1931), n.p.; K. S. Ahmed, 'Eid in England', *Islamic Review*, 26:2 (1937), 42–4; Khwaja Nazir Ahmad, 'Islam and socialism', *Islamic Review*, 10:2 (1922),

81–8, and 10:3, 137–44; 'Eid-ul-Azha (1349 AH) at the Mosque, Woking', *Islamic Review*, 19:6 (1931), 217–19; 'The importance and acuteness of the race problem' and 'Christianity and race antagonism', *Islamic Review*, 16:2 (1928), 47–8; Abdul Muntaqim, 'Islam and European civilization', *Islamic Review*, 10:2 (1922), 72–80.

101 Note to subscribers and contributors, *Islamic Review*, 38:1 (1950), 1.

102 See, for example, Muhammad Yakub Khan, 'Religion and politics', *Islamic Review*, 10:10 (1922), 19–22.

103 BL, India Office Collection, MSS Eur F143/80; 'The birthday of the Holy Prophet Muhammad', *Islamic Review*, 22:3 (1934), 69–74.

104 List of contributors, *Islamic Review*, 38:1 (1950), 1.

105 Ansari, '*The Infidel Within*', p. 127.

106 *Ibid.*, pp. 158–9, 152–3.

107 *Ibid.*, pp. 206, 342.

108 *Ibid.*, p. 206.

109 Abdullah Hussein, *Émigré Journeys* (London: Serpent's Tail, 2000).

110 Ansari, '*The Infidel Within*', pp. 210–11, 344–5.

111 *Ibid.*, pp. 343, 235, 178, 211–14.

112 *Ibid.*, p. 344.

113 *Ibid.*, pp. 344–6, 150–1.

114 Kenan Malik, *From Fatwa to Jihad: The Rushdie Affair and its Legacy* (London: Atlantic Books, 2009), p. 39.

115 Sivanandan, *Different Hunger*, p. 23.

116 *Ibid.*, p. 22.

117 *Ibid.*, pp. 15–16, 11.

118 *Ibid.*, p. 40.

119 Ansari, *East London Mosque*, pp. 35–7.

120 Institute of Race Relations, Black History Collection (hereafter IRR, BHC), Periodicals: *Anglo Asian Magazine, Asian Hackney, Asian Post, Asian Voice in Hackney, Asian Youth Association News, Asian Youth News, Bradford Black, Fowaad!, Free the Bradford 12, Indian Worker, Indian Workers Association GB Newsletter, Kala Tara, Liberation Mukti, Mukti, Newham Youth Movement, New Monitor, Newsletter of National Association of Muslim Youth UK, Northern Black, Paikaar*; Malik, *From Fatwa to Jihad*, ch. 2.

121 IRR, BHC, Periodicals: *Free the Bradford 12*, Bulletin of the July 11 Action Committee (1981).

122 See, for example, IRR, BHC, Periodicals: *Indian Workers Association GB Newsletter*, 3 (July/August 1978), 4; *Bradford Black* (July 1978), 4–5, 12.

123 IRR, BHC, *Asian Voice in Hackney*, 2 (January 1983), 3.

124 IRR, BHC, 'Other racial violence campaigns': The Steering Committee of Asian Organisations newsletter (January 1981), 2.

125 IRR, BHC, Periodicals: 'The missing link', *Newsletter of National Association of Muslim Youth UK*, 11 (March 1987), 1–2.

126 IRR, BHC, Periodicals: 'Racism in Britain', *Paikaar*, 1:1 (Winter 1984), 7–8.

127 IRR, BHC, Periodicals: 'The British state and the resistance of black people', *Paikaar*, 2:4 (Autumn 1985), 12–14; 'Black resistance and state funding', *Paikaar*, 3:1/2 (1986), 15–18; 'Activities of PWA (B) in 1983', *Paikaar*, 1:1 (Winter 1984), 9–10, 9.

128 IRR, BHC, Periodicals: 'Racism and Rushdie affair', *Paikaar*, 6:2/3 (1989), 6–10, 10. According to Ansari, the East London Mosque's inability to offer leadership during this period was one reason for the community's organisation along secular lines (*East London Mosque*, pp. 49–50).

129 Malik, *From Fatwa to Jihad*, pp. 49–50, 47, 63.

130 *Ibid.*, p. 52.

131 Modood, *Multicultural Politics*, p. 30.

132 *Ibid.*, p. 32.

133 *Ibid.*, p. 108.

134 Malik, *From Fatwa to Jihad*, p. 59.

2

Anti-racism, liberalism and class in *The Satanic Verses* and the Rushdie affair

Even in Europe and the United States, the stormtroopers of various 'sensitivities' seek to limit our freedom of speech. It has never been more important to continue to defend those values which make the art of literature possible. (Salman Rushdie[1])

It is surely not Muslims alone who oppose the libertarianism which sees the artist as a Nietzschean *ubermensch*, towering above conventional morality with perfect liberty to publish imaginative explorations regardless of social consequences. For, indeed, the artist without social responsibility who provokes anger instead of dialogue threatens the field of discourse itself. (Tariq Modood[2])

'FIGHT RACISM, NOT RUSHDIE': THE *SATANIC VERSES* CONTROVERSY

The *Satanic Verses* controversy has been described as a transitional event for Britain's South Asian Muslim minority. Their protest against the novel's publication, operating alongside (and often conflated with) Ayatollah Khomeini's fatwa and closely succeeded by the First Gulf War and further British Muslim anger, led to their 'dramatic visibilization' within the public sphere.[3] This protest must be contextualised within an extended socio-historical narrative. As Yunus Samad shows, the British Muslim protest against the novel was fiercer and more prolonged in the west Yorkshire city of Bradford than anywhere else in the UK, including London, which was, at the time, home to some sixty thousand Bangladeshi Muslims.[4] He locates a reason for the uneven geography of the protest and its concentration in Bradford in the specificities of the city's social history of the late 1970s and the 1980s: the exacerbation of Asian–white antagonisms that resulted from the widespread unemployment after the 1977 recession; the subsequent increase in the activities of the British National Party and the National Front within the town; the trial and subsequent acquittal of the Bradford Twelve in 1981; the halal meat controversy in 1984; and the Honeyford affair shortly afterwards in 1984–85. The latter was particularly divisive, entrenching the isolation of the Pakistani Muslim community (whose origins lie predominantly in the Kashmiri district of Mirpur) from the white majority.[5] Thus the anti-Rushdie agitation is presented as the culmination of a chain of social and racial antagonisms, as well as a product of religious sensitivities.

Illuminating here is Samad's description of the anger of Bradford's Mirpuri youth at the publication of *The Satanic Verses* in the wake of the Honeyford affair:

> It was the perception that they were again humiliated which was responsible for making religious consciousness dominant over other identities. But there was no increase in religiosity and restaurants still served alcohol and attendance for prayer in the mosques remained thin … The youth were resorting to Islamic idioms and metaphors to express their discontent against society which refused to accept them on an equal footing. Symbolically this was epitomised by their exclusion from the Yorkshire Cricket Club, despite being excellent cricketers who were born and bred in Bradford.[6]

This account sheds light on the dialectical relationship between class, race and religious affiliation. The manifestation of their anger in 'Islamic idioms and metaphors' is a product not of their Islamic piety but of their sense of oppression *as Muslims*. It is not just that the dimensions of the antagonism must be seen as social and racial as well as religious, as Samad shows, but that these dimensions cannot be conveniently separated. The distinction between Islam as a personal, private faith and Islamism as a political ideology – a distinction that is reiterated by Rushdie in his essays and journalism and that is current among cultural commentators across the political spectrum – is thus exposed as problematic.[7] There is a strong probability that Muslim identity will become politicised and enter the public sphere when it is under attack, and this politicisation is not necessarily the same as Islamism.

On the larger scale of Britain as a whole, the poverty of South Asian Muslim communities at the time of the affair and during the preceding years also serves to highlight the interconnection of class and religious affiliation and the significant class dimension of the protest. Modood writes that

Throughout the 1980s, of the nine non-white groups identified in the Labour Force Survey, Pakistanis and Bangladeshis have suffered the highest rates of unemployment, have the lowest number of educational qualifications and the highest profile in manual work; and this is true in each respect not just for women but also men, and not just for the middle-aged (the first generation) but also the young.[8]

These facts suggest that if, as Samad argues, it was the local history of Bradford which led to the heightened tensions there at the time of the Rushdie affair, this local politics was also partly symptomatic of structures of disadvantage that operated on a much broader scale. Further, the recorded rise in prejudice against Asians, as opposed to Afro-Caribbeans, during the 1980s suggests the increasing centrality of cultural and religious practices to racism in Britain at the time, underlining the vulnerability of South Asian Muslims in Britain and reconfiguring the protest as part of a multi-faceted anti-racist struggle.[9] Hanif Kureishi, in his 1986 essay 'Bradford', configures the city as a microcosm of multicultural Britain. For him, the events of the preceding years made Bradford a place that had to be seen 'because it seemed that so many important issues of race, culture, nationalism, and education, were evident in an extremely concentrated way … These were issues that related to the whole notion of what it was to be British and what that would mean in the future. Bradford seemed to be a microcosm of a larger British society that was struggling to find a sense of itself.'[10] Kureishi's comments here are prescient: many of the issues he explores in the essay were to become prominent on a national level in subsequent decades, in particular the so-called segregation of working-class Muslim communities and their primary identification in terms of their faith. His clear discomfort with the community's mobilisation for a public recognition of their faith (discussed in Chapter 3) points to the tensions that were to come to the fore during the Rushdie affair. Further, the antagonism shown by one of the actively anti-racist Bradford Twelve towards Kureishi because of his controversial film *My Beautiful Laundrette*,[11] which some British Pakistanis perceived as a denigrating representation of their culture,[12] gestures towards the gaps within and fracturing of a 'universal' anti-racism that became starkly visible during the controversy.

This fracturing is evident in the city's Community Relations Council's ambivalent response to the protest against *The Satanic Verses*. When Bradford's Council for Mosques asked the CRC to support the protest, the CRC was, as Philip Lewis writes, 'caught in a dilemma: Salman Rushdie was respected for his views on anti-racism and his written and video materials were widely used'.[13] They therefore decided to remain neutral, justifying this decision by claiming that since 'the specific issues relating to the concerns of the Muslim community ... are of a religious nature ... the best people to represent [their] concerns ... are the properly constituted religious organizations in the city'.[14] But, as Lewis points out, this position was in contradiction to their open support for the Council for Mosques on the provision of halal meat in schools – also an issue of a 'religious nature'. Whereas the halal meat controversy hinted at the limits of a secularist liberal anti-racism by raising the issue of religious rights, the Rushdie affair threw into sharp relief its limits and contradictions by positioning a committed and vocal anti-racist against a racialised and particularly vulnerable minority group (and one to which Rushdie is affiliated). Liberal commentators resolved this contradiction either by denouncing the protesters as misguided, ignorant or even barbaric ('illiberal', in short), or, at the very best, with the exhortation 'Fight racism, not Rushdie', thereby demonstrating their 'desire to be on the same side as the Muslims' and simultaneous failure to allow a minority group to define their oppression according to how they experienced it.[15]

This tension became particularly prominent over a decade later, in the wake of the 2001 race riots in Bradford, Burnley and Oldham as well as 9/11, when a number of left-wing commentators with anti-racist credentials denounced multiculturalism as the cause of 'self-segregation' and divisions and dissent between communities.[16] Kenan Malik roots the protest as well as more recent events, such as the 2005 clashes between Afro-Caribbeans and Asians in Lozells, Birmingham, in policies that recognise and support collective minority cultural identities.[17] For Malik, multiculturalism 'created' a Muslim community and detached it from majoritarian Britain, eventually leading to the radicalisation of Muslim youth. In his thesis, racism becomes an effect of multiculturalism rather than one cause of the formation of so-called segregated communities. Further, while anti-racist activism (including 'opposing discrimination in the workplace, organisation against racist attacks, preventing deportations and ending political brutality') is political, 'religious and cultural issues' (faith schools, the provision of halal meat in schools, and the protest against Rushdie's novel) are not.[18] This problematic distinction underpins Polly Toynbee's response to the 2005 proposals for the incitement to religious hatred bill: 'Race is something people cannot choose and it defines nothing about them as people. But beliefs are what people choose to identify with: in the rough and tumble of argument to call people stupid for their beliefs is legitimate (if perhaps unwise), but to brand them stupid on account of their race is a mortal insult.'[19] Toynbee's stark polarisation of 'race' and 'beliefs' is predicated on an erroneous and outdated understanding of racism as focused uniquely on colour rather than culture. Her flawed attempt to maintain this distinction is necessitated by a liberalism that requires a problematic combination of anti-racism with a valorisation of the individual. An engagement with colour racism does not threaten the status of the individual ('race defines nothing about [people] as people'), whereas an engagement with cultural racism entails a recognition of the collective and potentially of values that stand opposed to liberalism. Hence Toynbee's rejection of the very idea of Islamophobia, which is echoed by Rushdie himself who declares it a word that has been created 'to help the blind remain blind' and, like Toynbee, differentiates between 'a race' and 'a religion' on the grounds that the latter is no more than 'an idea'.[20] Hence also the general discomfort felt by the liberal left, including Malik and Rushdie, at the gradual erosion of the alliance between Afro-Caribbeans and Asians over the last decade or so of the twentieth century,[21] an erosion that was precipitated or at least exacerbated by *The Satanic Verses* itself, which, with its perceived attack on 'communal symbols', worked to separate 'Muslims as a community of suffering from the "Black" community'.[22]

In his essay 'Sport' (2000), Rushdie elaborates on his understanding of the term 'culture': 'Culture is what we now have instead of ideology. We live in an age of culture wars, of groups using ever narrower self-definitions of culture both as a shield and a sword. Culture is touchy. Use the wrong word and you'll be accused of racism by some cultural commissar or other.'[23] As well as dismissing the place of culture within racism here, Rushdie goes on to counterpose 'culture' to 'something else, something to do with art, imagination, education and ethics ... which enables us to see beyond national stereotypes to the richer complexity of real life'.[24] This polarisation of culture as art and culture as rules finds an echo in Mahmood Mamdani's critique of the two-fold application of the word that underpins imperialist constructions of the world:

> Is our world really divided into two, so that one part makes culture and the other is a prisoner of culture? Are there really two meanings of culture? Does culture stand for creativity, for what being human is all about, in one part of the world? But in the other part of the world, it stands for habit, for some kind of instinctive activity, whose rules are inscribed in early founding texts, usually religious, and museumized in early artefacts?[25]

Mamdani goes on to explain that this polarised understanding of culture is predicated on a refusal to understand the actions of those who inhabit the 'other part of the world' as deriving from concrete historical experiences of oppression or injustice. The binary opposition between creativity and rules that underpins Rushdie's understanding of the world can be similarly deconstructed through an understanding of narrow 'self-definitions of culture' as a function of subordination and resistance. Rushdie's working-class British Muslim opponents can then be rescued from his militaristic metaphors (especially that of 'stormtroopers', with its added twist of Nazism) through an understanding of their need to protect their rule-bound faith and culture within Britain. The 'free' artist's position (Rushdie's) can also be understood as predicated on a set of 'rules'– those of a liberal individualism, which sutures the notion of universal freedom to its particular ideological understanding of freedom.[26]

As Anshuman A. Mondal writes, 'while liberal rhetoric during the controversy positioned itself as a defender of fragile freedoms by speaking truth to power, the blithe dismissal of all Muslim objections (not just the fatwa) was, in fact, a performance of its actual cultural hegemony'.[27] It was the working-class British Muslim objection in particular that unsettled liberalism's self-positioning as 'speaking truth to power'. It is not insignificant, then, that in his many speeches, letters and articles written during the fatwa, Rushdie turns repeatedly to the issue of artistic freedom, but rarely with reference to the British protest against his novel. Of course the British protest may not have been such a source of preoccupation for him as it did not constitute a threat to his life, but there are moments in his writings where its absence is suggestive of its awkward refusal to fit his reductive binary configuration of freedom and censorship. For example, in his 1989 interview for *Bandung File*, when asked if he thought 'the opposition to the book [was] based on people feeling weak or feeling strong', a question which would seem to imply the vulnerable British Muslim minority, Rushdie avoids any mention of the latter, focusing instead on Islam as a whole (thereby despatialising the religion) and the general need to dissent from orthodoxy. Britain does appear in his response, but only in the form of 'Conservative politics', one of the orthodoxies that he is keen to dismantle, so that he retains a comfortably subordinate and oppositional position.[28] The notion of dissent from the orthodoxy of free speech (a possible description of the British-based anti-Rushdie agitation) can have no place within Rushdie's vision. In *Joseph Anton*, the narrator articulates explicitly the awkward fit of working-class protest in such a schema, quoting the South African writer Paul Trewhela's description of the campaign against the novel as a 'bursting forth of mass popular irrationalism', and alerting the reader to the difficult questions this poses for the left: 'how should one react when the masses were being irrational? Could "the people" ever be, quite simply, wrong?' Yet he follows this with a swift dismissal of those writers 'for whom the idea that the masses could be wrong was unpalatable' (John Berger, John le Carré and Germaine Greer) (124), and moves on to equate the Bradford book-burnings with the Nazi book-burnings in Hitler's Germany (128–9). This is just one example of several in the memoir where the power asymmetries of the British protests are swallowed up in the reductive construction of art as a 'counterweight to power' (78), and victimhood is reversed, becoming the prerogative of the beleaguered artist (117, 120, 188).[29] The censorship of writers in Islamic states also recurs throughout Rushdie's writing, reinforcing the equation of censorship with the powerful state and art with the disempowered.[30] Again, the inversion of these equations in the British context is not considered. Mobilisation in the name of a religion is detemporalised as well as despatialised, moreover. According to Rushdie, religion enters the public and political domain by choice and not as a consequence of power dynamics; indeed, the quest for power becomes a consequence of religion as such: '[religions] continue to emerge from the world of private life, where they belong ... and to bid for power', he writes.[31]

Rushdie's recurrent reduction of the opposition to his novel and artistic freedom in general to homogenising notions of 'Islam', 'orthodoxy', 'fundamentalism', 'policemen', 'Thought Police' and 'totalitarianism' and his near-silence on the British-based protest are also indicative of the awkward position that working-class collective protest occupies in liberal thought more generally.[32] Central to Noam Chomsky's *Objectivity and Liberal Scholarship* is a critique of liberal intellectuals' view that 'the masses are "objects, incapable of political expression or allegiance, to be 'controlled' by one side or the other"'.[33] Anthony Burgess articulates this vision in his understanding of the British-based protest: 'I gain the impression that few of the protesting Muslims in Britain know directly what they are protesting against. Their Imams have told them that Mr Rushdie has published a blasphemous book and must be punished. They respond with sheeplike docility and wolflike aggression.'[34] The contradictory combination of 'docility' and 'aggression' in representations of South Asian men has a history, as shown in Chapter 1. But the representation of the British Muslim dissenters as unable to think for themselves, gullible sheep under the spell of evil Imams – repeated in *Joseph Anton* where they are described as 'Bradford clowns' and 'cater-wauling … murderous children' – is also symptomatic of the failure of liberal commentators to recognise mass protest (184, 441). Dictators and totalitarianism are a requirement of neoliberalism – its necessary evil. Slavoj Žižek's reconfiguration of fundamentalisms as a *function* of liberal capitalism's 'postpolitical' foreclosure of dissent, which forces capitalism's exclusions into extreme positions, is a crucial corrective to this individu-alising ideology.[35] The dissent of Rushdie's protesters can then be seen as an effect of a limited liberal pluralism, which, by configuring them as illiberal and illegitimate in order to present itself as neutral, forced their difference into extreme forms of opposition (book-burning, expressions of support for Khomeini's fatwa). Rushdie's British dissenters are liberal capitalism's 'symptom', its necessary outside.[36]

THE *SATANIC VERSES* AND MULTICULTURAL POLITICS

My reading of *The Satanic Verses* argues that the novel carries illumi-nating traces of the tensions of British multiculturalism that have become increasingly visible over the last twenty-five years. I am aware that by critiquing a 1988 novel in the context of a set of social and cultural antag-onisms that were made visible by the dissent that it provoked and that are increasingly visible today I run the risk of 'presentism'. However, my contention is that the protest was symptomatic of ideological tensions that already existed in British society. To argue that these tensions are in fact present in a repressed form within the novel itself is, then, simply to consider *The Satanic Verses* as necessarily imbued by its social condi-tions of production, or as a 'worldly' text.[37] Reading the text and context together can productively illuminate complexities both in the textual representation of multicultural Britain and in multicultural Britain itself. In going beyond the literary text to the social or historical, I bring out the absences or silences which are structural to or constitutive of the novel's manifest speech. Pierre Macherey suggests that such a reading will reveal 'the reverse side of what is written [as] history itself'.[38] In the light of this, I reveal the protest against the novel as it transpired within Britain to be the 'reverse side' of the novel, a presence within the novel in its very absence. As Aijaz Ahmad says of Rushdie's earlier novel *Shame*, 'Rushdie has so often declared himself a socialist of sorts that it is both legitimate and necessary to see what this book might look like if we were to read it from the standpoint of – no, not socialism, simply some determinate energies of an emancipatory project.'[39] In this sense, then, considered in the context of his leftist, anti-racist non-fiction and journalism of the 1980s, Rushdie's novel invites a reading that positions social justice at its centre. I consider class as a 'structuring absence' or silence in *The Satanic Verses*, and the Rushdie affair as a means of 'mak[ing] this silence speak'.[40]

In their reading of *The Satanic Verses*, Graham Huggan and Tobias Wachinger declare the novel's Brickhall immigrant community 'impoverished'.[41] Yet the majority of the members of this community do not fit this description. Muhammad Sufyan is a highly educated former teacher. Despite his professional demotion on migration to Britain, as the owner of the Shaandaar restaurant and bed and breakfast he is (with the help of his ruthlessly exploitative wife) a successful businessman. Jumpy Joshi is a well-educated martial arts instructor and college friend of Saladin's, and Hanif Johnson is a lawyer ('a local boy done good'[42]). The only obviously impoverished immigrants in the novel are those who are lodging in the Shaandaar as 'guests' of the local council. They are nameless, faceless and silent. Like Mrs Karim and her daughter and son, victims of the 'unimportant fire' in a Camden bed and breakfast and silent protagonists of one of Rushdie's earlier essays, they have no chance of escape: they cannot scream (they have 'no mouths' (463)).[43] But while these anonymous, silenced beings may be the only glimpse that the novel offers us of Britain's underclass or capitalism's 'symptom', the latter does emerge, no longer silent, beyond the text at the point of the novel's reception – not in Rushdie's fictional Brickhall but in the city of Bradford. The silencing of such voices (working class, Muslim and potentially challenging to the 'end-of-ideology' ideologies of an 'unreconstructed liberalism'[44]) is necessary to the novel's 'speech'.[45] Reading for the silencing of class as dissent reveals the novel's liberalism and the limits of this liberalism for an anti-racist politics.

Further, a focus on the obvious parallels between the protest and the Jahilia, Imam and Titlipur strands of the novel reveals the absences and contradictions within the remainder of the novel, set in contemporary multicultural Britain. As Michael Gorra, among others, has pointed out, the novel anticipates the global Islamic response to it in many instances.[46] One of the most striking examples of this is the prescience of the exhortation of Bilal X, the exiled Imam's muezzin, to the people of 'Desh' via radio broadcast: 'Burn the books and trust the Book; shred the papers and hear the Word' (211). As well as anticipating the protest and the paradigm through which the affair was interpreted (books versus Book, words versus Word), these words also capture from within the space of London the central theme of the Jahilia parts of the novel. Thus the London-based Imam can be aligned with Jahilia's Mahound as well as with Khomeini and his fatwa beyond the space of the text. The figure of Ayesha and her pilgrimage, located in twentieth-century India, also symbolise a religious absolutism that resonates with the Imam and Mahound as well as the Islamic protest against the novel. Ostensibly, they can then be counterposed to the diversity and chaos of Brickhall and to Rushdie and his supporters as creative artists and thinkers, determinedly unconstrained, as well as to Salman the Persian's blasphemous corruption of the prophet's revelation and to the transgressive poet Baal. Yet, just as an understanding of the protest that foregrounds class undoes a simplistic binary of absolutism versus pluralism, so too the representation of multicultural Britain in Rushdie's novel is more complex than this paradigm would allow. The tension between the anti-racist narrative that forms the central focus of the Brickhall narrative and the conflicting requirements of a limited liberalism, which I explore below, requires a number of strategic displacements in the novel including the displacement of a binary of absolutism/collective versus uncertainty/individual, which occupies an uneasy relationship with the anti-racist narrative core of the Britain-based strand, onto the ancient and distant space of Jahilia, the enclosed space of the exiled Imam's Kensington apartment, and a religious pilgrimage in India.

Talal Asad suggests that Salman the Persian's reference to Islam's regulation on the slaughter of animals (part of his diatribe against the rules of Islam) would, for British readers, recall the various halal meat controversies that had taken place over the previous two decades (363–4). He mentions the notorious media campaign of 1984 against this Islamic practice and the consequent government commission which recommended that halal slaughter be rendered illegal.[47] For Asad, the presence of this particular detail within the Jahilia strand of *The Satanic Verses* is an oblique sneer directed by Rushdie at Britain's Muslims.[48] Leaving aside Rushdie's intentions here, an effect of this interpellation of a highly sensitive issue within contemporary Britain from a location that is distanced both spatially and temporally (Jahilia) is to reveal the contrasting absence of such an issue within the contemporary British space of the novel (Brickhall). Similarly, the issue of sexual segregation appears in the Jahilia strand of the novel (in Salman's diatribe against 'Submission', and in the 'brothel' episode which culminates in the showdown between poet and prophet and finally the death of the poet (366–7, 376–92)), interpellating western conceptions about the treatment of women in Islam generally, as well as the more specific hijab debate that has become such a politically sensitive issue in Europe in recent years. A revealing – and revealingly tenuous – link between Jahilia/Britain-beyond-the-text and Brickhall or Britain-within-the-text can, however, be glimpsed in this instance. Gibreel Farishta, delusional and plagued by jealousy, tells Saladin Chamcha of his lover Allie: 'She is a very private person, the most private person in the world. We have to protect her from lust' (436). In the context of Gibreel's archangel fantasies and his will to 'redeem' London, eradicating the city's sin and instituting instead the Word of God, the link between his behaviour towards Allie and western understandings of Islamic gender relations becomes apparent while also remaining somewhat elliptical. Similarly, Gibreel's donning of a burqa before his return to the stage in London references debates surrounding Muslim women's clothing but in a safely satirical manner (350). Thus, the issue of sexual segregation (and the binary of rules versus freedom) is present within contemporary Britain but in a transfigured, elliptical or comedic form, displaced onto the elite and mad figure of Gibreel. Issues that are at the centre of minority cultural politics in Britain are present in the narrative at a safe remove. They represent the point at which minority rights potentially clash with liberalism: mobilisation in the name of a religious faith by an oppressed minority group for the right to practise their radical cultural difference within the public sphere disturbs the central tenets of a secularist liberalism.

The point at which the Jahilia narrative does resonate strongly with the London narrative is in the Imam's story, which is significantly discrete, almost constituting a separate space in so far as it enters the narrative through Gibreel's dreams and only seems to connect with the other British narratives through its location (205–15). While this episode is a somewhat odd, disjunctive presence in Britain, it is also one that is determinate and necessary. Through this privileged, isolated and temporary figure, and his confinement to private space, radical dissent can be displaced from contemporary multicultural Britain onto the margin.[49] Further, such a displacement onto the Imam allows the significance of a religious identity for minorities in Britain to remain detached from class. It can therefore be dismissed as irrational or extreme, foreclosing any threat to the interests of liberalism while also enabling an anti-racist narrative to form a core theme of the novel. Liberalism permits, or even requires, Khomeini's presence in the Britain-based narrative, but disallows that of the Bradford protesters, which would threaten its interests by introducing the issue of class.

The tension between an anti-racist politics and liberalism that so disturbed Bradford's Community Relations Council lies at the heart of the Brickhall strand of *The Satanic Verses*. Perhaps influenced by Rushdie's own defensive analysis of *The Satanic Verses* in 'In good faith', or indeed the many analyses of the affair in terms of the binary of religious purity/ absolutism versus secular hybridity/doubt, critics have read the novel's two protagonists as emblematising the different sides of this binary. In such a reading, Gibreel Farishta, 'an untranslated man', becomes the voice of absolutist religious fervour and rigid resistance to change, while Saladin Chamcha, 'a creature of selected discontinuities', is aligned with flexibility, change and secularist doubt (427). When this somewhat reductive opposition is considered both in the context of Rushdie's own denouncement of the concept of the 'Pure' (particularly when it takes the form of religious faith) and advocacy of 'melange' and doubt, and in the context of the novel's conclusion which sees Gibreel driven to murder and suicide and Saladin find love, reconciliation and the possibility of self-fulfilment, it suggests a reading of Gibreel as 'bad migrant' and Saladin as 'good migrant' (394). Following this logic, Saladin becomes an idealised figure of 'hybrid' Britain and a vehicle through which 'newness' can 'enter the world'. Of course Saladin's overt Anglophilia, which leans towards an imperialistic nationalism (typified by his support for Margaret Thatcher's imperialistic battle for the Falkland Islands) and a racist view of 'his own people', would immediately problematise such a reading (257, 268). But this obstacle can be circumvented by configuring Saladin's trajectory in the novel as a process of learning.[50] By this analysis, Saladin's grotesque physical transformation and his consequent residence among the immigrant community of Brickhall effect a positive change in him: he learns to like 'his own people' and comes to terms with the 'Indianness' that he has tried so hard to shed.

Yet both Saladin and his counterpart Gibreel play more contradictory roles in the novel as a whole than such a reading would allow. Far from participating in community life, as John Clement Ball maintains, Saladin remains largely indifferent to his hosts and to the regulars and other inhabitants at the Shaandaar Café and lodgings. Indeed, it is his observer status that is foregrounded both when he looks down at the 'Street' from the confines of his attic room and when he voyeuristically and cynically dissects the community meeting that he attends after his return to human form (283–4, 412–16). Back in gentrified Notting Hill, his mounting unease is a product not of a newfound respect for the community that nurtured him in his goatish form or a recognition of the hollowness and hypocrisy of the ultra-English life he had carved out for himself, but of a yearning for revenge on the man he believes to be responsible for his arrest by the immigration police and subsequent misfortunes (417–19). His unlikely return to the community for a meeting in which inhabitants of Brickhall discuss and mobilise against the wrongful arrest of black activist Uhuru Simba is configured predominantly as a product of his desire for Mishal Sufyan (412). His heroic but failed attempt to save his former hosts Muhammad and Hind Sufyan from the fire at the Shaandaar could be read as a delayed gesture of gratitude and recognition of 'his own people'. But the text also suggests a rather different interpretation as we are told that Saladin's 'humanity is sufficient form and explanation for his deed'. This 'human' explanation is reinforced with the words '"Mishal! Sufyan! Hind!" cries evil Mr Chamcha' (466). An absolutist notion of 'evil' is deconstructed as the monstrous persona of revenge-filled Saladin is offset by his compassionate cries and heroic act. Rather than suggesting a narrative of progress from a yearning to inhabit a 'ye-olde dream-England' to a reconciliation to the 'fluid space of a demographically transformed metropolis' on the part of Saladin, this incident implies a generalised and liberal notion of the flawed individual, or the imperfect human being (180). And it is of course this humanist notion that many critics have located at the centre of the novel's controversial representation of the Prophet, whose moment of doubt when offered the temptation of compromise in the form of the 'satanic verses' is read as an assertion of his humanity and as consistent with the novel's 'faith in man as the source of rational creativity', thereby suggesting the possibility of a 'liberal, more "open" Islam'.[51]

If the Brickhall community does not function as a means of reacquainting Saladin with his Indianness, then how does the story of its inhabitants – specifically that of their struggle against Thatcher's racist state and its apparatus – relate to the stories of Saladin and Gibreel? Why route Saladin's trajectory through the Brickhall community? I would suggest that Saladin's ambiguous relationship with the Brickhall community is symptomatic of the narrative's simultaneous engagement and disengagement with the politics of race in Britain. The narrative does suggest a link between Saladin's residency in the Shaandaar and his eventual reconciliation to his cultural heritage but it is a tenuous and ill-fitting link – and it is this that is revealing. Saladin himself sets up this link when he first finds himself at the Shaandaar: 'What mean small-mindedness was this, to cast him back into the bosom of *his people*, from whom he'd felt so distant for so long! – Here thoughts of Zeeny Vakil welled up, and guiltily, nervously, he forced them down again' (257). Here, the Asian community with which he reluctantly finds himself identified is associated with Zeeny Vakil in India. This uneasy association of an East End British Asian community with India is sharply ironised when the Sufyan daughters Mishal and Anahita remind Saladin that, like him, they too are British (259). Yet the two spaces remain tenuously linked through their mutual opposition to Saladin's monocultural construction of Britishness, while Saladin's 'pluralisation' ultimately involves a return to India rather than an engagement with multicultural Britain. In this sense, India seems to stand in for multicultural Britain and to serve as a means of averting an engagement with a minority community or collective in Britain. As long as Saladin is a victim of the racist state he can remain an individual (against the categories they construct for him) and within the limits of liberalism; but for him to identify or engage with a collective against the racist state and thereby attain fulfilment would be for the narrative to step beyond these limits. The narrative must then maintain an uneasy link between the spaces of Brickhall and India in order to attempt to resolve its own contradictions. Liberal humanism and anti-racism are combined and in tension.

The narrative foregrounds the tension between a politicised collective response to Saladin's predicament and Saladin's own personalised response. His Brickhall allies, for whom his transformation is a materialisation of the racist abuse he has suffered, wish to claim him as an icon for the struggle against racial oppression. Mishal Sufyan, alerting him to the fact that he has now become a hero for the community, tells him: 'It's time you considered action' (287). She is referring to political action, but when Saladin's anger reaches its climax and he insists on leaving the Shaandaar to seek out Gibreel, he repeats the phrase to refer to the personal, individual action that he intends to take against his enemy (291). In similar vein, Hanif Johnson tells Saladin, the reluctant 'race-hero': 'You've got to realize how important you could be for us, there's more at stake here than your personal needs' (295–6). While constantly referencing this

politicised construction of Saladin's trajectory, the narrative simultaneously constructs a decidedly personal narrative for Saladin's metamor-
phoses. It is by becoming angry and refusing to accept his predicament
that Saladin regains his human form, yet his rage seems clearly focused
on Gibreel and the latter's failure to speak out and prevent Saladin's arrest
(294). The individualisation of Saladin's hatred, moreover, is captured by
the image of the hot breath of his anger melting all of the waxworks at
the Club Hot Wax so that the community's enemies (Thatcher, Enoch
Powell, Oswald Mosley) and its 'race-heroes' (Ignatius Sancho, Mary
Seacole, Grace Jones) merge: racist oppression and anti-racist resistance
become one and in place of this opposition there emerges a binary of
Saladin's individualised anger versus the collectives on which both racism
and anti-racism depend (292–4).

A focus on Saladin's counterpart Gibreel reveals a similar ambiguity.
While the absolutist zeal with which he attempts to redeem the city from
its sins in his archangel persona is aligned with a religious extremism
which is critiqued in the Jahilia and Ayesha strands of the novel and which
Rushdie would surely condemn, an interpretation of Gibreel simply as
'bad migrant' is problematic. For Gibreel is identified with an anti-racist
position as well as with religious zeal. While Saladin is drawn to the 'faded
grandeur' of the metropolis, Gibreel, by contrast, sees 'a wreck, a Crusoe-
city, marooned on the island of its past, and trying, with the help of a
Man-Friday underclass, to keep up appearances' (439). Gibreel's refusal
to be impressed by the ex-colonial power could be traced to his sense of
superiority as a Bollywood star, yet the politicised allusions to Britain's
continued adherence to its imperial past and its hypocritical dependence
on a black labour force suggest an overtly anti-colonial, oppositional
position at odds with Gibreel's uneducated, naive and indulged persona.
Similarly, while Gibreel's wish to tropicalise and 'redeem' London, whose
lack of clarity and 'truth' he deplores, is aligned with absolutism, the
city's ambiguity and mutability, appreciated by Saladin, are not simply
valorised but identified also with a lack of substance, a subordination
of meaning and value to commodification, combined with a nostalgic
yearning for an imperial past (320). Gibreel's vision of a tropicalised
London, moreover, incorporates, alongside 'increased moral definition'
and 'religious fervour', such elements as a 'renewal of interest in the intelligentsia … Emergence of new social values: friends to commence drop-
ping in on one another without making appointments, closure of old
folks' homes, emphasis on the extended family' (355). These social values

suggest a critique of the reification of human life under late capitalism and thus of Thatcherism on the part of the novel. The construction of Gibreel – like that of Saladin – is characterised by ambiguity, and this ambiguity, valorised in and of itself in the novel, occludes an ideological contradiction: that between a liberal individualism which would label Gibreel's position as 'illiberal' and an anti-racism which relies on the idea of the collective and on the grand narratives in which Gibreel is caught.

Uncertainty and ambiguity are highlighted through the two protagonists whose contradictions challenge the reader's interpretative certainties. Not only do both protagonists embody similar ideological contradictions, but the polar opposites that they appear to represent – angel and devil, good and evil, right and wrong, even black and white – are constantly conflated and confused. The two are 'forever joined ... their arms locked around one another's bodies, mouth to mouth, head to tail, as when they fell to earth' (353). They are one another's mirror image, adversaries that reflect each other (458). Indeed, the narrative suggests that it is through the conflation of their apparent oppositeness that the potential for love could emerge as each challenges the other's absolutism, and 'pluralism' results. When Gibreel is faced with the option of leaving his enemy to die in the burning Shaandaar or rescuing him, thereby compromising his absolutism, his choice to carry him to safety (their bodies significantly conjoined) is described as a 'small redeeming victory for love'. Gibreel's act of humanity, moreover, mirrors Saladin's attempted rescue of the Sufyans, thereby emphasising their conjoined status. This conjoining, compromise and humanity is then directly contrasted to the 'war ... enmity and rage' of the riots (468). The humanist discourse cannot countenance collectivity and oppositionality – and must therefore ultimately delegitimise communal resistance. Despite this paralleling of the two protagonists, however, there is a growing implication that it is Saladin who will in the end be the novel's 'hero'. As the final Brickhall section of the novel draws to a close, Saladin's weapon against Gibreel takes the form of poetry: cruel rhyming verses displaying an intimate knowledge of Allie and recited by Saladin in the guise of an adulterer (443–6). The characterisation of Saladin as poet in opposition to Gibreel's prophet clearly echoes the binary of poet versus prophet that underpins the Jahilia narrative. Here, Baal the poet (along with Salman the scribe, another artist in so far as he alters the Word of God with profane words of his own imagining) symbolises freedom of expression and transgression and is clearly opposed to the Prophet with his absolutist 'rules, rules, rules'

(363–8).[52] It is significant that Saladin's valorisation becomes more explicit through this paralleling with the Jahilia narrative, where the binary of individual secularist freedom versus religious oppression is located in a remote time and place, far from multicultural Britain where it would potentially threaten the anti-racist narrative. There is a double layer of contradiction and resolution in Rushdie's novel: first, class antagonisms, or the contradictions of capitalism, are contained and resolved through a liberal discourse that valorises ambiguity, uncertainty and freedom from categories; second, the contradictions between liberalism and anti-racism are resolved by strategic displacements.

Perhaps the most striking displacement in *The Satanic Verses* is a physical one – that of the novel's ending from Britain to India where the dangers of religious communalism can be exposed without further compromising the anti-racist, counter-hegemonic thrust of the Britain-based narrative. In India, the fallout of religious clashes has been particularly stark. Especially at the time of the novel's publication, the place names Meerut and Gujarat were almost metonymic of communal violence, with riots tearing each of the cities apart in the 1980s.[53] In the final part of *The Satanic Verses*, when Saladin is leafing through newspapers and magazines on his flight 'home' to India, an image of the Meerut massacre catches his eye, along with various related articles featuring 'Islamic fundamentalists' and an opportunist Imam:

> Communalism, sectarian tension, was omnipresent: as if the gods were going to war. In the eternal struggle between the world's beauty and its cruelty, cruelty was gaining ground by the day ... 'Fact is,' [Sisodia] said without any of his usual bonhomie, 'religious fafaith, which encodes the highest ass ass aspirations of human race, is now, in our cocountry, the servant of lowest instincts, and gogo God is the creature of evil.' (518)

This focus on secularism versus communalism continues shortly afterwards: Saladin meets Zeeny's friends, all of whom are differently involved in the struggle against religious extremism, and the oppressive power of religion in mainstream Indian culture is once again highlighted (536–7). Interestingly, here, as in responses to the *Satanic Verses* controversy, class plays an unsettling role, fleetingly disturbing a simple alignment of religion with power. In response to Swatilekha's denouncement of all grand narratives, including religion, the Marxist poet Bhupen Gandhi declares: 'We can't deny the ubiquity of faith. If we write in such a way as to pre-judge such belief as in some way deluded or false, then are we not guilty of elitism, of imposing our world-view on the masses?' This disturbance is swiftly dismissed, however, by Swatilekha's confident assertion that 'Battles lines are being drawn up ... Secular versus religious, the light versus dark. Better you choose which side you are on' (537). Ultimately, moreover, it is through his reconciliation with Zeeny, a symbol of Indian secular hybridity and opposed to the oppressive power (in Bombay, the extremist Hindutva Shiv Sena party), that Saladin gains happiness. He joins Zeeny and her friends in forming a human chain of protest across the city. Fulfilment is comfortably compatible with oppositional politics as well as with a secularist liberalism (537–8).

Swatilekha's words reappear in an *Observer* article written by Rushdie in the wake of the controversy, and again in *Joseph Anton*. Here, Rushdie brings the monochromatic binary of religion versus secularism into contemporary Britain, where religion occupies a significantly different position, and reasserts the necessity of choice: 'Now that the battle has spread to Britain, I can only hope it will not be lost by default. It is time for us to choose' (129–30). Despite the fact that the Christian church and the state remain formally connected in Britain, religious culture is now relatively powerless and clashes between different religious groups rarely figure in the news or media. It is rather when religious culture clashes with secularist British culture that it enters the public domain – and, especially in the case of minority religious culture, almost always in a position of powerlessness.[54] Indeed, in these instances, the rights of a religious group frequently become indistinguishable from the rights of a racialised minority group, and where the minority in question is structurally disadvantaged in social and economic terms, the issue of religious rights becomes inseparable from the issue of class as well as from that of race. The configuration of religion as an oppressive structure is therefore often in tension with an anti-racism which is concerned with the rights of racial minorities in Britain. In *The Satanic Verses*, an overt valorisation of Saladin/secularism (as opposed to Gibreel/religion) within contemporary Britain, especially given that these poles are also aligned respectively with assimilation and rejection, would come dangerously close to valorising hegemonic British culture and disturbing the anti-racist core of the Brickhall narrative. Ideological contradictions are resolved through a form of spatial displacement, to India, which provides a less awkward means of exposing the dangers of religious communalism and privileging a binary of secular freedom versus religious oppression. This tension between minority religions and liberal secularism is arguably more visible today than it was in 1988. However, the contradictions of a liberal anti-racism that cannot valorise the communal were immanent in 1980s Britain. The novel ideologically reflects and attempts to manage these immanent contradictions, which were then unearthed in violent form by the novel's publication.

In *The Satanic Verses*, Afro-Caribbeans and Asians are firmly allied against racism and 'black' is used as an umbrella term (286–7, 451). This enables a construction of the Brickhall inhabitants as individuals who are united not by virtue of shared cultural practices or codes for living, but simply by the fact that they are not white and are therefore victims of the racist state. Just as 'attacks against individuals' (as opposed to 'communal symbols')[55] enable a broad alliance across non-white groups, so the notion of a broad alliance enables a construction of its members not as a cultural collective but as disparate individuals united against an oppressive force. Indeed, characters who occupy the foreground of the community are highly individualised first- and second-generation immigrants, sometimes with uncategorisable racial or cultural identifications: Hanif Johnson has an Asian mother and a white father; John Maslama is a non-denominational 'True Believer', an Indian from Guyana; and, most strikingly, Pinkwalla is 'a seven-foot albino, his hair the palest rose, the whites of his eyes likewise, his features unmistakably Indian ... An Indian who has never seen India, East-India-man from the West Indies, white black man. A star' (292). Here again, the Rushdie affair can be used to make the novel's silences speak. The rupturing of the alliance between Afro-Caribbeans and Asians that took place within the social text was, as Werbner suggests, a consequence of the communal nature of the protest. The protest destabilised the liberal anti-racist binary of individual freedom versus a constraining structure or grand narrative; in this instance, an oppressed collective formed through identification with a grand narrative (that of Islam) was struggling against an individualist liberalism.

Sufyan's wife Hind is perhaps the only member of the community who seems to wish to adhere to the cultural values and codes for living that she has transported with her from Bangladesh. But, unlike her husband and many of the other community members, she is almost impossible to like, barely developed beyond the stereotype of the repressive, retrogressive and unforgiving British Asian matriarch. The material greed, prudery and patriarchy for which she stands are counterposed to Sufyan's poetry, oppositional politics and what Hind considers to be his obsession with sex. Sexual transgression is aligned with an oppositional politics as well as creativity (247), just as it is aligned with creativity and art in the Jahilia strand of the novel. 'Whores and writers,' Baal tells Mahound, 'We are the people you can't forgive.' And Mahound replies: 'Writers and whores. I see no difference here' (392). The implication that poetry or art is necessarily oppositional echoes constructions of the Rushdie affair as a battle waged by the beleaguered artist fighting repressive forces for freedom of expression. Hind clearly occupies the wrong side of this binary – and with an added twist of racism ('she was stuck in this country full of Jews and strangers who lumped her in with the Negroes') and Thatcherite entrepreneurism, any suggestion that her behaviour is symptomatic of the cultural dislocations that she has undergone and the oppressive social structures in which she is caught is attenuated almost to the point of disappearance (289, 264, 290). Hind functions as a kind of repository for cultural difference within the community, just as the Imam enacts this function in London as a whole. Liberalism's necessary Other is absorbed in an elite individual figure located at the city's, and novel's, peripheries (the Imam); the silenced, anonymous and temporary tenants of the Shaandaar; a stereotype of the Asian matriarch (Hind); and a mad elite visitor to Britain (Gibreel). The difference that is located at the centre of Brickhall remains largely confined to colour difference and so within the limits of liberalism. These limits are in danger of transgression when the individuals cohere into a community or collective in order to protest against the death in police custody of black activist Uhuru Simba. James Procter describes the narrative's highly abstract and aestheticised representation of the riots, configured through the eye of a camera.[56] This aestheticisation of collective protest works to contain the threat that it poses. Collective resistance is also delegitimised in the novel through the configuration of the community cohering around a series of false heroes – Saladin, Gibreel and, to an extent, Uhuru, discredited for his womanising (412) – just as the British protest against the novel was delegitimised through the reduction of the protesters to victims of false leaders. Furthermore, resistance is reduced to the level of commodity: badges, t-shirts and plastic horns and haloes are manufactured to capitalise on the community's protest, while John Maslama pays arch-capitalist Hal Valance to market Gibreel as the community's anti-racist saviour (286, 447). The representation of the protest is, then, shaped by the difficulty of detaching anti-racist resistance from an essentialism or absolutism with which the narrative is clearly uneasy.

John McLeod comments on the significance of the trope of hot temperatures in the novel. He argues convincingly that this trope links the 'pious certainties' of the Imam to the religious certainties displayed by Gibreel in his will to tropicalise the city and to the certainties of a violent struggle against Thatcher's racist state, claiming that the generalised discrediting of 'the "hot certainties" of truth' in the novel works to delegitimise violent anti-racist resistance and to equalise oppressor and oppressed.[57] The confusion of the fire started by the police that burns down the CRC with the fire of the protesters further emphasises the alignment of oppressor and oppressed and the repression of power. The parallels between the fire at the Shaandaar and that of Rushdie's 1984 essay, 'An unimportant fire', in which he describes the deaths of Mrs Abdul Karim and her two young children in a Camden bed and breakfast, are notable.[58] Yet, while in the essay Rushdie makes explicit the connection between the deaths and unequal social structures and deplores the rumours that the unhoused families started the fire themselves,[59] in the novel there is the suggestion that Hind – one of the victims of the fire and of racism – is partly responsible for the crime, as well as a conflation of the violence of the powerful and disempowered (it could be attributed to the police; to their antagonists, the rioters; or to Gibreel). Indeed, the overtly politicised nature of Rushdie's essay contrasts starkly with the representation of the Shaandaar fire – which is in the end reduced to the status of an 'unimportant fire' in so far as it functions largely as a stage-set for Saladin and Gibreel's redeeming acts of 'human love', its ramifications remaining unspoken as the narrative shifts swiftly to India. McLeod omits another fire from his analysis – that of the Bradford book-burnings. Forced beyond the margins of the legitimate political spectrum into a position of absolutist, extreme dissent, the Bradford book-burners are capitalism's 'symptom' and the protests the point at which Žižek's 'politics proper' can be located.[60] It is revealing that the fire Gibreel blows from his trumpet is motivated by a combination of a rejection of England with a religious conviction, the two elements of the British Muslim protest that facilitate a construction of it as 'fanatic', 'irrational', 'fundamentalist', and so on. An engagement with the Bradford fires of protest highlights the absence of class as a factor in Gibreel's fire, enabled by the displacement of rejection/religion onto an elite and mad individual, and exposes the contradictions in the novel that are managed through strategies of containment and displacement.

'DO NOT KNOW YOUR PLACE': CONCLUDING REMARKS ON SPACE

In the wake of 9/11, Rushdie's position veered from a recognition 'that it would be wrong to bomb the impoverished, oppressed Afghan people' and an acknowledgement of the need for a 'resolution of some of the world's thorniest problems' to an open support of US military action in the 'war on terror' accompanied by a scepticism towards the deeply religious Bush administration.[61] There is, however, much that is consistent throughout his articles on the global political situation. He repeatedly individualises terrorism, attributing responsibility primarily to the individuals who commit the acts of violence. For Rushdie, 'The terrorist wraps himself in the world's grievances to cloak his own true motives.'[62] While his secularist aversion to the metaphysical leads him to criticise Bush for using terms such as 'evil' in his anti-terror rhetoric, Rushdie's terms of criticism reveal an individualisation which is similarly depoliticising:

> the greatest difficulty with [Bush's religious rhetoric] is that it dehistoricizes these events, depoliticizes and even depersonalizes them. If evil is the devil's work ... then that, to my unbeliever's way of thinking, actually lets the terrorists off the hook. If evil is external to us, a force working upon us from outside ourselves, then our moral responsibility for its effects is diminished.[63]

He replaces Bush's implication that 'evil' is an external force with an implication that 'evil' is within us, part of our human nature, a notion that is clearly present in *The Satanic Verses*.[64] He thereby despatialises the events of 11 September and all acts of terror, detaching them from the structures of power that are entrenched in global space, so that they become 'out-of-geography' events.[65] The world becomes little more than an empty container, Henri Lefebvre's 'passive receptacle', in which we are all moral (or immoral) actors.[66]

Derek Gregory cites New Labour's former principal adviser on foreign affairs calling for a new kind of imperialism – 'one acceptable to a world of human rights and cosmopolitan values'.[67] As Gregory explains, this is a form of imperialism that can legitimately operate within the contemporary world through an ideological repression of the world's divisions and exclusions – or its 'power-topologies'.[68] In other words, 'cosmopolitan values', a liberal-pluralist respect for racial and cultural difference, can be accommodated within neo-imperialism – or indeed, as former prime minister Tony Blair suggested on the verge of Britain's invasion of Afghanistan, they can only be accommodated through neo-imperialism:

'We are ... defending values about democracy, freedom, the ability to respect people of different faiths, races and creeds, and a belief that we will create a better world.'[69] Rushdie's support for the 'war on terror', then, is not inconsistent with the liberal anti-racist position that emerges in *The Satanic Verses*. In *Joseph Anton*, too, Rushdie sets 'human nature' and 'the universality of its rights and ethics and freedoms' against the terror attacks and 'the fallacies of relativism that were at the heart of the invective of the armies of the religious (*we hate you because we aren't like you*)' (626). Implicit here is an echo of Kenan Malik's critique of the thesis that demotes Enlightenment values from their status as a universal necessary for the advancement of 'political rights and social justice' to a 'weapon in the clash of civilizations'. On the grounds of their supposed shared relativism, Malik links the 'clash of civilizations thesis' to the 'multiculturalist argument' that suggests that 'every community should be encouraged to express its own identity, explore its own history, formulate its own values, pursue its own lifestyles'.[70] Like Malik, Rushdie claims the necessity of a universal: liberal humanism with its basis in Enlightenment rationalism. Yet, the assertion of this universal can only result in the creation of an exception,[71] which will inevitably lead back to a 'clash of civilizations' or a 'clash of fundamentalisms'.[72] Rushdie's universal has its exclusions which are invisibilised in his dematerialised cosmopolitan understanding of the world, just as a limited liberal-pluralist approach to Britain's cultural diversity obscures the inequalities of the public sphere which exclude working-class religious minorities.

In his commencement address for Bard College, New York, Rushdie tells his audience: 'Do not know your place.'[73] This echoes the title of the collection in which this essay appears, *Step across This Line*, and captures a repeated theme throughout his work: the transgression of boundaries. A spatial metaphor is frequently used to describe disobedience against a generalised notion of rules, which incorporates, at its extreme, religious fundamentalism and terrorism. The idea of disobedience or freedom is abstracted to include elements as diverse as 'kissing in public places, bacon sandwiches, disagreement, cutting-edge fashion, literature, generosity, water, a more equitable distribution of the world's resources, movies, music, freedom of thought, beauty, love'. This shopping list of freedoms, which equates transgression as a value as such with an apparently socialist belief in equality, hints at the tension between liberalism and a more materialist oppositional stance that can be traced in *The Satanic Verses*.[74] Just as Rushdie lifts acts of terror out of their context, so he lifts the individual who doesn't 'know his place' out of the social conditions of privilege which enable his or her freedom of choice. For it is mainly those who benefit from capitalism who have the freedom to opt out of collective identities through individual consumption.[75] In Rushdie's use, then, spatial metaphors remain largely disconnected from the material, while in the social context of *The Satanic Verses* and the protests it sparked (east London and Bradford) divisions of class are entrenched in space and a dematerialised understanding of transgressive boundary-crossing or of the multicultural metropolis is hard to sustain.[76] To 'free' the working classes of the East End or Bradford from the boundaries that separate them from the wealth or 'regeneration' that surrounds them and that are materialised in the gated communities or country homes of the rich, it is not enough to tell them to 'step across this line' or to refuse their 'place'. The idea of not knowing or refusing one's place also informs the work of Slavoj Žižek which advocates the rejection of one's 'subordinated place in the social-political edifice' and an identification with 'the point of exception' of the social order – that is, with those who do not benefit from capitalism. For Žižek, it is by identifying with this exception that a 'true universality' can be attained.[77] This construction of a rejection of one's place materialises the notion of spatial transgression. Rushdie and his supporters represented *The Satanic Verses* as breaking taboos and transgressing boundaries. But, in a material sense, it is rather the working-class Bradford protesters who transgressed boundaries by refusing to accept their 'subordinated place' within neoliberal capitalism's structures.

NOTES

1 Salman Rushdie, *Step across This Line: Collected Non-Fiction 1992–2002* (London: Random House, 2002), p. 62.

2 Tariq Modood, *Multicultural Politics: Racism, Ethnicity and Muslims in Britain* (Edinburgh: Edinburgh University Press, 2005), p. 112.

3 Pnina Werbner, *Imagined Diasporas among Manchester Muslims: The Public Performance of Pakistani Transnational Identity Politics* (Oxford: James Currey, 2002), p. 7; Modood, *Multicultural Politics*, p. 14.

4 Yunus Samad, 'Book burning and race relations: political mobilisation of Bradford Muslims', *New Community*, 18:4 (1992), 507–19, 511.

5 *Ibid.*, 512–14.

6 *Ibid.*, 516. Samad points out that at first British Muslim leaders were asking simply for the insertion in the novel of a short statement reasserting its status as fiction. It was only after the media's demonising response to the Muslim dissent, and the Muslim community's realisation that their religion was not

protected by British blasphemy law, that the stakes were raised (514).

7 See, for example, 'Is nothing sacred?' in Rushdie, *Imaginary Homelands: Essays and Criticism 1981–1991* (London: Granta, 1992 [1991]), p. 422; and 'Not about Islam?' in Rushdie, *Step across This Line*, p. 396.

8 *Today*, 14 March 1990, cited in Modood, *Multicultural Politics*, p. 103.

9 Modood, *Multicultural Politics*, pp. 7, 38–41.

10 Hanif Kureishi, *Dreaming and Scheming: Reflections on Writing and Politics* (London: Faber, 2002), p. 58.

11 *Ibid.*, p. 64.

12 Review of *My Beautiful Laundrette*, *Paikaar*, 4:1 (1987), 18, 23.

13 Philip Lewis, *Islamic Britain: Religion, Politics and Identity among British Muslims* (London and New York: I. B. Tauris, 2002 [1994]), p. 159.

14 Cited in *ibid*.

15 Modood, *Multicultural Politics*, p. 103; Lewis, *Islamic Britain*, p. 159.

16 See, for example, comments by David Blunkett, Kenan Malik and Trevor Phillips in: Tahir Abbas, 'British South Asian Muslims: before and after September 11', in Tahir Abbas (ed.), *Muslim Britain: Communities under Pressure* (London and New York: Zed Books, 2005), pp. 3–17, p. 12); Tariq Modood, *Multiculturalism: A Civic Idea* (Cambridge: Polity, 2007), p. 11.

17 Kenan Malik, *From Fatwa to Jihad: The Rushdie Affair and its Legacy* (London: Atlantic Books, 2009), pp. xviii–ix, 38, 63–79.

18 *Ibid.*, p. 78.

19 Polly Toynbee, 'My right to offend a fool', *Guardian* (10 June 2005), p. 27.

20 *Ibid.*; Salman Rushdie, *Joseph Anton* (London: Jonathan Cape, 2012), p. 344. All subsequent citations are given within the body of the chapter and are to this edition of the text.

21 Modood, *Multicultural Politics*, pp. 32–3; see also Tariq Modood, 'Political blackness and British Asians', *Sociology*, 28:4 (1994), 859–76; Rushdie, *Joseph Anton*, p. 142; Malik, *From Fatwa to Jihad*, pp. xi–xii, 50–2. Malik cites Tariq Mehmood whose novel *While There is Light* (Manchester: Comma, 2003) depicts the fracturing of a secular anti-racist alliance. References to Linton Kwesi Johnson's poem 'Inglan is a bitch', the Black Panthers and Malcolm X, as well as to the Socialist Workers Party, the Valley Strikers' march and *The Manifesto of the Communist Party*, convey a shared sense of oppression and resistance with white workers and those of Afro-Caribbean heritage (pp. 197, 195, 52, 195, 159–60, 168, 139–40, 121–2, 175).

22 Werbner, *Imagined Diasporas*, p. 71.

23 Rushdie, *Step across This Line*, p. 345.

24 *Ibid.* Unsurprisingly, *Step across This Line* is dedicated to New Atheist Christopher Hitchens.

25 Mahmood Mamdani, 'Good Muslim, bad Muslim – an African perspective', *10 Years after September 11* (October 2001), http://essays.ssrc.org/10yearsafter911/good-muslim-bad-muslim-an-african-perspective/ (last acces-

sed 6 November 2014), cited in Derek Gregory, *The Colonial Present* (Oxford: Blackwell, 2004), p. 22.

26 Slavoj Žižek, 'Multiculturalism, or, the cultural logic of multinational capital', in *The Universal Exception: Selected Writings*, vol. 2 (London and New York: Continuum, 2006), pp. 152, 180 n. 1.

27 Anshuman A. Mondal, 'Revisiting *The Satanic Verses*: the *fatwa* and its legacies', in Robert Eaglestone and Martin McQuillan (eds), *Salman Rushdie* (London: Bloomsbury Academic, 2013), pp. 59–71, p. 60. Mondal offers a brilliantly compelling reading of *The Satanic Verses*, arguing that ultimately, despite its ostensible aim to 'challenge "orthodoxies of all kinds"', it 'reinforces a secularist orthodoxy which believes that religion no longer has anything to contribute to human development' (pp. 67–8).

28 See Lisa Appignanesi and Sara Maitland (eds), *The Rushdie File* (London: Fourth Estate, 1989), p. 29.

29 Similarly problematic alignments occur in the comparison of the Bradford and Bolton book-burnings to those carried out by Hitler's National Socialists, and in the comparison of British Muslim calls for the book to be banned to the book bans carried out by the state in apartheid South Africa (see *ibid.*, pp. 67, 43–4). In Rushdie's first children's book, *Haroun and the Sea of Stories* (London: Granta, 1990), published shortly after the fatwa was announced, the binary of creative freedom versus a totalising authoritarianism is pronounced.

30 Rushdie, *Step across This Line*, pp. 62, 274–5, 442; Rushdie, *Joseph Anton*, pp. 303, 331.

31 Salman Rushdie, 'In bad faith', *Guardian* (14 March 2005), www.theguardian. com/politics/2005/mar/14/labour.religion (last accessed 6 November 2014); see also 'God in Gujarat', in *Step across This Line*, pp. 401–3.

32 Rushdie, *Step across This Line*, pp. 61, 62, 146, 154, 156, 233.

33 Martin Duberman, 'Foreword', in Noam Chomsky, *Objectivity and Liberal Scholarship* (New York: New Press, 2003 [1969]), pp. v–ix, p. ix.

34 Anthony Burgess, 'Islam's gangster tactics', *Independent* (16 February 1989). Burgess's remarks are predictably followed by a comparison of the Bradford book-burners to those of Hitler's Nazi regime.

35 Slavoj Žižek, 'A leftist plea for "Eurocentrism"', in *The Universal Exception*, vol. 2, p. 205.

36 See Žižek, 'Multiculturalism', pp. 173–4.

37 Edward W. Said, *The World, the Text, and the Critic* (Cambridge, MA: Harvard University Press, 1983), pp. 34–5.

38 Pierre Macherey, *A Theory of Literary Production*, trans. Geoffrey Wall (New York and London: Routledge, 1996 [1978; French original 1966]), p. 94.

39 Aijaz Ahmad, *In Theory* (London and New York: Verso, 1992), p. 143.

40 Macherey, *Literary Production*, p. 86.

41 Graham Huggan and Tobias Wachinger, 'Can newness enter the world? The

Satanic Verses and the question of multicultural aesthetics', in Liselotte Glage and Ruediger Kunow (eds), *'The Decolonizing Pen': Cultural Diversity and the Transnational Imaginary in Rushdie's Fiction* (Trier: Wissenschaftlicher Verlag Trier, 2001), pp. 25–38, p. 29.

42 Salman Rushdie, *The Satanic Verses* (London: Random House, 1999 [1988]), p. 185. All subsequent citations are given within the body of the chapter and are to this edition of the text.

43 Rushdie, *Imaginary Homelands*, pp. 139–42.

44 Homi Bhabha, 'Unpacking my library ... again', in Iain Chambers and Lidia Curti (eds), *The Post-Colonial Question: Common Skies, Divided Horizons* (Abingdon and New York: Routledge, 1996), pp. 109–11, cited in Ruvani Ranasinha, 'The *fatwa* and its aftermath', in Abdulrazak Gurnah (ed.), *The Cambridge Companion to Salman Rushdie* (Cambridge: Cambridge University Press, 2007), p. 49. Bhabha describes an 'unresconstructed liberalism' as one 'that presupposes an uneven playing field, a utopian notion of the self as sovereign and "free" choice as inherent in the individual'.

45 Terry Eagleton, *Ideology: An Introduction* (London: Verso 1991), p. 4.

46 Michael Gorra, *After Empire: Scott, Naipaul, Rushdie* (Chicago and London: University of Chicago Press, 1997), pp. 149–50.

47 It was Jewish lobbyists who finally persuaded the government not to follow up this recommendation (Talal Asad, 'Ethnography, literature, and politics: some readings and uses of Salman Rushdie's *The Satanic Verses*', *Cultural Anthropology*, 5:3 (August 1990), 239–69, 254).

48 *Ibid.*, 254.

49 Significantly, the Imam is against history and measuring time (211–15), echoing constructions of Muslims as lagging behind their secular European counterparts rather than as coeval others (see Doreen Massey, *For Space* (London: Sage, 2005), especially pp. 68–70).

50 See John Clement Ball, *Imagining London: Postcolonial Fiction and the Transnational Metropolis* (Toronto: University of Toronto Press, 2004), pp. 203–4.

51 Pnina Werbner 'Allegories of sacred imperfection: magic, hermeneutics and passion in *The Satanic Verses*', *Current Anthropology*, 37, Supplement: special issue on 'Anthropology in public' (1996), 55–86, 57, 69. See also the response to Werbner's article by Akbar Ahmed who critically cites Ian McEwan's reading of the novel according to this humanist paradigm (in Werbner, 'Allegories', 69).

52 Baal is also aligned with the transgressive, secular and politically oppositional poet Faiz Ahmed Faiz (334–5), described by Rushdie in 'Step across this line' (*Step across This Line*, pp. 432–4).

53 See also 'God in Gujarat'.

54 The Anglican Church was the only component of the British establishment to maintain a dialogue with British Muslims during the Rushdie affair (Philip Lewis, 'Arenas of ethnic negotiation: cooperation and conflict in Bradford',

in Tariq Modood and Pnina Werbner (eds), *The Politics of Multiculturalism in the New Europe: Racism, Identity and Community* (London: Zed Books, 1997), pp. 126–46, p. 142).

55 Werbner, *Imagined Diasporas*, p. 71.

56 James Procter, *Dwelling Places: Postwar Black British Writing* (Manchester: Manchester University Press, 2003), p. 115.

57 John McLeod, *Postcolonial London: Rewriting the Metropolis* (London and New York: Routledge, 2004).

58 Rushdie, *Imaginary Homelands*, p. 142.

59 *Ibid.*, p. 141.

60 See Žižek, 'Multiculturalism', p. 162; 'A leftist plea', pp. 192–4, 203–4.

61 Rushdie, *Step across This Line*, pp. 392, 398–9; 'How to fight and lose the moral high ground', *Guardian* (23 March 2002), www.theguardian.com/books/2002/mar/23/salmanrushdie; 'The altered states of anti-Americanism', *Guardian* (31 August 2002), www.theguardian.com/books/2002/aug/31/iraq.politics; 'Fight the good fight', *Guardian* (2 November 2002), www.theguardian.com/books/2002/nov/02/iraq.salmanrushdie (all accessed 6 November 2014).

62 Rushdie, *Step across This Line*, pp. 392–3; see also pp. 396, 438.

63 *Ibid.*, p. 438.

64 In an interview about *Shalimar the Clown* (London: Jonathan Cape, 2005), while acknowledging that political unrest in Kashmir contributes to the path his protagonist takes, Rushdie reiterates and emphasises the primacy of internal and individual factors (Edward Stourton, interview with Salman Rushdie, *Today*, BBC Radio 4 (broadcast 29 August 2005)). For an astute reading of the novel, see Peter Morey, 'Mourning becomes Kashmira: Islam, melancholia, and the evacuation of politics in Salman Rushdie's *Shalimar the Clown*', in Rehana Ahmed, Peter Morey and Amina Yaqin (eds), *Culture, Diaspora, and Modernity in Muslim Writing* (Abingdon and New York: Routledge, 2012), pp. 215–30.

65 Gregory, *Colonial Present*, p. 19.

66 Henri Lefebvre, *The Production of Space*, trans. Donald Nicholson-Smith (Oxford: Blackwell, 1991), pp. 55, 90. Derek Gregory provides a useful corrective to this despatialisation: 'All political violence – including transnational terrorism and state terrorism – is intimately involved in the local: it requires a matrix out of which volunteers or informants can be recruited and through which material and ideological support can be provided' (*Colonial Present*, p. 143).

67 Gregory, *Colonial Present*, p. 254.

68 *Ibid.*, pp. 136, 143.

69 Cited in Paul Gilroy, *After Empire: Melancholia or Convivial Culture?* (Abingdon: Routledge, 2004), p. 68.

70 Malik, *From Fatwa to Jihad*, pp. 207–8.

71   Žižek, 'Multiculturalism', pp. 178–9.

72   Tariq Ali, *The Clash of Fundamentalisms: Crusades, Jihads and Modernity* (London: Verso, 2002).

73   Rushdie, *Step across This Line*, p. 152.

74   *Ibid.*, p. 393.

75   See Jonathan Friedman, 'Global crises, the struggle for cultural identity and intellectual porkbarrelling: cosmopolitans versus locals, ethnics and nationals in an era of dehegemonisation', in Pnina Werbner and Tariq Modood (eds), *Debating Cultural Hybridity: Multi-Cultural Identities and the Politics of Anti-Racism* (London: Zed Books, 1997), pp. 70–89, p. 88.

76   For the socio-spatial inequalities of east London, see Doreen Massey, *Docklands: A Microcosm of Broader Social and Economic Trends* (London: Docklands Forum, 1991); Kenneth Leech, *Brick Lane 1978: The Events and their Significance* (London: Stepney Books, 1994 [1980]).

77   Žižek, 'Multiculturalism', pp. 178–9.

3

The limits of liberalism in the work of Hanif Kureishi

While some strangers can be assimilated, as their strangeness is 'seen' as only a matter of appearance, other strangers can only be assimilated as the unassimilable. Their strangeness is represented as a matter of being, and hence betrays the very appearance of difference within the discourse of multiculturalism itself ... We can only welcome those others who allow us to be ourselves and be different, at one and the same time. (Sara Ahmed[1])

FROM A THATCHERITE MONOCULTURALISM TO A LIBERAL MULTICULTURALISM

Critics commenting on Hanif Kureishi's earlier fiction have rightly focused on his attempts to explode hegemonic notions of a monoracial Britain as a vital aspect of his work. Anuradha Dingwaney Needham has praised Kureishi's endorsement of hybridity, claiming that it is necessarily oppositional – 'For it is against (or in place of) the demand for a pure (white) British subject that he offers the hybrid, multicultural, multiracial subject as the more appropriate bearer of a contemporary "Britishness".'[2] In his powerful 1986 essay 'The rainbow sign', Kureishi himself overtly states the need for a redefinition of Britishness: 'It is the British, the white British, who have to learn that being British isn't what it was. Now it is a more complex thing, involving new elements. So there must be a fresh way of seeing Britain and the choices it faces: and a new way of being British after all this time.'[3] Like Salman Rushdie's *The Satanic Verses*, this essay, along with Kureishi's first novel *The Buddha of Suburbia* (1990) and early screenplays, must be contextualised in their historical moment: that of Margaret Thatcher's government and the purist, Powellite vision of Britain that underwrote her policies and rhetoric on race and immigration. Thatcher's much cited speech of May 1978 in which she spoke of immigrants 'swamping' Britain and the Falklands War, with its accompanying rhetoric of nostalgia for empire, helped to strengthen the identification of Britishness with an exclusionary whiteness and to construct Britain's minorities as a threat to the cohesion and well-being of the nation.[4] The tightening of immigration controls, particularly through the British Nationality Act of 1981, eroded the rights of non-white Commonwealth citizens to enter Britain; and an increasingly coercive authoritarian state targeted minorities through highly repressive police tactics – a context that is captured powerfully in Rushdie's controversial novel.[5] The 1990s, and particularly the election of a Labour government in 1997, saw a partial shift to a more inclusive notion of Britishness. Tony Blair's government's commissioning of the Macpherson inquiry into the murder of Stephen Lawrence, which declared Britain's police force 'institutionally racist', can be seen as a significant marker of this shift.[6]

While Thatcher's politics combined an exclusionary, racialised British nationalism with an economic neoliberalism, New Labour integrated multiculturalism into a neoliberal economy, and cultural difference and hybridity became exploitable commodities in a globalised marketplace. Thus British subjects could be individualised and equalised, regardless of their racial or cultural affiliation, while their structural position within society, shaped partially by their racial or cultural affiliation, could be occluded. Further, as discussed in the Introduction, a symbolic appreciation of cultural diversity can work to screen these inequalities as well as the exclusions of a liberal multiculturalism. With a focus on Australia, Sara Ahmed describes how 'in some multicultural constructions of the nation, the "we" itself emerges through the very gesture of claiming difference. Those who appear as different are incorporated as difference – a process that allows the nation to imagine itself as heterogeneous (to claim their differences as "our difference").'[7] Ahmed continues: 'While some strangers can be assimilated, as their strangeness is "seen" as only a matter of appearance, other strangers can only be assimilated as the unassimilable. Their strangeness is represented as a matter of being, and hence betrays the very appearance of difference within the discourse of multiculturalism itself.'[8] When members of a minority group enact, or seek to enact, cultural practices which threaten the ideology of autonomous individual 'choice' or 'freedom' (for example, arranged marriages; the wearing of the hijab; protests against creative works that offend), thereby positioning themselves beyond liberal tolerance, they become 'unassimilable' and the exclusions of a liberal multiculturalism are exposed.[9]

Those cultural practices and their adherents that fall outside the 'limits of multicultural hospitality' are then constructed as threatening to social cohesion,[10] especially but not only since 9/11 and the rise of Islamophobia.

Kureishi's long oeuvre spans the transition from a Thatcherite mono-culturalism to a liberal multiculturalism and the backlash against multi-culturalism of the post-9/11 period. It is in the context of a hegemonic liberal multiculturalism that Kureishi's work of the mid- to late 1990s and early to mid-2000s – the subject of most of this chapter – should be read. Following his second novel, *The Black Album* (1995), his focus on issues of race and ethnicity apparently ceded to an interest in masculinities, rela-tionships, families and fatherhood, in the context of a predominantly white Britain. But four stories in his collections *Love in a Blue Time* (1997) and *The Body and Seven Stories* (2002) do focus explicitly on race: 'We're not Jews', 'With your tongue down my throat', 'My son the fanatic' (all *Love*) and 'Touched' (*Body*). In addition, one story in his collection *Midnight All Day* (1999), 'Girl', and one in *The Body and Seven Stories*, 'Hullabaloo in the tree', have, as in his novella *Intimacy* (1998), Asian or (possibly in all cases) mixed-race male protagonists – who are, however, barely marked by their racial difference.[11] This chapter begins with an exploration of Kureishi's treatment of racial difference in a selection of his short stories and *Intimacy*, focusing particularly on its frequently ellip-tical, coded presence. I ask whether Kureishi's protagonists' autonomy from minority culture and community functions as a politicised critique of these prescriptive codes for living, or whether, by contrast, the subver-sion of conventional codes and categories tends towards an individualism that actually operates comfortably within exclusionary liberal social formations. This discussion illuminates the more focused consideration of Kureishi's engagement with Islam in *The Black Album* as well as the short story and screenplay versions of 'My son the fanatic' (1997) and his semi-autobiographical work *My Ear at his Heart: Reading my Father* (2004). The chapter ends with a brief discussion of his novel *Something to Tell You* (2008).[12]

OCCLUDING RACE

Almost exactly midway through Kureishi's 1998 novella *Intimacy*, the reader comes to learn that the narrator Jay is not white – or not quite. Through his exploration of the tensions between family life and indi-vidual desire, a detail emerges, casually voiced, as if its significance does not exceed its function as a vehicle for contemplating the complexities of desire from another angle: 'In India', we learn,

> they don't seem to put the same emphasis on romantic love. Couples copulate when necessary and get on with their separate lives. In Lahore my uncle lives in one part of the house with his sons, three brothers, male friends ... My aunt, the daughters, female servants, and the children, live in another part ... Perhaps it is a fine idea to have the women close but not too close. Presumably, over there they suppress their desire, but I am of a generation that believes in the necessity of satisfying oneself. (60)

We discover, then, that at least some of the narrator's close family are Pakistani, and this partial knowledge disrupts the reading process. Suddenly, there are prior textual moments that could be configured retroactively as offering glimpses of the narrator's racial difference. These moments begin to appear as barely tangible hints, highly coded references that all but disappear into the normative whiteness of Britain that shapes the assumptions we bring to our readings of fiction. So, a description of the narrator's friend Victor as 'speak[ing] slowly, as some *English* men do' could now be read as gesturing to a broader field of comparisons and contrasts, enabled by Jay's experience of another culture (6; emphasis mine). Jay's description of constant childhood fears – 'of parents, aunts and uncles, of vicars, police and teachers, and of being kicked, abused and insulted by other children' – could be partly reconfigured in terms of his racial difference (27). Given the autobiographical content of *Intimacy*, any knowledge of Kureishi's own experiences of racism as a child would also encourage the reader to read race into the text at this point. Other textual moments start to appear curiously elliptical. Racial difference seems glaringly absent from the detailed description of Jay's father (40–4). The lack of any mention of his racial difference when we learn that he worked as a clerk in a police force that is self-confessedly racist at an institutional level appears as an occlusion of the structure of race in Britain and a detachment of the father from his social context and conditions (43). Similarly, the elision from the description of Jay's parents' marriage of the factor of racial difference seems awkward. Assuming that Jay's father is Pakistani and his mother English, their marriage in the 1950s would have transgressed boundaries that were firmly entrenched in British culture. Again, the invisibility of race here blurs the social context of their relationship: the stigmatisation of mixed-race relationships in Britain is obscured.[13] This apparent occlusion of race is highlighted further with the allusion to 'dark Beethoven' that briefly interrupts Jay's musings on their marriage (44). Why this curious reference to revisionist claims that the composer may not have been white in a narrative where the central character's racial difference is barely mentioned – and at a moment where the deracialisation of Jay's descriptions is, arguably, at its most striking?

The degree of uncertainty in *Intimacy* – the partial, fleeting knowledge that the reader is allowed – alerts us to the categories that underpin difference. First, when we read the revelatory passage and rethink moments in the narrative, it is difficult not to feel unease about our half-knowledge – our inability to 'place' the central characters in cultural and racial terms. A recognition of this unease highlights the difficulty of thinking beyond essentialised, bounded notions of culture and race. Further, as we reconfigure textual moments as coded allusions to the narrator and his family's cultural difference, or as occlusions of this difference, we become aware of the stereotypes that are influencing this process of reconfiguration. For example, if we read Jay's father's culture difference into the description of his unquestioning adherence to 'family values', we are, at least in part, reading the latter as a function of his probable identification as Indian Muslim/Pakistani and thereby stereotyping South Asian Muslim culture. The narrative silences, then, have the effect of challenging the assumptions that we make as readers of cultural difference, forcing us to think across and beyond categories instead. Indeed, such an interpretation would be in line with that of many of Kureishi's commentators who locate a political resistance in the author's constant subversion of categorising and essentialising notions of culture.[14] Kureishi's own comments on this aspect of his work would suggest an interpretation along similar lines. 'You expect to recognise ethnicity but no one says that a white character is white', he says of *Intimacy*.[15] If he is, as he suggests, challenging the normativity of whiteness, its 'exalted position of transcendental signifier', by raising other ethnicities to this position of transparency, then this gesture can be read as transgressing the hierarchising boundaries that map out categories of racial difference.[16] In the light of this, it is worth noting that Kureishi does, on a number of occasions, mark whiteness ('In a blue time', *Love*, 11; 'That was then', *Midnight*, 85; *Intimacy*, 59). Conversely, however, the effect of this self-conscious erasure of minority ethnicities could be to obscure the status of whiteness as 'transcendental signifier' rather than to dislodge it, thereby repressing racial hierarchies. Should we read the elliptical presence of racial difference in *Intimacy* as a means of challenging our assumptions about cultural difference and the categories that these assumptions involve? Or should we, conversely, read this near-absence as a narrative repression symptomatic of a liberalism that co-opts 'assimilable' difference into the normative culture and screens inequalities behind a rhetoric of individual choice? If we read race as an occlusion, are we then falling into the trap of prescription, of setting up a normative model of how race *should* figure in the narrative of an Asian or mixed-race Briton?

Pierre Macherey warns of the danger of what he calls the 'normative fallacy' – the reduction of a literary text to its relationship with a model that has an *a priori* existence, and a method that, if taken to its logical conclusion, renders the text redundant.[17] Measuring *Intimacy*, its speech and its silences, against a yardstick that determines what should be said is, then, to be avoided. Indeed, much of Kureishi's work has been praised by critics for its very refusal to say what it should say, to assume what Nahem Yousaf, quoting from Kureishi's *The Black Album*, calls the 'brown man's burden' – or the burden of countering negative ideologies surrounding Asian communities with equally ideological positive images that homoge-nise and constrain.[18] In the light of this, Kureishi's departure from the issue of race can also be seen as a refusal to meet his readership's expectations of a minority writer. As Ruvani Ranasinha notes, the media response to *Love in a Blue Time* was characterised by a focus on the few stories in this collection that do deal with race, thus highlighting the unease that can be generated when an Asian writer locates his fiction firmly and exclusively within white Britain.[19] In the light of this, the absence of the issue of race from his later work could be seen as a subversive, even playful, deviation from prescribed representations – and indeed Kureishi's own comments on his recent work might endorse such a reading. He says of his play *Sleep with Me* (1999), which has an all-white cast: 'all the characters are white and English. And they're sort of trotting around in this beautiful house. And that amuses me very much, as an Indian, writing about that.'[20] But Macherey suggests a more constructive way of measuring the silences of a work of fiction: rather than configuring 'the silence of the book' as 'a lack to be remedied, an inadequacy to be made up for', we must, he suggests, 'distinguish the necessity of this silence', showing it to be 'the juxtaposition and conflict of several meanings which produces the radical otherness which shapes the work'. He goes on: '[The silence of the book] is not the sole meaning, but that which endows meaning with a meaning: it is this silence ... which informs us of the precise conditions for the appearance of an utterance, and thus its limits, giving it real significance, without, for all that, speaking in its place.'[21] If we follow Macherey's theory, then, the absence of race in *Intimacy* becomes constitutive of the narrative itself, not as a part of the narrative that can be recuperated as a positive presence but as a condition of the narrative's speech. By making the narrative's silences speak, or showing that 'what the work *cannot say*' is also, paradoxically, 'what the work is *compelled* to say in order to say what it *wants* to say', we can illuminate the text's relationship to the politics of multiculturalism in Britain.[22]

In *Intimacy*, the narrator's friends Asif and Najma represent tradition and order. The couple live in Kureishi's iconic suburban space, the heart of conventionality and stasis; they married young and prioritise a commitment to family life; and, when confronted with Jay's decision to leave Susan, Asif's reaction is to say, 'I suppose what you are doing is the modern way' (29, 100). This final example echoes the curious slippage from culture as a differential to generation as a differential in Jay's description of his family in Pakistan: 'Presumably, over there they suppress their desire, but I am of a generation that believes in the necessity of satisfying oneself' (60). The temporalising gesture here is suggestive of an Orientalist relegation of Islamic culture to an earlier stage in the history of modernity. Similarly, Asif's objection to the 'modern way' positions him on the wrong side of the binary of tradition versus modernity. But the substitution of the temporal for any explicit articulation of Asif and Najma's cultural affiliation as a means of contextualising their domestic choices also appears as a curiously coded allusion to their difference. Further, while Asif's resolute immersion in family life evokes the stereotyping narrative of the Asian family as close and committed, or inherently oppressive, this narrative is destabilised through the narrator's individualisation and universalisation of Asif's choices in the following question: 'But why do *people who are good at families* have to be smug and assume it is the only way to live, as if *everybody else* is inadequate?' (32; emphasis mine). The fact that Kureishi withholds race from the descriptions of Asif and Najma lets him off the hook in a sense, deflecting potential accusations of stereotyping from himself onto the assumptions of his reader who is confronted with his or her own implication in the reductive categories that underpin discourses of difference.

Through its apparent refusal to articulate a connection between ethnicity and practice, *Intimacy* can be seen to destabilise assumptions and displace boundaries that map out ethnic 'groups'. However, the categorisation of ethnicities is not just a mechanism for oppression but also a means to political mobilisation. Yunus Samad highlights the damaging consequences of erasing cultural categories in his description of the decision of Bradford city's authorities to return to culture- and colour-blind social policies in the late 1980s;[23] and Bhikhu Parekh details the dangers inherent in the misleading or misguided liberalism that labels the oppositional use of categories of ethnicity or race as necessarily erroneous because predicated on the very structures utilised by racist ideology.[24] Warning against a wholesale rejection of essentialist conceptions of ethnicity, Pnina Werbner writes that 'citizenship rights and multiculturalist agendas are as much dependent on collective objectifications as are racist murders or ethnic cleansing'. While the latter reify through distortion and silencing, the former objectify by foregrounding cultural identities situationally.[25] If difference must remain visible as a means to social praxis, then, an interpretation of the highly coded and ambivalent references to cultural difference in *Intimacy* as necessarily oppositional is problematised.

An analysis of Kureishi's short story 'Hullabaloo in the tree' (*Body*), where the reader encounters a pair who are not dissimilar to Jay and Asif, enables further consideration of how the occlusion of racial difference functions in *Intimacy*. 'Hullabaloo' opens with its protagonist, known simply as 'the father', recalling a recent incident as he makes to leave the park with his young family:

> A week ago, in this park, they had run into an Indian friend, a doctor, who'd been shocked by the disrespect and indiscipline of the father's children. The second seven-year-old twin ... had said to the doctor friend, 'What are you – an idiot?'
>
> The father had had to apologize.
>
> 'They are speaking to everyone like this?' the friend had said to the father. 'I know we live here now, but you have let them become Western, in the worst way!'
>
> No English friend would have presumed to say such a thing, the father had commented, later at home.
>
> 'The problem is,' the kid had replied, 'he's a brown face.' (131)

This brief allusion to the father's 'Indian friend' quickly disappears into a simple narrative that focuses on the father and another father's retrieval of a ball from a tree. The allusion is, however, mirrored at the close of the story, where the father wishes for the presence of his Indian friend so that he can show him the value of a degree of disorder and 'indiscipline', and that 'If children, like desire, broke up that which seemed settled, it was a virtue' (139). In both cases, then, the Indian friend represents 'strict rules or a system', illiberal order and stasis – and indeed, most significantly, the suppression of desire, which recalls the references to South Asian Muslim culture in *Intimacy* where suppressed desire is aligned with 'over there' and, by inference, 'back then'.

The opening incident clearly marks the father and his sons as Asian – not through a hegemonic white gaze which exposes them as Other, but through the gaze of the Indian doctor who sees them as 'the same' or as 'one of us'. But this recognition is swiftly undermined through the father's petulant dismissal of the Indian man's comments and his categorisation of the doctor as 'an Indian friend' (which disassociates himself from 'Indianness'), as well as through one of the twin's (mis)recognition of the doctor as entirely other to him ('he's a brown face'). The dynamics of the racial gaze that freezes the non-white man into objecthood, excluding him from the self–other exchange that enables subjectivity, are displaced in this encounter where recognition functions as a source of fear of constraint, not subordination.[26] The source of fear is located not in the relationship of power that is grounded in racial categories but in a homogenising purist construction of ethnicity that demands of the father conformity to a certain notion of 'Indianness'. The implied critique of cultural categories becomes detached from the hierarchical structure of race that creates such categories. This critique of categories appears even more detached from relations of power when the Indian doctor's demand for cultural conformity is aligned with a generalised notion of order at the close of the story. Cultural hierarchies are dissolved into an abstract and universalising binary of order (stifling, repressive) versus disorder (subversive, liberating).

In 'Hullabaloo', the process of revelation reverses that of *Intimacy*, where an eventual disclosure of racial difference disrupts an assumed whiteness. In the short story, far from being occluded, racial difference seems to frame the narrative. The revelation is rather of the father's and his sons' disassociation from this racial or cultural difference, which seems to be explained, in part, by their incremental generational distance from the father's Asian father (whose grandsons are 'pale' and no doubt pass as white). Just as the characters dissociate themselves from racial difference, moreover, so the story disassociates itself from the issue of race. The narrative frame can be reconfigured as a margin to the story – a repository for difference, detached from the protagonists and the adventure that forms the focus of their story. Cultural difference, in the form of the stereotyped Indian doctor, is pushed beyond the boundaries of liberal Britain – an 'over there' within the nation's borders. It is also pushed beyond the narrative present, in another temporalising gesture, into the father's father's generation of newly arrived immigrants (137–8). It is interesting to note here that two out of the four stories in Kureishi's collections where race is a focus, 'We're not Jews' (*Love*) and 'Touched' (*Body*), are set in an earlier historical moment (probably the 1950s). Both protagonists are the children of mixed-race marriages and their fathers are immigrants from the Indian subcontinent. The racial antagonism that is thematised in these stories is, then, consigned to the past – the time of the father's immigrant father in 'Hullabaloo' – and the stories themselves are consigned to the margins of Kureishi's collections. Difference seems to function as a means of establishing the mixed-race subject in a de-raced or post-race liberal British space.

Given the number of mixed-race characters in Kureishi's work, his elliptical treatment of racial difference must be considered in the context of debates concerning the difficulties and necessity of developing a discourse of race that is adequate for more complex racial identities. Suki Ali's study of mixed-race junior school children is persuasive in its expo-sure of the tension between the fluidity of the children's self-perceptions and the rigidity of the discourse available to them. Despite her awareness of the need for 'strategic essentialism', she concludes: 'The only way to move beyond racialised constraints is to begin a process of deconstruction (one that is often charged with being a-political), and to engage with the possibility of post-race futures.'[27] Reading Kureishi's work through such an approach to race – one motivated by a drive to accommodate iden-tities that strain the current available discourse – could suggest a more socially grounded framework for interpreting the persistent refusal of cultural categories. Ali also emphasises the performative nature of ethnic identification for mixed-race subjects.[28] As well as featuring in *The Buddha of Suburbia*, the notion of the performative, as a means of destabilising essentialist identity categories and debunking notions of authenticity, is a focus of the short story 'With your tongue down my throat' whose protagonist, like *Buddha*'s Karim, is half-Pakistani and half-English. In contradistinction to the coded references to racial difference in *Intimacy*, 'Hullabaloo' and 'Girl' (*Midnight*), race emerges as a clear theme here – a contrast that can be attributed to its original publication as early as 1987. When the protagonist Nina's half-sister Nadia visits from Pakistan, she brings with her a shalwar kameez for Nina, who uses it to 'perform' a Pakistani woman:

> With the scarf over my head I step into the Community Centre and look
> like a lost woman with village ways and chickens in the garden. In a second,
> the communists and worthies are all over me. I mumble into my scarf.
> They give me leaflets and phone numbers. I'm oppressed, you see, beaten
> up, pig-ignorant with an arranged marriage and certain suttee ahead. But
> I get fed up and have a game of darts, a game of snooker and a couple of
> beers with a nice lesbian. (*Love*, 69)

On one level, Nina's performance exposes the stereotypes of Asian women
that inform opinions on the left as well as the right. But her detachment
from the role she plays and the exaggerated manner in which she discards
her role turn her performance into parody. Nina's identification as mixed
race, while enabling her performance, does not serve to deconstruct the
'racialised constraints' that fix subjects into unitary categories. Instead, the
'free', 'outsider' mixed-race Nina emerges as a polar opposite to the cliché
of the traditional Pakistani woman as victim of her culture. A binary of
the liberal individual (Nina) versus the illiberal, unliberated social subject
emerges, anticipating those traceable in *Intimacy* and 'Hullabaloo', as well
as 'Girl', where the eponymous Nicole has rejected the bigoted white
suburban neighbourhood of her childhood for her mixed-race lover
Majid and the freedom he can offer her in the metropolis.

Nina lives on a run-down council estate, has had two abortions,
done a stint as a sex worker and been addicted to crack, all of which
would not immediately position her as a convincing symbol of liberal
individualism. However, the long and cliché-ridden catalogue of 'social
problems' that have plagued her again smacks of parody. Class appears
as a performance rather than a material imposition. Furthermore, her
mother, despite her own deprived background, is a teacher, and, while
the area they live in is poor, Nina is able to navigate her way through
'honeyed London for the rich', transgressing social boundaries with
relative ease (61–2, 72).[29] Her marginal social position emerges increasingly as a function of a generalised 'youth angst' and rebellion. Despite
(or perhaps because of) her characterisation as rebellious and dysfunc-
tional and her mixed-race identity, Nina is not a disruptive presence.
Her half-sister Nadia, while visibly Pakistani, is a rich cosmopolitan on
holiday, her incongruous presence on a council estate traceable only to
the burst condom that led to the accidental conception of Nina (89).
The real 'outlaw' in the story, the real disjunctive presence in normative
Britain, is the working-class Pakistani immigrant woman who is unable
to cross the borders which separate her run-down estate from 'honeyed

London' – the woman whom Nina acts badly and who, reduced to two-dimensional imitation, all but disappears beneath the narrative's layers of performance. We learn towards the end of the story that Nina's narrative is actually being ventriloquised by Howard, Nina's mother's white middle-aged, middle-class, non-committal lover. In this second layer of performance, the performer, Howard, is entirely detached from his role, and Nina is exposed as a constructed identity. The implication is that all identity is performance, and the notion of the individual as social subject, and of identity as socially conditioned, is reduced almost to caricature. Traceable here is the 'infinite regress' that Tariq Modood warns of when discussing the limitations of an endless deconstruction of category: 'this argument for internal differentiation and heterogeneity can have the character of an infinite regress ... we could go on and on till all we have are individual biographies ... Yet most people would acknowledge that this or a Thatcherite-"there-is-no-such-thing-as-society"-individualism is a very poor understanding of the social world.'[30]

Kureishi's hyper-deconstruction, then, and his own slippery and barely discernible presence in his work, obscured by narrative layers or an ironically distant narrator, can be productively reconfigured as what Sara Upstone calls a 'postmodern didacticism'; far from evading an ideological position, his fiction valorises a very particular, individualist and secularist, mode of living, which is, paradoxically, not entirely incompatible with Thatcherism.[31] To return to Macherey's theory of narrative silences, the occlusion of race illuminates a limited liberalism in Kureishi's work which privileges the 'free' individual over identity categories and the communal, and obscures hierarchies of power. As Upstone and Ranasinha demonstrate, this hardline liberalism entails a rejection not just of cultural or ethnic categories, but also of the family as a stifling and repressive unit constraining individual desire, a theme which forms the focus of many of the stories collected in *Love in a Blue Time* and the 2003 screenplay *The Mother*, as well as *Intimacy*.[32] The implications of this for Kureishi's representation of Islam and Muslims in the context of multicultural Britain are explored in the next section.

REPRESENTING MUSLIMS

In his 1986 essay 'Bradford', Kureishi details the frequent racial attacks faced by taxi drivers in the city, the story of the Bradford Twelve, the prominence of the National Front and the Ray Honeyford affair, and takes care to relate these tensions to poverty and class.[33] Despite this, however, a revealing ambivalence appears in the discussion of the issue of 'Islamic separatism', triggered by the author's visit to neighbouring Batley's Islamic Zakariya Girls School. Some of his criticism of this particular school might well be valid, but it descends into a series of questions that accuse more than they explore: 'Did the Asian community really want this kind of separate education anyway? And if it did, how many wanted it? Or was it only a few earnest and repressed believers, all men, frightened of England and their daughters' sexuality?' (*Dreaming*, 68). Here, the notion of a faith school as a means of protecting and preserving a minority religious culture in the context of a largely secular public sphere is quashed beneath a stereotype of a separatist Islamic patriarchy, and the context of religious, racial and social marginalisation that contributes to so-called separatism fades almost to invisibility.[34] Kureishi's discussion of Chowdhury Khan, then president of the Bradford Council of Mosques, is also illuminating. Pronouncing Khan's views 'extremely conservative and traditional', he goes on to claim that 'they are also, isolated from the specifics of their subcontinental context, the values championed by Ray Honeyford' (69). He fails to consider Khan's views as in part a product of their location in Britain and indeed in Bradford. By obscuring this context, he equates a reactive, minority, working-class conservatism (Khan's, arguably) to a then hegemonic conservatism (Honeyford's). Not only does the subcontinent become the constitutive Other of a despatialised Britain, but a universalised conservatism becomes the constitutive Other of liberalism. While a separatist view and practice of ethnicity is not reducible to class, it cannot be detached from social conditions. As Jonathan Friedman points out, the attempt to establish hybridity as the normative discourse is carried out from the top, by the social and cultural elite, who define the identities of others in these terms: 'The contrast between hybrid/creole identifications and the essentialisation that is common to lower-class and marginalised populations, as well as what are referred to as "redneck" leaders of ethnic mobilizations, *is a contrast in social position.*'[35] Interestingly, shortly after his discussion of the school and Khan, Kureishi outlines the views of Tariq, a young politically active Muslim inhabitant of Bradford, who, while not a 'separatist', is able to understand that 'the problem of integration was adjacent to the problem of being poor in Britain' (71). While Kureishi articulates Tariq's views, he fails to apply them to his own discussion of separatism. The poverty of the Asian community is clear in Kureishi's essay, but the relationship between the 'separatism' and social position of the Muslims he meets is obscured.

In 1986, when 'Bradford' was written, a challenge to the racist-nationalist exclusions of Thatcher's Britain by an endorsement of cultural diversity was a priority for an oppositional politics. In the light of this, Kureishi's antipathy towards monoculturalism 'from below' (or the cultural 'separatism' of some of Bradford's Muslims) is in part a product of the historical moment, and the tension between this antipathy and his anti-racism in 'Bradford' is comparable to a similar tension in Rushdie's *The Satanic Verses*. Yet, the equation of 'dominant' and 'defensive' essentialisms for Muslims[36] – especially working-class Muslims – in the context of post-fatwa late twentieth-century and early twenty-first-century multicultural Britain is more troubling. Here, I explore the author's representation of British Muslims and Islam in four of his post-fatwa but pre-9/11 works – his novel *The Black Album*, his short story and screenplay versions of 'My son the fanatic', and his semi-(auto)biographical *My Ear at his Heart* – to ask how far they reach beyond the limits of a liberal multiculturalism.

In a 1999 interview, in response to a question about his feelings of responsibility as a writer in the wake of the Rushdie affair, Kureishi makes the following revealing comments: 'In so far as a writer has any responsibility, it's to their own imagination ... but also the responsibility of being sceptical, of asking questions ... And part of [serious culture] is that it is irresponsibility ... It is asking questions of authority. And not being ... respectful to ideologies.'[37] His comments are usefully contrasted with those of Modood who, discussing the Britain-based protests that followed the publication of the book, writes critically of Britain's unwillingness

> to acknowledge in its institutional and legal arrangements the existence of a Muslim community which ... can be deeply hurt and provoked to violence by forms of literature that the majority of citizens have become used to tolerating ... Is it not obvious that different cultural groups will value irreverent literature in different degrees depending on their history and the vulnerabilities of their position?[38]

The crucial contrast between these two views lies in their understandings of what constitutes opposition in the particular set of circumstances that obtained in the wake of the novel's publication. For Kureishi, Rushdie's 'irreverent' novel was oppositional in terms of its challenge to religious ideology and its transgression of the constraints imposed on 'free speech' by religious doctrine. For Modood, by contrast, it was the grassroots protest against the novel that was oppositional. As Modood points out, the protagonists in the Britain-based demonstrations and book-burnings were predominantly working-class South Asian Muslims. While Rushdie's novel was not just accepted but feted by the liberal secular intelligentsia in Britain, the demonstrators' anger could not be accommodated anywhere within Britain's political spectrum. It could not find a place within a metropolitan anti-racism which refused to recognise political mobilisation by a disempowered minority group *in the name of a religion*. If Kureishi is concerned with an opposition to religious 'dogma', Modood sees beyond this binary. His concern is with opposition as the struggle for a political voice by a marginalised group, whether this struggle is mobilised via a secularist anti-racism or an anti-materialist doctrine (religion) – but especially when it is mobilised via the latter because this form of opposition is largely delegitimised within the political spectrum and is therefore particularly lacking in agency.

Not only does *The Black Album* depict a book-burning in protest against Rushdie's *The Satanic Verses*, but the theme of censorship and creative freedom threads its way through the novel as a whole. The politicised piety of Riaz the Islamist is frequently counterposed to protagonist Shahid's fascination with literature, art and music, inspired and encouraged by his lover Deedee Osgood. Shahid boasts a collection of Prince albums (including the eponymous *Black Album*), the walls of his college room are adorned with art postcards, and his extensive collection of books include 'studies of Freud, along with fiction by Maupassant, Henry Miller, and the Russians' (29). By contrast, Riaz's acolyte Chad, a convert to Islam, has weaned himself off music which, he claims, enslaved him (79). Riaz, too, despite his zealotry, has artistic leanings, considered by some in the community to be at odds with his piety – but unlike Shahid's, his writing 'always [has] a standpoint' or a clear message (67–9, 174). Conversely, for Shahid, creative culture has the capacity to unsettle and to disturb; it is the very antithesis of the single-mindedness of religious belief (75, 183). While Riaz and his group 'would admit no splinter of imagination into their body of belief', for Shahid the world was 'more subtle and inexplicable' and his friends' belief a story which, like all stories, 'could not be true or false ... human, aesthetic, fallible' (133). Further, creative culture provides a space for the articulation of the taboo. It is after seeing a play by Spanish dramatist Federico García Lorca that Shahid begins to realise 'that there was a multitude of true things that couldn't be said because they led to uneasy thoughts. Disruption of life, even, could follow; the truth could have serious consequences. Clearly the unsaid was where it all happened' (75). These 'uneasy thoughts' are what his mother sought to suppress when she attempted to censor Shahid's short story about racism which disrupted her vision of their upwardly mobile position in Britain (73). It is this uneasiness, moreover, that Shahid's sexual corruption of Riaz's pious poetry – redolent of Salman's corruption of Mahound's verses in *The Satanic Verses* and the final act which cuts his ties with the group – engenders (233–6).

In many respects, then, Kureishi's post-fatwa novel appears to corroborate his own somewhat myopic response to the Rushdie affair, echoing the binary opposition of a censoring and rigid Islam versus an iconoclastic, liberating and liberal creativity, as Ranasinha argues.[39] Yet, there are alternative voices in the novel which dislodge such a reductive opposition – and which do so, moreover, by highlighting the role of class. When Shahid challenges Riaz about his punitive attitude towards the author of the controversial book, Riaz's response is to alert Shahid to their poverty and lack of voice: 'Look at [your people], they are from villages, half-literate and not wanted here. All day they suffer poverty and abuse. Don't we, in this land of so-called free expression, have to give them a voice?' (173). Shahid echoes these words in his attempt to defend the aubergine worshippers to Deedee (209), while both Riaz and Andrew Brownlow, Deedee's estranged socialist husband, emphasise the privileged status of writers (182, 215), and Brownlow explicitly reframes the free-speech controversy in terms of class: 'But you don't believe the liberals – who are working themselves up into a pompous lather – are fighting for literary freedom, do you?', he asks Shahid: 'They're just standing by their miserable class. When have they ever given a damn about you – the Asian working class – and your struggle? Your class is arguing back' (215). Thus, an abstract notion of freedom of speech is debunked along with that of an equal public sphere, and the binary opposition of liberal individualism versus communal repression, on which normative constructions of the Rushdie affair were predicated, is complicated. Indeed, this binary is also challenged by Shahid's construction of Riaz's stubborn adherence to the principles of his faith as individual, unorthodox behaviour that is directly opposed to the conformity of 'rebellious' youth. As he remarks: 'Where everyone else had zigged, Riaz had zagged' (109). And while Deedee – who emblematises secular free-thinking and creativity, with her love of literature and music and her bohemian lifestyle – is swift to challenge Shahid's defence of Riaz, she frequently emerges as misguided and myopic, while her subversive lifestyle and her problems are configured as a product of class privilege and middle-class self-indulgence, respectively (44, 57).

The counter-arguments offered by both Islamist Riaz and socialist Brownlow are, however, undermined by the ironisation of these characters. While Riaz is portrayed as increasingly sinister, Brownlow's drunkenness, misogyny and self-contradiction render him an object of ridicule (98, 119, 151, 240, 97, 94, 238). The development of a stutter at the collapse of communist states, and its return when he attempts to talk about the book-burning, emblematise the breakdown of his black-and-white political principles when confronted by more complex social realities (32, 242). His collapse of voice could be read as a form of self-censorship routed in his political conviction: he becomes mute when the latter is undermined. In this sense, Brownlow's socialism, like Riaz's faith, is shown to be limited and limiting, in contradistinction to the unfettered complexity and productive transgressions of creative culture. It is also configured as a performance which breaks down under duress, as is religious belief. When Chad brandishes a burning copy of the controversial book, we are told: 'the former Trevor Buss and Muhammad Shahabuddin Ali-Shah, alias Brother Chad ... laughed triumphantly' (225). This emphasis on the multiple personae adopted by Chad in his attempt to find a sense of belonging at the very point that he is engaged in a passionate act of protest in the name of his religious faith undermines the sincerity of his commitment to an idea, and hence the very notion of commitment. Instead, Chad is exposed as a layering of different identities which can be peeled back infinitely (106–8), as is suggested by the strata of personae in 'With your tongue down my throat'. There is no inner core or 'fixed self' and so there cannot be a coherent belief system: 'How could anyone confine themselves to one system or creed? Why should they feel they had to?' (274).

While a positive notion of communitarianism does emerge in the novel when the group organises to defend a working-class Asian family against racist attacks, their cohesion and the purpose of their action are questioned, and the communitarian aspect of religious culture appears increasingly as a source of division and oppression as well as a performance (89–90, 129–30). As Shahid understands it, believing is a matter of 'joining', and joining leads to divisions: 'He had noticed, during the days that he'd walked around the area, that the races were divided ... But where did such divides lead to, if not to different kinds of civil war?'(133).

A faith-based communitarianism becomes a divisive communalism. As Bart Moore-Gilbert argues, ultimately the novel privileges individual rights over community or group rights, and represents the latter as entrenching or creating the disadvantages of others (women, individuals within the community, or the white majority).[40] Further, just as Riaz's anti-racist group fails to understand the disaffection of the white working class, Brownlow, despite his socialist desire to be an ally of the oppressed minority group that Riaz and his friends seek to represent, is unable to bridge the secularist/religious divide, pronouncing Riaz a 'slave of super-stition' and religion 'bondage' (94–5, 96–7). Thus, socialism and religious minority mobilisation remain in tension with one another. With this, the novel arguably points to the blindspots of secularist left-wing poli-tics when it comes to religion and Islam in particular. Yet, the fact that a multiculturalist respect for religious difference and a materialist aware-ness of class and of the unevenness of the public sphere remain disjunc-tive and irreconcilable in *The Black Album* can be read differently. These gaps in understanding between Muslims and socialists are ideologically necessary so that the novel can remain finally compatible with liber-alism, despite its articulation of a range of different political positions through its characters.[41] Keeping a Muslim identity politics separate from and disjunctive with a class-based politics enables a liberal critique of the former to remain intact and uncomplicated by class.

Through its ironisation of Deedee – with her 'boutique multicultur-alism' which draws her towards her young Asian lover but cannot tolerate the worship of an icon and seeks to 'rescue' Asian girls from their 'culture' (208–10, 155, 29)[42] – the novel gestures towards the failure of a certain brand of western feminism to encompass cultural difference.[43] Yet, there are no convincing alternative female voices in the novel. While the most prominent female member of Riaz's group, Tahira, has the potential to act as a foil to Deedee, perhaps most notably when she challenges the lecturer's notion of equality for its predication on the erasure of difference (229–30), she remains a minor, underdeveloped character who considers the likeable protagonist 'an egotist with an evil smile' (235). Ultimately, there is little space in the novel for a recognition of cultural difference that strains at the limits of a secularist liberalism, or for an understanding of Islam that departs from stereotype. While Shahid concludes that there 'had to be innumerable ways of being in the world', *religious* ways are all but reduced to posturing, rigidity and censorious behaviour, and Deedee's questions to her lover when he defends the aubergine worship

– 'Is it your culture? Is it culture at all?' – remain unchallenged (274, 209).
On the surface, the dialogic form of the novel, which gives voice to the
free-thinking hedonistic liberal and the fundamentalist Muslim, satirising
both in the process, obfuscates a clear ideological position.[44] Indeed, the
multiplicity of perspectives works as a smokescreen, obscuring Kureishi's
political position. And yet, this very refusal to adopt a clear position – at
least until the end of the novel when Shahid makes his tentative choice
– is itself a political position. It is an 'end of ideology' ideology, or an
anti-ideology ideology,[45] whereby an endless process of deconstruction
leaves only the individual subject intact as a transcendental or, paradoxically, a fundamental.

In Kureishi's 1997 short story 'My son the fanatic' (*Love*) the liberal
British Pakistani Parvez, who 'avoided all religions', is counterposed to his
son Ali, the eponymous Muslim fanatic or fundamentalist (123). Indeed,
this tension between liberalism and fanaticism is the logic on which the
narrative turns. Despite the twist at its close (where Parvez is so enraged
that he beats his son, provoking the calm response of 'So who's the fanatic
now?'), the narrative privileges and valorises the father's liberal views,
configuring him as the victim of his son's behaviour (131). The dichotomy
of father versus son is overwhelming, all but foreclosing a consideration
of the social context that might shape their contrasting choices. The
oppression of Muslims, both on a global scale and within Britain, is fleetingly alluded to; but this important context is voiced by Ali and thereby
reduced to the aggressive, irrational assertion of a dehumanised fanatic.
When Ali tells his father 'All over the world our people are oppressed',
this point is diverted by Parvez's confusion as to 'who "our people"
were' (129). Thus the binary of homogeneous collective ('our people')
and heterogeneous confusion – what Sukhdev Sandhu describes as Kureishi's 'messthetics' – emerges.[46] Indeed, this binary is visible at the very
opening of the story, where we share Parvez's curiosity and confusion as
to why his son's bedroom should suddenly be so 'neat and ordered', why
'spaces [were] appearing where before there had been only mess' (119).
Paradoxically, however, the heterogeneity of the Muslim community,
which Parvez's confusion at Ali's remark evokes, is rendered invisible, and
the two poles of fanatic and secular liberal do not leave room for other
living practices of Islam. The poverty of Britain's Muslim community is
sketchily visible when Parvez and his friend Bettina, a sex worker, spot Ali
in a run-down Muslim area, but the reader's sympathy is channelled away
from this hint at the destitution that characterises Muslim communities

in some northern cities to Parvez's own struggle to give his son opportunities that he lacked and to Bettina, another of society's victims (129).

In his essay 'The road exactly', an introduction to the screenplay
My Son the Fanatic, Kureishi demonstrates his awareness of the poverty
and disenfranchisement of a large proportion of Asian Muslims and
roots some Muslims' turn to radicalism in this context.[47] Certainly, this
context is more evident in the screenplay than in the short story. Shots of
run-down streets in a northern city form a backdrop to the drama in the
film, and Parvez frequently experiences racial abuse; the wooden club he
carries in his taxi, and the moniker of 'little man' bestowed on him by the
German capitalist Schitz, are suggestive of a general climate of fear and
belittlement which is punctuated by abuse or attacks, such as the vicious
jibes of the comedian and crowd in the club he visits with Schitz and
Bettina (*Collected Screenplays 1*, 289–90, 334, 305, 306, 130–1). Further, the
son, named Farid in this version, explicitly roots his turn to Islam in this
context, chastising his father for his lack of pride and inability to stand
up for himself in the face of racial abuse (334, 337), while both Bettina
and an anonymous worshipper at the mosque express understanding and
respect for Farid's rejection of capitalist values and determination to challenge his subordination (325, 318). Indeed, Parvez is depicted as a weak
and deeply flawed individual, riven with contradictions: sympathetic to
and protective of Bettina's fellow sex workers, he nevertheless secures
their services for Schitz, assuming the duties of a pimp; furious that the
maulvi's residence in his home has resulted in his wife Minoo's retreat
into the role of servile housewife, he is happy to exploit her domestic
services while beginning an adulterous relationship with Bettina and –
in the screenplay but not the film itself – attempting to rape her when
drunk (366–9, 297, 351–2, 346–7). Thus, the valorisation of the secular
liberal father against the fanatical son is to some degree undermined. Yet,
as Ranasinha points out, in stark contrast to his father, Farid is not much
more than a two-dimensional stock figure, parroting clichés to defend
his choices (333).[48] Further, while he represents his rejection of his career
in accountancy as a critique of capitalism, the discovery that he in fact
stopped studying when he started using drugs, together with his misogynistic and anti-Semitic comments and abusive behaviour, undermine an
understanding of his choice as an ethical one (337, 344, 338, 365–6, 378).

Ranasinha argues that a primary concern of the screenplay is a critique
of patriarchy.[49] Indeed, aside from Parvez, it is Bettina who is drawn
with the most complexity and subtlety, while her fellow sex workers are

configured as feisty and rebellious victims of patriarchy and capitalism. When the maulvi and his coterie violently demonstrate against Bettina and her fellow workers, the fundamentalists and sex workers form another dichotomy in the film, with the latter humanised and the former reduced to cardboard cut-outs (377–8). In contrast to Bettina, the only Muslim woman, Minoo, is little more than a stereotype of the obedient yet resentful Asian housewife, and the alliance she and Farid form in resistance to Parvez's philandering is divested of legitimacy by Farid's own misogyny (299, 312–14, 245–6, 338). Ultimately, the screenplay's concern with gender works to stigmatise Farid and his friends, whose version of Islam is, again, the only one present. Parvez's admonition to his son that 'there is nothing of God in spitting on a woman's face' briefly detaches Farid's behaviour from his religion (379), but the words are spoken by a non-believer and so a glimpse of an alternative understanding of Islam fades away (324–5). As in Kenny Glenaan and Simon Beaufoy's television film *Yasmin*, there is little room for an understanding of a British Muslim masculinity that departs from the stereotypes of drug addict and fanatic. Yet, while in *Yasmin* the father is portrayed as a sad, retreating figure, unable to offer a viable alternative to his son's turn to Islamism in the face of rising prejudice after 9/11, in Kureishi's film the father, despite his weakness, remains an enlightened figure of hope and possibility.[50] Despite his flaws and foibles, including his violent attack on Farid, which ostensibly bring him down from the pedestal on which liberalism is so often placed, the viewer's sympathy is drawn towards Parvez. Indeed, it is precisely the messiness of Parvez – his apparent lack of fit to any singular ideology – and of his alliance with Bettina, which transgresses boundaries of race as well as propriety, that humanises him. Counterposed to the son's 'purity', it is this messiness or inconsistency, which is entirely consistent with an individualist liberalism, that is valorised.

In *The Black Album*, 'My son the fanatic' and, to a lesser degree, the screenplay of the same name, we can trace the opposition that underpins Slavoj Žižek's configuration of late-capitalist liberal democracy, 'the tension between "open" post-ideological universalist liberal tolerance and particularist "new fundamentalisms"', which 'imposes itself as the main axis of ideological struggle' and must be rejected for any real engagement with the social inequalities that capitalism produces.[51] Put differently, by configuring identity categories, essentialisms or, as Terry Eagleton puts it, 'the parochialism of the traditional order', as obstructing the 'freedom' of 'an abstract "mankind"', liberalism screens the real source of constraint

– the social inequalities that are structural to capitalist power and operate along lines of gender, race, religion or ethnicity.[52] As discussed in Chapter 2, Žižek configures the 'fundamentalisms' of the contemporary world as a *product of* the hegemonic status of 'post-ideological universalist' liberalism, which forecloses dissent, thereby forcing it into illegitimate and extreme forms.[53] To broaden these terms, the monocultural, communal identification of a British Muslim (that of Kureishi's fanatical son, Riaz, or even Asif or the Indian doctor) is arguably reinforced by its marginalisation or delegitimisation by a secular liberal culture. Modood points out that the experience of marginalisation or 'exclusion' sustains 'group identity', which then enables the group in question to transmute its negative representations by mainstream society to a positive self-assertion of a collective identity. Given that Muslims experience a relatively high degree of exclusion in contemporary Britain,[54] a communal identity is more likely to be important to more of them.[55] If neoliberalism gives rise to monocultural essentialisms, then a straightforward valorisation of liberal multiculturalism against monoculturalism, both in Kureishi's texts and in certain theories of cultural hybridity, is problematised.

As in Rushdie's *The Satanic Verses*, in *My Ear at his Heart: Reading my Father* Islam frequently jars with an anti-racism that was oppositional in the context of Thatcherism but cannot accommodate the religion of the author's paternal heritage. References to Islam recur throughout; indeed, the frequency and length of these references is often surprising, suggesting a continued and uneasy preoccupation on the part of Kureishi with the religion. Kureishi describes how a Muslim Somalian acquaintance, Abdullah, and the Bengali manager of his local takeaway experience London:

> The manager refers to 'the white man'; Abdullah has just been talking about 'the whites', and I realize that they know they live under a reconstituted colonialism; this is not only a matter of racism but a question about how people like them live in a world dominated by white political, social and cultural power ... According to this picture, the white man possesses everything and will not part with it willingly; not only that, everything white is better than everything non-white ... the non-white seems to exist, can only exist, in the gaps of the white world. (107)

Despite his understanding that power structures are 'not only a matter of racism', Kureishi's repeated opposition of the 'white' world to the 'non-white' world has the effect of reducing hierarchies to a question of race, thereby screening the capacity of 'white ... power' to accommodate certain kinds of 'non-whiteness'.[56] Interestingly, while the men he chooses to focus on here are probably both Muslim, he does not explicitly relate their acute feeling of oppression within London to their religious identity at a time when Islamophobia had become pronounced. Moreover, Kureishi goes on to parallel the 'white man' of today, who is 'in charge', with Enoch Powell, a figure who is a significant presence in this text, as in much of Kureishi's non-fiction (32, 103–7). Of course, it is arguable that the references to Powellism are necessitated by the time span that the book covers and triggered by Kureishi's father's manuscript 'The redundant man', set in 1960s London. However, the effect of this intermittent retreat into the past, which enables a powerful contestation of Powellism and Thatcherism, is to deflect attention away from the exclusions through which liberalism operates and which it conceals beneath a multiculturalist rhetoric.

When discussing the racist climate of the late 1970s and 1980s, a period when the National Front was a visible and threatening presence, Kureishi observes: 'Among the most significant oppositions … was Rock against Racism – the disaffected and liberal young, those whom Islam could only reject' (105). This brief, unexpected and seemingly arbitrary allusion to Islam is revealing. Its somewhat incongruous presence hints at an awareness of the tensions between a secular anti-racism and Britain's Muslim minority. Especially given its presence in the middle of a long passage concerning the overtly racist climate of Kureishi's youth and immediately before a moving account of the racist abuse that the author suffered personally, it also works to discredit Islam in so far as the latter is configured as incompatible with, or even disenabling of, a crucial mobilisation against racism. The burden of responsibility is placed uniquely on Islam, which is doing the rejecting. There is no recognition that the accommodation of two incompatible forms of opposition and dissent must be mutual, as Modood shows in his response to the Rushdie affair.[57] Furthermore, the counter-opposition of the 'liberal young', who are 'disaffected', to 'Islam' carries the implication that those who adhere to Islam are *not* among the 'disaffected'. Indeed, in the context of Kureishi's oeuvre and when placed alongside 'liberal', the word 'disaffected' takes on overtones of bohemianism, implying a rebellious opting out of the system rather than a structural exclusion. The fact that the 'disaffected and liberal young' are cast in a subordinate position to Islam works to screen the disempowerment of the adherents of this religion within Britain and globally. Particularly when read in conjunction with the many allusions in the narrative to Islam, and all religion, as stifling, repressive and wholly incompatible with any form of 'culture' or 'combative imagination', a dichotomy of freedom versus constraint emerges here, positioning Islam on the same side of the binary as the essentialising discourse of race and racism (55–6, 92, 117–18, 167–8).

The narrative's frequent, uneasy return to the trope of Islam could be understood as symptomatic of an inability not only to reconcile the place this religion occupies within his family history to his understanding of his relatives as 'liberal' (92, 167), but also to accommodate Islam within a view of a culturally diverse Britain which is informed by a secularist liberalism. Yet, the retreat into the past, facilitated by the explicit focus on Kureishi's father (the title, the cover photographs, the opening and close of the book), enables a withdrawal from this tension. Often, what might appear as an oddly evasive change of subject or loose thread in the narrative can be conveniently explained by attributing the shape of his narrative, with its detours and shifts, to the conditions supplied by the stories of his father or uncle. For example, when we learn that Omar's reaction to his nephew reading V. S. Naipaul's *Among the Believers* is to tell him 'All Naipaul does is insult us', the curiosity that this might provoke in the reader about Kureishi's own position on this matter is immediately disappointed as the narrative moves swiftly on to a barely related discussion of his cousin Nusrat (57). The various intertexts from which *My Ear* is woven function not only as launch-pads for an exploration of a particular issue or moment but also as decoys; the opinions that he traces within these texts fill the author's own silences on certain issues (race and Islam, in particular) and deflect attention away from these silences.

AFTER 7/7

Kureishi's novel *Something to Tell You* closes in 2005, shortly after the 7/7 terror attacks. The narrator, Jamal, a psychoanalyst of mixed Pakistani–white British heritage, laments the devastation of Bloomsbury's Tavistock Square, not just for the lost lives but also for its symbolic meaning:

> That beautiful London square was where Ajita, Valentin and I had attended many philosophy lectures … It was where Dickens wrote *Bleak House*, and Woolf *Three Guineas*; where Lenin stayed, and the Hogarth Press published James Strachey's Freud translations in the basement of number 52. There is also a plaque to commemorate conscientious objectors in the First World War, as well as another for the victims of Hiroshima, along with a statue of Gandhi. (313)

This urban space is identified with the cultural iconoclasm and political radicalism of the Bloomsbury Group. As Sara Blair has shown, the
geographical area of Bloomsbury was a zone of class and race instability
and transgression before the literary group had formed; indeed, it was this
very instability that made it fertile ground for the group's cultural oppositionality.[58] In Kureishi's vision of the space, there is a familiar contrasting
of literature (Dickens, Woolf, Hogarth Press), as well as critical thought
(Lenin, Freud, philosophy lectures), with the Islamism and terror signified by the bombing. The attack, it is implied, is on critical culture as
well as on the freedom emblematised by the conscientious objectors in
the First World War and M. K. Gandhi. The allusion to Hiroshima, as
well as to Gandhi and the war, together with the cultural diversity of the
three student friends inhabiting the square – Jamal, Ajita and Valentin
(who is Bulgarian) – underlines the transnationalism of the space. This
in turn recalls the frequent counter-opposition in the wake of the 7/7
bombings of the multicultural character of London and the victims, seen
to emblematise 'our' inclusive, open and diverse culture, to the bombers'
singular, homogenising bid to destroy the capital's 'easy-going mix'.[59] In
such a construction, London's diversity (as well as the victims') repels any
suggestion that the capital and its relation with the rest of the world are
shaped by and operate through oppressive neo-imperial hierarchies.

In Kureishi's super-diverse London of the new millennium – 'a world
city' of 'exiles, refugees and immigrants' where the brothels are multicultural and the protagonist's son listens to Mexican hip-hop (10, 40, 157, 14)
– there are frequent allusions to culture and art as a force against authoritarianism and death, particularly through the focalisation of Henry, a
renowned playwright of leftist leanings. For Henry, creative culture
is 'the only negation of the human desire to murder' (51) while art is
the 'still point – a spot of sense' in the 'thrashing world' of 'bloodied,
shredded bodies under Bush-Blair' (303) and a means of examining 'the
Other' with 'imagination and intelligence' (281). Further, Henry likens
the conflict between 'Islam and the West' to that 'between puritans and
liberals, between those who hate the imagination and those who love it ...
between repression and freedom'. The multiculturalism he celebrates and
advocates has limits – and Muslim women who wear the veil fall outside
them (272). While Henry is a much more likeable character than *The
Black Album*'s Brownlow, the exclusions of his socialism where religion
is concerned bring to mind the Marxist academic of the earlier novel: it
is 'these guys' faith rather than their social position which makes them

appear infantile', Henry claims of Muslim waiters at an Indian restaurant he frequents with Jamal, thereby deflecting any potential accusation of class snobbery as the source of his condescending remarks (93). Henry is by no means the moral compass of the novel, yet, as is typical of Kureishi's fiction, Jamal, the narrator and Henry's interlocutor, frequently withholds an opinion, leaving his friend's views barely challenged. Jamal himself, despite his withdrawal from a clear political position, betrays a discomfort with his former lover Ajita's post-7/7 adoption of an explicitly Muslim identity (320). Upstone finds in the novel a more positive characterisation of the appeal of religious belief. For her, the character of Ajita, sympathetically drawn, provides an 'interrogation of Jamal's middle-class liberalism'.[60] But Ajita's newfound interest in Islam remains little more than a performance, redolent of Nina's in 'With your tongue down my throat'. Initially she wears the burqa on the Underground to test Londoners' reactions to it after the bombings, and, despite intimations that her interest goes further, the mismatch between a privileged, apolitical adopted New Yorker and a serious engagement with Islam suggests the latter is mere play-acting, or at best a passing phase (319–22). 'Muslimness', then, is largely relegated to the margins of the narrative, remaining distinctly Other to the secular narrator and central characters.

Arguably, the novel ironises all of the characters and their views on Muslims and multiculturalism, which are anyway contradictory and hard to pin down. Omar Ali, the protagonist of *My Beautiful Launderette* – now a wealthy middle-aged businessman as well as a 'stalwart of the anti-racist industry' and a Labour peer – supports the post-9/11 British bombings of Iraq, voicing the neo-imperial rhetoric of 'civilisation' as his rationale. Yet he immediately retracts his most extreme comments, which are fuelled by an urge to provoke Henry and attenuated by a 'cheeky face' (160). Further, seemingly clearly defined political views are exposed as riven with contradictions: Henry's privileged daughter Lisa's radical socialism collapses when confronted with the working-class lifestyle of her father's lover Miriam (148–9). Unlike in some of Kureishi's short fiction, class, and its intersection with race and migration, does play a significant role in *Something to Tell You*. The poverty of west London's newly arrived immigrants is underlined, as is the Islamophobia that scars the lives of the Muslim inhabitants of the working-class neighbourhood where Miriam lives (10, 14–15). Similarly, the chasm between the wealth and decadence of the celebrities who gather at Ajita's brother Mustaq's rural pile and the deprivation of the people who inhabit the nearby town is sharply drawn (195–8). In this respect, the narrative eschews the liberal multiculturalism that can be traced in Kureishi's earlier work and that underpinned some responses to the 7/7 bombings. Yet, ultimately the deconstructive impulse in the novel, which fractures any clear political narrative, privileges an individualism that helps to relegate cultural otherness to the margins of the novel. Raymond Williams questions the radicalism of the Bloomsbury Group by arguing that their opposition to 'poverty, sexual and racial discrimination, militarism and imperialism' was conditioned by its upper-middle-class position so that it was 'not any alternative idea of a whole society' or solidarity with the working classes that Bloomsbury espoused, but rather 'the supreme value of the civilized individual'.[61] Similarly, it is the iconoclasm of the individual that both forms and, crucially, limits the oppositionality of Kureishi's narrative, so that the division between the critical culture that shapes the history of Tavistock Square and the collectivism, moral strictures and fundamentalism that are normatively identified not just with the act of terror that destroyed it, but also with Islam and Muslims, remains.

NOTES

1 Sara Ahmed, *Strange Encounters: Embodied Others in Post-Coloniality* (London: Routledge, 2000), p. 113.

2 Anuradha Dingwaney Needham, *Using the Master's Tools: Resistance and the Literature of the African and South Asian Diasporas* (Basingstoke: Palgrave Macmillan, 2000), p. 121.

3 Hanif Kureishi, *Dreaming and Scheming: Reflections on Writing and Politics* (London: Faber, 2002), p. 55.

4 *Ibid.*, pp. 27–9.

5 John Solomos, *Race and Racism in Contemporary Britain* (Basingstoke: Palgrave Macmillan, 1999), pp. 59–60; John McLeod, *Postcolonial London: Rewriting the Metropolis* (London and New York: Routledge, 2004), p. 130.

6 Les Back, Michael Keith, Azra Khan, Kalbir Shukra and John Solomos, 'The return to assimilation: race, multiculturalism and New Labour', *Sociological Research Online*, 7:2 (2002), www.socresonline.org.uk/7/2/back.html (last accessed 6 November 2014).

7 Ahmed, *Strange Encounters*, p. 113.

8 *Ibid.*

9 Bhikhu Parekh's description of the limits of liberalism is instructive here: 'It is an inspiring political doctrine stressing such great values as human dignity, autonomy, liberty, critical thought and equality. However, it has no monopoly of them ... it is insufficiently sensitive to and cannot give

coherent accounts of the importance of culture, tradition, community, a sense of rootedness and belonging, and so on' (*Rethinking Multiculturalism: Cultural Diversity and Political Theory* (Basingstoke: Palgrave Macmillan, 2nd edn, 2006 [2000]), p. 339).

10   Ahmed, *Strange Encounters*, p. 113.

11   Hanif Kureishi, *Love in a Blue Time* (London: Faber, 1997); *Intimacy* (London: Faber, 1998); *Midnight All Day* (London: Faber, 1999); *The Body and Seven Stories* (London: Faber, 2002). All subsequent citations are given within the body of the chapter and are to these editions of the texts. None of Kureishi's most recent short stories, published in his *Collected Stories* (London: Faber, 2010), focuses on race or cultural difference in Britain, although 'Weddings and beheadings', first published in 2006, is set in a location that is suggestive of Iraq and narrated from the point of view of a photographer who is obliged to document beheadings of hostages.

12   Hanif Kureishi, *The Black Album* (London: Faber, 1995); *My Son the Fanatic*, dir. Udayan Prasad (1997); *Collected Screenplays 1* (London: Faber, 2002); *My Ear at his Heart: Reading my Father* (London: Faber, 2004); *Something to Tell You* (London: Faber, 2008). All subsequent citations are given within the body of the chapter and are to these editions of the texts. Kureishi's most recent novel, *The Last Word* (2014), was published too late for inclusion in this book.

13   Yasmin Alibhai-Brown, *Mixed Feelings: The Complex Lives of Mixed-Race Britons* (London: Women's Press, 2001); Suki Ali, *Mixed-Race, Post-Race: Gender, New Ethnicities and Cultural Practices* (Oxford: Berg, 2003).

14   See, for example, Needham, *Using the Master's Tools*; Sukhdev Sandhu, *London Calling: How Black and Asian Writers Imagined a City* (London: Harper-Collins, 2003).

15   Nahem Yousaf, *Hanif Kureishi's* The Buddha of Suburbia: *A Reader's Guide* (New York and London: Continuum, 2002), p. 10.

16   Diana Fuss, 'Interior colonies: Frantz Fanon and the politics of identification', in Nigel C. Gibson (ed.), *Rethinking Fanon: The Continuing Dialogue* (New York: Humanity Books, 1999), pp. 294–328, p. 297.

17   Pierre Macherey, *A Theory of Literary Production*, trans. Geoffrey Wall (New York and London: Routledge, 1996 [1978; French original 1966]), pp. 19–20, 77.

18   See, for example, Yousaf, *Hanif Kureishi*; Needham, *Using the Master's Tools*; Bart Moore-Gilbert, *Hanif Kureishi* (Manchester: Manchester University Press, 2001), among others. In *The Buddha of Suburbia*, this idea is explored when Karim and fellow minority actor Tracey dispute the politics of representing an Asian character – Uncle Anwar – who conforms to stereotype (London: Faber, 1990).

19   Ruvani Ranasinha, *Hanif Kureishi* (Tavistock: Northcote House, 2002), p. 103.

20   Colin McCabe, 'Interview: Hanif Kureishi on London', *Critical Quarterly*, 41:3 (1999), 37–56, 49.

21 Macherey, *Literary Production*, p. 86.

22 *Ibid.*, pp. 87, 94.

23 Yunus Samad, 'The plural guises of multiculturalism: conceptualising a fragmented paradigm', in Tariq Modood and Pnina Werbner (eds), *The Politics of Multiculturalism in the New Europe: Racism, Identity and Community* (London: Zed Books, 1997), pp. 240–60, pp. 251–3.

24 Parekh, *Rethinking Multiculturalism*, p. 24.

25 Pnina Werbner, 'Essentialising essentialism, essentialising silence: ambivalence and multiplicity in the construction of racism and ethnicity', in Pnina Werbner and Tariq Modood (eds), *Debating Cultural Hybridity: Multi-Cultural Identities and the Politics of Anti-Racism* (London: Zed Books), pp. 226–56, p. 229.

26 Frantz Fanon, *Black Skin, White Masks*, trans. Charles Lam Markmann (New York: Grove, 1967).

27 Ali, *Mixed-Race, Post-Race*, p. 180.

28 *Ibid.*, pp. 9–16.

29 For a discussion of Kureishi's treatment of class in relation to metropolitan space, see Sara Upstone, *British Asian Fiction: Twenty-First-Century Voices* (Manchester: Manchester University Press, 2010), pp. 48–9. Upstone argues convincingly that the apparently working-class culture and spaces Kureishi portrays are frequently distanced from real poverty and that his prose when describing them is often characterised by 'more than a hint of detached modernist *flâneurie*' (p. 49).

30 Tariq Modood, *Multiculturalism: A Civic Idea* (Cambridge: Polity, 2007), p. 120.

31 Upstone, *British Asian Fiction*, p. 44.

32 *Ibid.*, pp. 42–4; Ranasinha, *Hanif Kureishi*, ch. 5.

33 Kureishi, *Dreaming*, pp. 57–79. All subsequent citations are given within the body of the chapter and are to this edition of the text.

34 Kureishi's views on faith schools seemed broadly similar nearly two decades later ('The carnival of culture', in *The Word and the Bomb* (London: Faber, 2005), pp. 95–100).

35 Jonathan Friedman, 'Global crises, the struggle for cultural identity and intellectual porkbarrelling: cosmopolitans versus locals, ethnics and nationals in an era of dehegemonisation', in Werbner and Modood (eds), *Debating Cultural Hybridity: Multi-Cultural Identities and the Politics of Anti-Racism*, pp. 70–89, p. 88 (emphasis mine). See also Slavoj Žižek, 'Multiculturalism, or, the cultural logic of multinational capital', in *The Universal Exception: Selected Writings*, vol. 2 (London and New York: Continuum, 2006), pp. 174–5.

36 Needham, *Using the Master's Tools*, p. 127. Such a gesture can also be seen in the parallel Sandhu draws between Kureishi's representation of the property developer's attitude towards London in *Sammy and Rosie Get Laid* (*Collected Screenplays 1*, pp. 91–176), and the attitude of *The Black Album*'s Riaz. According

to Sandhu, both aim to 'clean up London', the former for the swifter flow of capital and the latter to lead people to Allah, and both disregard 'individuality' (*London Calling*, pp. 245–7). Sandhu uncritically highlights Kureishi's own equation of two very different ideologies – the one hegemonic and the other counter-hegemonic.

37 McCabe, 'Interview', 53.

38 Tariq Modood, *Multicultural Politics: Racism, Ethnicity and Muslims in Britain* (Edinburgh: Edinburgh University Press, 2005), p. 11.

39 Ranasinha, *Hanif Kureishi*, p. 91.

40 Bart Moore-Gilbert, 'From "the politics of recognition" to "the policing of recognition"', in Rehana Ahmed, Peter Morey and Amina Yaqin (eds), *Culture, Diaspora, and Modernity in Muslim Writing* (Abingdon and New York: Routledge, 2012), pp. 183–99, pp. 189–90.

41 Macherey, *Literary Production*.

42 Stanley Fish, 'Boutique multiculturalism, or why liberals are incapable of thinking about hate speech', *Critical Inquiry*, 23 (Winter 1997), 378–95, 382.

43 See Moore-Gilbert, *Hanif Kureishi*, pp. 140–3.

44 Moore-Gilbert notes that the distance between the omniscient narrator and the protagonist 'diminishes as the latter increasingly approximates to the authorial vision of what is appropriate to the identity and identifications he constructs for himself' – a secular individualist detachment from the Islamic group ('From "the politics of recognition"', p. 190).

45 Terry Eagleton, *Ideology: An Introduction* (London: Verso, 1991), pp. 4, 39, 42.

46 Sandhu, *London Calling*, pp. 245–7.

47 Kureishi, 'The road exactly', in *Dreaming*, pp. 219–20.

48 Ranasinha, *Hanif Kureishi*, pp. 94–5.

49 Ibid., pp. 93, 96–7.

50 Simon Beaufoy (writer) and Kenny Glenaan (director), *Yasmin* (2004); see Rehana Ahmed, 'British Muslim masculinities and cultural resistance: Kenny Glenaan and Simon Beaufoy's *Yasmin*', *Journal of Postcolonial Literature*, 45:3 (2009), 285–96.

51 Žižek, 'Multiculturalism', p. 177.

52 Eagleton, *Ideology*, p. 61.

53 Žižek, 'Multiculturalism', p. 177.

54 Madeleine Bunting, 'This is about real victims', *Guardian* (11 December 2004), www.theguardian.com/world/2004/dec/11/race.religion (last accessed 6 November 2014).

55 Modood, *Multiculturalism*, pp. 106, 39–40, 61.

56 Ahmed, *Strange Encounters*, p. 113.

57 Modood, *Multicultural Politics*, pp. 105–6.

58 Sara Blair, 'Local modernity, global modernism', *English Literary History*, 71:3 (Autumn 2004), 813–38.

59 Trevor Phillips, 'Let's show the world its future', *Observer* (10 July 2005),

www.theguardian.com/uk/2005/jul/10/olympics2012.olympicgames   (last accessed 6 November 2014).

60 Upstone, *British Asian Fiction*, p. 55.
61 Raymond Williams, *Culture and Materialism* (London: Verso 2005 [1980]), p. 165.

4

Locating class in Monica Ali's *Brick Lane* and its reception

The giving and accepting of offence is a natural part of living in a plural world. If we want the pleasures of pluralism, we have to be grown-up enough to accept the pain too. (Kenan Malik, paraphrasing Monica Ali[1])

Context and history are all ... episodes such as *Behzti* or the Danish cartoons cannot be viewed in isolation but as one of a series of events, within Europe and beyond, in which Muslims (but not only Muslims) believe themselves increasingly under siege from a hostile 'West'. They are embedded in a long history of relationships between East and West, Muslims and Christians, colonizers and colonized, and one of the lessons from *Behzti* and other affairs is that the consequences of that history remain to be addressed. (Ralph Grillo[2])

THE NOVEL'S RECEPTION

Monica Ali's 2003 debut novel, *Brick Lane*, was published to considerable acclaim. Lauded by a host of literary critics and journalists, the novel was shortlisted for the Man Booker Prize, the Guardian First Book Award, the Commonwealth Writers' Prize and the US National Book Critics Circle award, and Ali was pronounced one of the decade's twenty foremost young British novelists by the highly regarded *Granta* magazine even before the novel was published. At the 'popular' end of the spectrum, *Brick Lane* won the WHSmith People's Choice Award and was the chosen title for the first Richard and Judy Book Club in 2004. While its story opens in Bangladesh, with the birth of the protagonist Nazneen, the majority of the novel is situated in the 'enclaved' East End Bangladeshi community to which Nazneen migrates when barely a woman to marry an older man.[3] Nazneen's physical, transcontinental journey underpins the novel, but it is her journey of self-development as a Muslim Bangladeshi woman negotiating the challenges of working-class immigrant life within the confines of a Tower Hamlets council estate that forms its focus. *Brick Lane* was not the first work of fiction to depict the lives of working-class South Asian Muslims; Salman Rushdie's *The Satanic Verses*, Syed Manzurul Islam's collection of short stories *The Mapmakers of Spitalfields* (1998) and Abdullah Hussein's *Émigré Journeys* (2000) all explore this territory in very different ways. It was, however, the first novel by a British writer of Muslim heritage to engage closely with such a community subsequent to and in the context of events, including the 2001 race riots and the 9/11 terror attacks, that have cast a spotlight on Britain's Muslim population. As such, the level of interest it generated in a media and reading public eager for a greater 'understanding' of British Muslims is perhaps unsurprising.[4]

No less surprising, this chapter suggests, was the impact of its publication, as well as its adaptation into film, on some Tower Hamlets Bangladeshis who read the novel as a representation of their already beleaguered community that had entered the public domain at a time of particular vulnerability and scrutiny by government, media and the majority public. In December 2003, shortly after the publication of *Brick Lane*, the Greater Sylhet Development and Welfare Council (GSDWC), a nationwide voluntary organisation which cites the welfare of Sylheti Bangladeshis in Britain as its primary concern, wrote an eighteen-page letter to Monica Ali protesting against the novel's depiction of their community. A copy of the letter was sent to John Carey, chair of that year's Booker Prize, and to the *Guardian*. Its main point was that their community had been represented in a 'shameful' way – that Bangladeshis (Sylhetis, in particular) had been portrayed as 'backward, uneducated and unsophisticated'.[5] Some three years later, filming of the novel on Brick Lane itself and the surrounding streets provoked further dissent. A group of around one hundred protesters, many of whom were businessmen and traders affiliated to the Brick Lane Business Association, marched through the streets shouting slogans such as, 'Community, community, Bangladeshi community' and 'Monica's book, full of lies'. The protest was spearheaded by Abdus Salique, a local sweetshop owner, Labour Party member and future mayor of Tower Hamlets (2008–9). The film company was eventually forced to withdraw and produce the final scenes of the film elsewhere.[6] The dissenters again pronounced the novel 'racist and insulting' and called for their community to be 'accurately and ethically portrayed, not … subjected to distortion, misrepresentation, sensation and stereotyping'.[7]

Largely dismissed as insignificant and even risible by commentators across the media as well as by the author herself, these small-scale protests were, however, given substantial publicity, resonating as they did with the British Muslim mobilisation against Rushdie's *The Satanic Verses*, as well as with other contemporaneous disputes which saw members of Britain's minority faith communities poised against the media and literary establishment in protest against a creative work. These include, most notably, the 2004 demonstrations by hundreds of Sikhs against the Birmingham Repertory Theatre's staging of Gurpreet Kaur Bhatti's play *Behzti* ('Dishonour') for its portrayal of sex abuse and murder in a gurdwara; the 2005–6 global protests against the publication of cartoons featuring the Prophet Mohammed in the Danish newspaper *Jyllands-Posten*; and the contrasting protest, also in 2005, by writers and artists against government proposals for legislation against incitement to religious hatred.[8] English PEN, who had lobbied energetically against the proposed legislation, were swift to denounce both Ali's detractors and the media hype. For them, the campaign against the filming of the novel in Brick Lane was to be dismissed as that of 'a tiny number or protestors' headed by a 'self-appointed' leader and 'unelected and unaccountable community "representatives"'.[9] Columnists were warned to avoid the paradigm of 'Free Speech absolutists vs an embattled minority' in reporting on the protests; instead, they were advised that the dispute was between 'a small group of authoritarians who don't understand the nature of fiction vs a much larger us that includes many progressive Bangladeshis and others in the Brick Lane area'.[10] PEN's sharp criticism of the notion that the protesters should be seen as representative of the Bangladeshi community was echoed in a number of articles highlighting the varied response to the controversy on the part of local Bangladeshis, many of whom were said to support the novel and its filming in the area. Jonathan Heawood asserted that the protesters should be stripped 'of their claim to "community" status',[11] while Ali herself cited the positive response to her novel from several female and younger east London Bangladeshis as well as the eagerness of hundreds of local men and women to act as extras in the film.[12] Ruby Films claimed to have involved large numbers of supportive members of the local Bangladeshi community as consultants or film crew,[13] and Natasha Walter sought to show that the 'book burners' did not 'speak for all of Brick Lane' by interviewing three Bangladeshi women, two of them residents of Tower Hamlets, about their more measured responses to the novel and its filming.[14] The gendered nature of the protest was cited repeatedly by critics, echoing representations of the *Behzti* controversy:[15] the reactionary male protesters, we were told, objected to the portrait of an emancipated woman that emerges in the novel and its film version.[16] Indeed, Mahmoud Rauf of the Brick Lane Business Association appears to corroborate this understanding of the protest when he highlights Nazneen's infidelity in his explanation of why the novel was offensive to him.[17]

These objections to the protest by the literary intelligentsia are persuasive. The GSDWC is just one of several Bangladeshi organisations in Britain and its representatives are predominantly men. Similarly, the protest against the film was composed almost completely of men, with just two women sighted.[18] Their voices, albeit largely dismissed across the media, dominated and obscured other dissenting voices from the same community, including those of some of its women. A homogeneous notion of a minority community will conceal hierarchies within this group and risk marginalising its more disenfranchised members (often its women and children) by listening only to the loudest voices. Ali herself has argued that the 'giving and accepting of offence' is not only inevitable but also important in a plural world, as to prohibit the giving of offence is also potentially to weaken the position of female members of minority religious groups.[19] Thus, it is indeed problematic to reduce the controversy to a simplistic paradigm of 'Free Speech absolutists vs an embattled minority'. Yet to substitute philistine 'authoritarians' for 'an embattled minority' in constructions of the dispute is also problematic for its apparent failure to take into account the social and racial position of Tower Hamlets Bangladeshis, including the community leaders.[20] While it is important to 'strip' the largely male and middle-aged protesters of their claim to a *representative* '"community" status', it is equally important not to strip them, in the process, of their status of belonging to a community that occupies a subordinate position in Britain, or indeed to strip the community itself of its status as a minority community by emphasising its heterogeneous nature at the expense of the social and cultural factors that bind it together. The emasculation that working-class Bangladeshi men might experience as a result of social and cultural exclusion can contribute to the aggressive assertion of their (limited) power over the community's women.[21] Arguably, therefore, the granting of a voice to minority community members, and of a degree of legitimacy to their offence, could work to enhance the community's position (including that of its women), rather than compound its vulnerability.

Natasha Walter makes the point that, unlike those triggered by Rushdie's *The Satanic Verses* or Gurpreet Kaur Bhatti's *Behzti*, the *Brick Lane* protests were against the so-called negative portrayal of the Bangladeshi people of Brick Lane rather than the religious content of the literary work: 'We had almost got used to regular threats against blasphemous art … by Christian, Muslim and Sikh fundamentalists. But this ugly trend has widened with the latest controversy, which takes the objection from religious grounds to grounds of cultural accuracy, or a nebulous "respect".'[22] While Walter shows minimal – if any – sympathy for objections to artworks on religious grounds, her attitude towards 'grounds of cultural accuracy' or 'respect' seems particularly critical. Sympathetic responses to protests against perceived offence to religious belief, moreover, have tended to highlight and defend the significance of the sacred to Asian faith communities – a significance which does not apply directly to the *Brick Lane* affair.[23] But what Walter describes as a widening of a 'trend' of protest from a focus on religion to a more generalised concern with cultural respect in fact serves to underline the social conditions of *both* minority religious *and*, more broadly, minority cultural protest and calls for censorship. In other words, objections to an artist's depiction of a minority religion or culture are in part rooted in the subordinate social position of the people objecting, which is determined by class and race as well as religion. This is not to dismiss the significance of the sacred by eclipsing faith with class or to elide the differences between the *Brick Lane* controversy and controversies that have been focused primarily on a perceived insult to religion. For example, the focus of the *Behzti* protest was specifically the play's location in a Sikh temple, as well as its use of Sikh symbols.[24] But while the gurdwara (or mosque) is a sacred space and Brick Lane a secular one, the former's significance extends beyond doctrinal religion to Sikh (or Muslim) culture and community, just as the latter's encompasses the faith of the community who live and work there. As demonstrated in my discussion of the Rushdie controversy, it is impossible to extricate religion from structures of class and race, and therefore vital to highlight the importance of a materialist, contextual approach to disputes between members of minority communities and creative artists. Thus it becomes possible to deconstruct liberal understandings of such disputes which tend to pit secularism, 'freedom of expression' and individual rights against (religious) authoritarianism, censorship and communitarianism, valorising the former and stigmatising the latter.

To embed religious protest in the material thus is also to counter the distinction between religion and race drawn by several writers and journalists to justify their campaign against the proposed legislation against incitement to religious hatred. In her essay for the English PEN volume on the legislation, Ali herself claims that an attack on a person on the grounds of their 'race' or ethnicity is an attack on their 'human dignity and common humanity'; religions, on the other hand, 'are sets of ideas and beliefs' and 'should not be privileged over any other set of notions'.[25] While Ali is sensitive to the importance of religion to the identities of Muslims, for her this is a reason to denounce the legislation, not to support it: it means that the boundary between criticism of a person's religion and criticism, or insult, to the person is dangerously blurred, increasing the risk of rendering criticism of religion illegal.[26] Polly Toynbee takes Ali's argument further in the distinction she draws between race as imposed (and therefore beyond insult) and religion as chosen (and therefore a legitimate target for insult), as discussed in Chapter 2.[27] Her reduction of race to a biological essentialism and religion to individual choice occludes the socially constitutive character of religious culture. If we argue, against Toynbee, that the public sphere is shaped by hierarchies of religion (as well as race and class, gender and sexuality), that religion (like race) contributes to the definition of one's social position, then religion and race cannot be seen as discrete categories as Toynbee and Ali would have it.[28] Hence, a protest by a group of working-class Muslim Bangladeshis against a perceived lack of cultural respect is not vastly different from such a protest on the grounds of religion. In both cases, they are responding to political and social vulnerability.

BRICK LANE (THE NOVEL)

The filming of the novel on location in Brick Lane, which sparked the second wave of protests, is anticipated by a scene in the novel itself. Midway through *Brick Lane*, the protagonist Nazneen and her husband Chanu make their way down the eponymous street:

> For a moment [Nazneen] saw herself clearly, following her husband, head bowed, hair covered, and she was pleased. In the next instant her feet became heavy and her shoulders ached.
>
> 'From a sociological standpoint, it is very interesting.'
>
> A young woman with hair cropped like a man's pointed an impressive camera at a waiter in a restaurant doorway. She wore trousers, and had she

been wearing a shirt her sex would have been obscured. To alleviate this difficulty she had dispensed with a shirt and come out in underwear. She turned round now and pointed the camera at Nazneen.

'You see,' said Chanu to the street, 'in their minds they have become an oppressed minority.'

Nazneen adjusted her headscarf. She was conscious of being watched. Everything she did, everything she had done since the day of her birth, was recorded. Sometimes, from the corner of her eye, she thought she saw them. Her two angels, who recorded every action and thought, good and evil, for the Day of Judgement. It struck her then ... that this street was filled with angels.[29]

Here, the direction of the anthropological gaze is inverted as the photographer becomes the subject of Nazneen's curious, quietly mocking gaze, and so too of the reader's gaze. The gaze that causes Nazneen's self-conscious adjustment of her headscarf, moreover, is not photographic but celestial. The Muslim woman's headscarf, pregnant with meaning in twenty-first-century Britain, loses its metonymic force as it figures neither as part of a western hegemonic discourse of female oppression nor indeed as part of a counter-hegemonic discourse of British Muslim assertion and resistance, but within a personal and individualised narrative of guilt and confusion at Nazneen's attraction to Karim, the middleman who brings her clothes to sew and will shortly become her lover. He is the source of Nazneen's preoccupation and of her fleeting pleasure at her 'modest' appearance, expressed in the opening sentence. While Chanu's words, 'From a sociological standpoint, it is very interesting', refer to the white working classes and the threat they feel from their brown compatriots, they also serve to highlight and gently ridicule the sociological framework within which Nazneen, complete with covered head, might be presented by the photographer. This, in conjunction with the repeated allusion to Nazneen's covered head, implies a self-conscious mockery, on the part of the narrative, of the anthropological discourse that freezes headscarved Asian women into the frame of 'oppressed victim'.

On the power of the image, Henri Lefebvre writes: 'Wherever there is illusion, the optical and visual world plays an integral and integrative, active and passive, part in it. It fetishizes abstraction and imposes it as the norm. It detaches the pure form from its impure content – from lived time, everyday time ... After its fashion, the image kills.'[30] If we read the image of the headscarved Muslim woman in these terms and the photographer's lens as the normative gaze that constructs this image, then the inversion of the gaze could be seen to fracture the image and expose the (literally) 'impure content' of Nazneen's life that lies beneath. The individual subject is revealed beneath the stereotyping image; the idea of the 'authentic' Bangladeshi woman, framed by the media or indeed from within the community (for Chanu Nazneen is an 'unspoilt' village girl, and for Karim 'the real thing'), is undermined. Here, too, the narrative appears almost to anticipate its reception: its mockery of the majoritarian public's thirst for knowledge of its Other and, elsewhere, of Karim's misconstruction of Nazneen as authentic can be read as anticipatory sideswipes at notions of authenticity that were to emerge in readings of the novel as 'failed realism' from both inside and outside the Bangladeshi community.[31] The detachment of the protagonist's gaze, which neither returns the photographer's in a gesture of defiance nor looks down in a gesture of self-consciousness, but rather absorbs itself in a vision of angels, pushes the photographer outside the frame of the narrative. Brick Lane evaporates as Nazneen is transported onto a metaphysical plane, which sits above the level of the street and the city. In this respect, the scene echoes her first excursion beyond the boundaries of her own estate, into the financial City. Here Nazneen remains largely invisible, but when she does eventually make eye contact with a female City worker clad in a scarlet coat, her thoughts immediately turn to God (45–6).

In the City scene, as throughout the novel, Nazneen's dominant gaze fractures her surroundings, frequently dismembering the figures or objects she encounters into metaphoric fragments. So, the City worker's coat is 'the colour of a bride's sari' and her ringed fingers 'weapons'; Nazneen watches 'heads above railings', and the entrance to a skyscraper is 'like a glass fan … sucking people in' (44–7). Her fading memory of her native village in Bangladesh is captured in the image of her 'pulling at the fine mesh' of a 'giant fisherman's net', 'squinting into the sun, vision mottled with netting and eyelashes' (179), but this image could also be applied to her vision of Britain, which atomises the visible world around her into isolated segments and creates an impression of detachment. Nazneen's partial vision and her absorption in her faith at moments of encounter are conceivable as a product of the difficulties she has with decoding the alien context of a western metropolis, a strategy for translating the foreignness she encounters into the familiar or perhaps for keeping it at bay. Yet a consequence of her detachment is a dilution of the conflictual social relations that fix her and her community into a subordinate position within Britain. Her detachment suggests placelessness; it de-places her and, to an extent, despatialises Britain. Thus, the profoundly uneven relationship between a Bangladeshi woman inhabiting a council estate in one of Britain's poorest boroughs and the 'leisure-rich salariat' who work in the financial City and play in the restaurants and bars of nearby Brick Lane is obscured as Nazneen's trajectory through the latter is almost frictionless.[32] Moreover, while the narrative positions itself on the other side of the lens, with Nazneen, an effect of this is a repression of the pressures and prejudices of majoritarian Britain on the working-class Muslim community of Tower Hamlets. Like that of the scantily clad photographer, the hegemonic gaze is pushed largely beyond the narrative frame throughout the novel. Indeed, Nazneen's excursions beyond the fictional Dogwood Estate and surrounding streets are rare, and while the novel's near-immersion in an impoverished, enclaved Muslim community, riddled with unemployment, drug addiction and gang warfare, suggests a materialist engagement with 'space as a (social) product', paradoxically the extent of its territorialisation forces a break between community and context, fragmenting the former and blurring the socio-spatial relations within which it is embedded.[33]

The abstraction of community from social context in a novel which has as its focus female Bangladeshi garment workers in Tower Hamlets has particular implications for its treatment of gender. Both Sukhdev Sandhu and M. K. Chakrabarti, in their reviews of *Brick Lane*, remark on the absence of external social pressures on Ali's Bangladeshi characters. For Sandhu, the 'campaign of violence and intimidation' that scarred the area in the 1970s and 1980s is a curious silence.[34] Similarly, Chakrabarti's primary concern is with the 'insularity' of the novel, its near-confinement to the domestic and interior world of its protagonist and consequent repression of what lies beyond: 'an entrenched class system, arcane property laws, legal double standards, exclusive educational systems, white flight, political doublespeak, fear, and racial loathing'.[35] Neither Chakrabarti nor Sandhu, however, connects the novel's occlusion of racial violence to its primary focus on the lives of women, notwithstanding Sandhu's praise for this aspect of the novel. Naila Kabeer, in her study of the lives of Bangladeshi female garment workers in Dhaka and London (an acknowledged source for Ali's novel), points to the infrequency of the factor of racism in the London-based women's accounts of their reasons for choosing to work within the home and for rarely leaving the home after dark. Indeed, a self-conscious concern of the novel is to give voice and vision to the private lives and labour of Muslim women that are so often silenced and submerged beneath the public narratives of racism, riots and Islamicisation. But while Kabeer takes care to locate the causes for the restricted movement of the London-based women in the exclusions of mainstream Britain as well as in the patriarchal structures of the Bangladeshi community, and to show that the latter cannot be isolated from the former,[36] in *Brick Lane* the interiority of Nazneen's world and the near-absence of racial antagonism (in part a product of gender) work to detach the patriarchal oppression operating within the community from external pressures, thereby inflecting the novel with an element of culturalism and introducing other silences.

The trajectory from constraint to freedom that Nazneen follows is shaped overwhelmingly by patriarchal structures within the community and their evasion or subversion. Notably, it is from within the curiously frictionless space of the financial City where she gets lost when newly arrived that Nazneen recalls the contrasting sense of constraint she and her friends experience within their community, captured by Razia's advice to her: 'If you go out to shop, go to Sainsbury's. English people don't look at you twice. But if you go to our shops, the Bengali men will make things up about you' (47). Almost from our very entry into the world of the Dogwood Estate, we are bombarded with a litany of patriarchal crimes against the community's women – whether Amina's subjection to her husband's violence and polygamy, Jorina's daughter's forced marriage, or Razia's impoverishment and near-imprisonment by her husband who sends his earnings to his extended family in Bangladesh (57, 38, 100–3). Conversely, there is little sense of the pressures that are exerted on the community's men from outside this space. While Chanu does emerge as a victim of racial prejudice and discrimination to some extent, the narrative seems to withdraw from any overt suggestion of structural antagonism. The hint that Chanu got sacked from his council job remains just that and the sense of his subordination is constantly attenuated by his ineptitudes, which come to figure as cause (109, 263, 265–6, 294). Much later, Nazneen becomes 'free' to act when the two men in her life have been displaced to Bangladesh – or, in the case of Karim, possibly to fight jihad somewhere. Razia's husband, too, is displaced from the novel and it is when he is killed that her flat finally becomes a home, losing 'the feel of a settler camp', as she describes it, 'a temporary pitch in hostile terrain where all resources had to be grabbed and held' (294). In this respect, the binary of cultural repression versus individual freedom in which the controversy surrounding *Brick Lane*'s publication and filming was frequently framed can be traced within the novel itself: a submission to patriarchal culture on the part of the Muslim woman is counterposed to an individual dissent and withdrawal from culture and community. To return briefly to Lefebvre, the destructive nature of the image lies for him in its fragmentation or 'dismemberment' of space. Indeed, images are 'fragments of space', and so it is through a re-membering of space, or a recontextualisation of the image, that their distorting properties can best be countered.[37] While the cultural stereotype (the headscarved Bangladeshi woman, caught in the photographer's gaze) is mocked and gives way to the individual subject, Nazneen and the Muslim community she inhabits remain largely adrift from their moorings in hierarchies of race, religion and class. Nazneen, then, emerges as the opposite pole of the oppressed Muslim woman, a liberated escapee from the patriarchal constraints of South Asian Muslim culture, leaving the polarity largely intact.

Despite the emphasis in *Brick Lane* on the patriarchal oppression within the Muslim community in focus, the central male figures, Karim and Chanu, are far from cardboard cut-out villains; in line with its fragmenting, deconstructive thrust, the narrative digs beneath their surface personae to reveal complex, contradictory subjectivities. When Nazneen becomes aware of the discrepancy between her idealised Karim (as lover and aspiring community leader) and the real Karim, whose socks are full of holes and speeches full of contradictions (284, 286), she recognises that she had 'patched him together, working in the dark … made a quilt out of pieces of silk, scraps of velvet, and now that she held it up to the light the stitches showed up large and crude, and they cut across everything' (380). The image is fractured; the labour exposed beneath the surface. Similarly, Karim's stammer can be read as a fragmented form of speech. At first it is interpreted by Nazneen (and so by the reader) as a product of his disaffiliation from his Bangladeshi heritage, affecting him only when he speaks in Bengali. As such it helps to explain his compensatory immersion in and defence of British Muslim politics as a response to his feelings of displacement (287, 375). But his stammer is soon reconfigured simply as a childhood habit that he has not quite outgrown, returning occasionally as a symptom of nervousness in the face of Nazneen as 'the real thing', the 'authentic' Bangladeshi woman, no matter which language he speaks in (378–9). This sudden subversion of Nazneen's interpretation seems anomalous, almost gratuitous. It functions only as another layer of deconstruction, further highlighting Nazneen's misreading of Karim and Karim's misreading of Nazneen (as 'the real thing'). The interpretation of Karim's stammer as signifying the fragmented, contradictory subject, without a 'place in the world', is itself fragmented or deconstructed so that fragmentation comes to signify little more than itself (54, 99, 218, 375).

In similar vein, the emphasis on Karim's inconsistencies and self-contradictions is such that the notion of collective political mobilisation becomes undermined. Nazneen's dissecting vision provides a vehicle for seeing past the eruptions of rage associated with 'political Islam' to the disaffection and social contradictions experienced by a poor minority community seeking to sustain their culture and religion in a place and time that do not readily accommodate these, especially in the context of the meetings of the Bengal Tigers. But, while the stereotyping image of the 'Islamic fundamentalist' is disturbed, in the process the young male British Muslim is deconstructed to the extent that he becomes delinked from any coherent social and political narrative. The proclamations of Karim and the character who goes by the name of 'the Questioner', Karim's foil in the community meetings, cancel each other out, reducing the content of the discussion to mere posturing: '[Nazneen] looked at Karim now: how absorbed he was in his manoeuvrings. If the Questioner had talked about the Lion Hearts, Karim would have talked of Afghanistan. If he said black, Karim would say white' (349). Not only is an immersion in Muslim politics represented as a problematically reductive, or black-and-white, response to the uncertainties of second-generation diasporic living, but it is also emptied of social meaning. Significantly, moreover, with Karim's literal displacement (has he gone to Bangladesh, or to fight jihad somewhere?), the politicisation of the community *as Muslims* is also displaced: at the end of the novel, the Questioner takes on Karim's role as community leader and tells Nazneen that his new group, which will replace the Islamic Bengal Tigers, is not religious. He says: 'It's going to be a political organization. Local politics' (407). Islam is confined to the private domain and the Islamic Bengal Tigers denounced as 'a mixed-up idea'. We can trace here the ideological distinction between Islam as a private faith (legitimate) and 'political Islam' or 'Islamism' (illegitimate), which dominates media and political discourses across the spectrum – and which precludes the politicisation of British Muslims *as Muslims*. With this liberal private/public division, assertive Muslim identities and practices – the wearing of the hijab or cultivation of a beard, the sale and consumption of halal meat, simply adopting the label 'British Muslim',[38] as well as mobilisation for equality in the name of Islam – can be collapsed into an extremist Islamism and marked as illegitimate.[39]

In fact, the possibility of a faith- and community-based mobilisation for justice against anti-terror legislation and widespread Islamophobia in Britain on the part of young Muslim men is evident in Tower Hamlets in the formation of faith-based community organisations, which, as Halima Begum and John Eade describe, offer young men a viable alternative to extremism: 'while "faith" has been a battle cry for international terrorists of different religious persuasions', they write, 'it has equally been a catalyst for community and social cohesion at the local scale in Tower Hamlets and other parts of East London'.[40] This scenario reconfigures faith and the communal as potential vehicles for resistance against structures of violence and constraint, and maps out for young men roles that go beyond stereotype. Muslim women, moreover, are considerably more advanced than their male counterparts in utilising their faith as a public source of empowerment and resistance: Gurchathen Sanghera and Suruchi Thapar-Bjorkert, writing of Pakistani Muslim women in Bradford, document a feminised form of Islamic politicisation which combats, in particular, patriarchal structures of oppression within their culture and community.[41] By contrast, at the end of *Brick Lane*, the community's struggle is firmly secularised; Nazneen enters the community and mainstream Britain as an agent ('I'll come [to the new meetings]. I'd like to', she says) – but she does so on mainstream Britain's terms (liberal and secular) (407).[42] Indeed, throughout Nazneen's faith is privatised. And so, while the novel's representation of Islam challenges neo-Orientalist stereotypes of a separatist, disjunctive, threatening and potentially violent religion, it simultaneously domesticates it, rendering it co-optable into liberal discourses. The evacuation of the two male protagonists at the end of the novel, leaving only the cipher-like figure of the Questioner, suggests a failure on the part of the novel to articulate a legitimate form of masculinity that combines Britishness with an assertive Muslimness. If Karim's stammer is no more than a minor speech impediment of childhood that he has not quite outgrown, this particular failure of speech on the part of *Brick Lane* marks the limits of dominant understandings of British Muslim masculinities, especially in the immediate wake of 9/11, the period when the novel is located and was completed.

While the community's struggle is ultimately secularised, in the scene of the Brick Lane riot, which Nazneen is forced to negotiate as she searches for her runaway daughter Shahana, it is internalised. In this scene, social struggle is materialised in space; the abstract space imposed by capitalism is torn apart.[43] A commercial space that relies on the power of the image (the 'green and red pendants [advertising] the Bangla colours and basmati rice', the 'exotic' Hindu gods incongruous in the window of a Bangladeshi restaurant), Brick Lane is no longer a receptacle for commodities or a commodity itself (208, 373). Instead, the social relations that shape this street and its relationship to the surrounding space emerge from beneath its surface:

> All the mixed-blood vitality of the street had been drained. Something coursed down the artery, like a bubble in the bloodstream. A police car was parked at a crazy angle in the road, the front doors wide open and the interior abandoned. The car rocked. A door swung shut. It rocked again. Nazneen looked at the boys pushing it ... The car went over and suddenly a noise licked around Brick Lane like a flame, crackling from every corner. (394)

But while the rioting disrupts the commodified surface of the street, the scene simultaneously fragments into a collection of images and objects that 'become more "real" than reality itself', where 'reality' stands for 'productive activity' or the social relations of production.[44] The rocking car becomes hyper-real, detached from the boys who are eventually exposed as responsible for its movement. Burning tyres become 'a coiled snake ... flam[ing] with acrid fury and shed[ding] skins, thick, black, choking, to the wind', familiar figures emerge out of the shadows into Nazneen's line of vision, and her atomising gaze picks out 'crouching shapes and whirling arms, the pale streak of trainers' (396). The disembodied shoes and limbs recall similar images throughout the novel, creating strings of images that refer to nothing beyond themselves.[45]

Just as the scene of the riot is fractured into a series of images, so the social spectrum is fractured as the rioters are revealed as Bangladeshi boys fighting themselves and their internal struggle becomes detached from their context in Britain: 'There were no white people here at all. These boys were fighting themselves. A dizziness came over [Nazneen] and she leaned against the glass. How long, she thought, how long it has taken me to get this far' (395). The last sentence is ambiguous: where exactly has she got to? The journey metaphor suggests she is referring to her position of participation, which enables her to see the 'reality' of the situation. It implies a newfound clarity of vision, which valorises her perspective and therefore its erasure of the *source* of the riot in the context of mainstream

Britain. A brown-on-brown riot is in fact a territorial act caused by the lack of ownership of place or space. This lack is a product of a specific subordinate position within the structures of neoliberal capitalism.[46] But while the effects of this position are present in the narrative (poverty, drug abuse and underachievement, as well as rioting), the near-invisibility of normative Britain obscures the location of their cause and therefore the cause itself. The representations of the struggle and the community are inflected with a circular logic: severed from social relations, they come to signify little more than themselves, so that power is endlessly deferred. This circularity is captured neatly in Karim's description of the riot: 'It's revenge. And revenge for revenge ... It's not even about anything any more. It's just about what it is' (398). Traceable here is the culturalism that characterised government reports on the 2001 race riots in Bradford, Burnley and Oldham. As critics noted, these reports focused on 'issues of segregation and social cohesion within a discourse that construct[ed] the segregated communities as "the problem"', and repeatedly represented the communities as 'disintegrating from within'.[47] Ali's brown-on-brown riot almost literalises this notion as the Bengal Tigers' white antagonists disappear beyond the frame. It is notable also that the one antagonistic relationship between 'inside' and 'outside' explored in the novel is between the Bangladeshi community and their white working-class neighbours, encapsulated in the 'leaflet war'; while the Lion Hearts importantly capture the shift to Islamophobia on the part of Britain's far right margin (and anticipate the English Defence League), the focus on them as the primary – even sole – source of external provocation quietly exonerates the liberal centre where in fact Islamophobia can and must be exposed.[48]

It is significant that the novel ends with a circular space: the ice rink that Nazneen will enter, having shed her peripherality and emerged as an agent (412–13). In this abstract space, everyone is autonomous, following their own trajectory across the ice, and everyone can be equal. If the image of Torvill and Dean skating through Margaret Thatcher's Britain in the 1980s suggests the nationalistic fervour of the Olympic Games, as well as a classically gendered, white Britishness where surface is value, that of Nazneen skating in her sari, accompanied by Razia's assertion that in England 'you can do whatever you like', suggests the liberal multiculturalist rhetoric of former prime minister Tony Blair's 'inclusive' Britain. Excluded from the former, Nazneen can enter the latter, where the glitzy costumes have been shed and everyone can be an individual, whether

dressed in jeans or a sari. In this abstract space, the sari becomes a signifier of an empty notion of difference as individualism, compatible with a
liberal multiculturalism whose limits are obscured. Reviewers have noted
this jarringly optimistic ending of the novel.[49] I submit, however, that the
relationship of the ending to the narrative that precedes it is not one of
disjunction. The abstraction of the circular ice rink parallels the abstraction of the community from its context. Through its fragmentation from
the surrounding space, it becomes a 'container' for individuals, a receptacle defined by what is inside it rather than by the dialectical relationship between inside and outside. The film ends with a different image:
Nazneen and her daughters lying in the freshly fallen snow outside their
tower block shortly after Chanu's departure. The ideological effect of
this scene, however, is similar: the implication is that Nazneen and her
daughters are now free to act; the snow is a *tabula rasa* on which they can
make their individual marks.[50] Sara Upstone counters criticisms of the
novel's optimistic ending by reading it as an articulation of a 'utopian
realism' that engages with existing, post-9/11 social realities for British
Muslims but simultaneously gestures beyond these to a renewed and
expanded multiculturalism that can encompass religiosity as well as secularism.[51] But, for this reader, the future projected is not one that exceeds
the limits of a liberal understanding of equality in terms of individualism
and cultural assimilation in order to accommodate assertive public British
Muslim identities.[52]

With its focalisation through a first-generation migrant, *Brick Lane* is
suggestive of narratives of the 1950s, 1960s and 1970s (Sam Selvon's *The
Lonely Londoners* (1956) or Buchi Emecheta's *In the Ditch* (1972)) rather than
of its 'black British' counterparts of the new millennium (Zadie Smith's
White Teeth (2000) or Nadeem Aslam's *Maps for Lost Lovers* (2004)). This is
not to imply that the novel lacks historical credibility; many of Britain's
Bangladeshis did arrive in the 1980s, later than other South Asian immigrants, and their distinctive demography meant that their integration
into British society was slow, especially for women.[53] But the migrant
perspective of the novel allows the narrative to retreat from the contesta-
tory cultural and religious assertiveness that is associated with British-
born South Asian Muslims; Nazneen wears saris and headscarves rather
than the hijab, and her peripheral, touristic perspective deconstructs the
essentialism that is necessary to subaltern forms of resistance. Contrary to
Upstone's assertion that it is Nazneen's disadvantage 'in terms of gender,
race, religion and class' that makes her positive claim on Britishness at

the end of the novel so significant – for, if she can do so, '*who cannot?*'
– despite her material disadvantage, her character *can* be accommodated
within normative liberal British culture without significant disruption.[54]
The thirteen or so years that are missing from the novel (1988 to 2001) can
be read as signifying the loss at the end of the first section of Nazneen
and Chanu's baby son, which defies language. But this period, bridged
by Nazneen's sister Hasina's letters from Bangladesh, contained events
that were highly significant for Britain's Muslim minority, notably the
Rushdie affair and the First Gulf War, which illuminated tensions in
multicultural Britain that had hitherto remained buried beneath the more
immediate need to combat the colour racism and nostalgia for empire of
earlier decades. As such, its absence could additionally be read as another
marker of the limits of the novel's speech.[55] In its simultaneous movement
towards and retreat from or quelling of the disruptive potential of Islam
in Britain, *Brick Lane* might be fruitfully considered as a *transitional* novel,
a product of the period immediately following 9/11 when an engagement
with the fraught politics of this contemporary moment was pressing and
yet stymied by the dominance of liberal secular discourses; an early post-
9/11 novel of a different character to those that dominate discussions of
this genre of fiction, but one that manifests similar failures of speech.[56]

BRICK LANE (THE STREET)

The isolation of the community from its wider social context within the
novel is reflected in Ali's own comments about it, as well as in a number
of reviews of the novel. In an interview with the writer Diran Adebayo,
Ali remarks:

> I'm ... interested in how people have received this book given some of the
> examples which you cited earlier – you know the idea of something like
> *Bombay Dreams* and aren't we all living in a lovely multicultural melting
> pot now. Well that isn't the picture I paint in the book and that's not how
> I see it happening. That's not a reality, at least for the people about whom
> I'm writing. What's interesting to me is that people are prepared to see this
> other side of Britain and recognize that it is a world apart but it's part of
> what makes England now.[57]

With these comments, Ali justifiably sets her novel apart from the easily
consumable 'multicultural melting pot' image of Britain, highlighting its
focus on the 'other side' – the disadvantaged, disaffiliated and bounded
minority communities who are not such an obvious resource for the

multicultural niche of the book market; the underside of the 'time-space compression' that enables the privileged consumer to sample different cultures – whether on Brick Lane itself, through purchasing the £75 bag that Chanu spies in a shop window or the fashionable clothing that Nazneen and Razia's clothing collective plans to sell, or through travel (209, 402–4).[58] But the novel's immersion in a poor Muslim community seems at odds with its considerable success, especially with some sections of the media. The right-wing *Evening Standard*, for example, which repeatedly distorts and stigmatises Britain's Muslim minority, lauded *Brick Lane* as revealing a 'rich, fresh and hidden world'.[59] A reason for the positive reception of *Brick Lane* can be located within the parallels between Ali's final sentence and the brief publicity quote from the *Standard*'s review: while 'this other side of Britain' is 'part of what makes England now', it is also 'a world apart' (in Ali's words) or a 'hidden world' (in the words of the *Standard*'s reviewer). These two phrases highlight the detachment of the community from normative Britain that can be traced within the novel itself. This detachment is implicit in the publicity quote from Margaret Forster, which appeared on the cover of the hardback edition of the book: 'It gave me everything I crave in a novel, taking me into a life and culture I know so little about.' Similarly, it underpins Geraldine Bedell's comment in the *Observer*: '[the novel] opened up a world whose contours I could recognise, but which I needed Monica Ali to make me understand'.[60]

Graham Huggan describes how the 'marketably authentic' Other is produced by removing that Other from its historical situation, or by decontextualising it, so that it becomes metonymic of the culture from which it originates.[61] What is relevant here is not the severance of a community as cultural Other from its place of origin (Bangladesh, for example) but its severance from majority Britain. The social relations that position it within Britain are concealed through its decontextualisation and its difference further domesticated through this exoticist representational mechanism.[62] Ali herself is convinced that it is not the 'anthropological' aspect of the novel that attracts readers but rather its ability to transcend boundaries of difference through a story of 'universal' appeal.[63] She tells Adebayo: 'I read London journalists saying, "It opened up a whole new world that I didn't know about that was so fascinating" … I don't actually think that's why they enjoyed the book. I think the fact that people will be reading it in Polish and all those other languages does say something about the real reason why some people relate to it.

I wrote it simply to tell those stories.' Yet, these two aspects of the novel (the 'anthropological' and the 'universal') operate symbiotically; it is paradoxically the near-impermeable nature of this boundary between the Brick Lane Bangladeshi community and its context of mainstream Britain (underpinning its 'anthropological' aspect) that enables the novel's reviewers, and conceivably much of its readership, to universalise the Bangladeshi community. This is supported by the publicity quote from the *Daily Telegraph* garlanding the paperback edition of the novel. It describes *Brick Lane* as 'A brilliant evocation of sensuality, which could occur anywhere'. The abstraction of the Bangladeshi community, which conceals the structures of power within which it is embedded, works to universalise it. It becomes metonymic: it is any community or every community; it stands in for the world.[64]

Members of the literary establishment dismissed the Bangladeshi protesters' reaction to the novel for their failure to read it *as fiction*.[65] Ian Jack, editor of *Granta* magazine, sums up the 'liberal consensus' on the novel as 'a novel is a novel is a novel, and not sociology' – a position that he shares. However, in his remarks on why Monica Ali was selected in 2003 as one of *Granta*'s Best of Young British Novelists, Jack articulates a contradictory impulse to read the novel in part as representative of a specific community, or precisely as 'sociology' or anthropology. He says: 'we [the judges of *Granta*'s Best of Young British Novelists awards] liked the book because we (none of us Bengalis from east London) felt that it showed us a glimpse of what life might be like among one of the largest and least-described non-white communities in Britain.'[66] Jack goes on to contemplate the effect of the fact that the title of the novel references a specific location, suggesting that 'the reality of the name heighten[s] the reality of the novel for the reader'.[67] I would add that it heightens the 'anthropological' reality of the novel for the reader, encouraging the latter to read Nazneen's story as that of an 'authentic' Bangladeshi woman living in Tower Hamlets, as did so many of its reviewers and, arguably, so much of the reading public, for whom it was and remains a popular choice. The following excerpt from a posting on a *Guardian* discussion forum about the *Brick Lane* protest emphasises this tendency and the impossibility of severing fiction from the sociological, as Jack would have us do:

> [*Brick Lane*] is a graphic description of the male domination of life enshrined in the Muslim religion and the gradual realisation of the mother and daughter that there is a quite independent life waiting for them to

forge for themselves. It also points to the origins of the current wave of young male Muslim terrorists, outraged and desperate at their loss of hegemony and the bitter realisation that there is no place for their type of medievalism in modern Western society ... the Muslims of Brick Lane may not welcome the mirror held up to their lives ... [but] I am [not] sure about their moral right to disrupt such filming in the hope of avoiding the spotlight on their misogynist lifestyles.[68]

This construction of the novel as a critique of Muslim misogyny, and the protest as a defence or cover-up of such misogyny, is reductive and tortuous but nevertheless significant because it shows how the reading of fiction is inevitably imbued with its context, with events and ideologies that prevail in the social world,[69] and how a fictional representation of Bangladeshi inhabitants of a Tower Hamlets council estate will easily be read as representative of *British Muslims* (as a homogeneous group defined in terms of their religious affiliation regardless of their self-definition) and co-opted into preconceptions about that community.

What is at stake is not just the fictional representation of a specific location on a map, inhabited by individuals (as Jack implies when he considers the effect of a novel titled *Rosevale Gardens, N4 6UT*, for example), but that of a specific community that occupies a subordinate class position in Britain and rarely has access to cultural discourse or self-representation. Added to this is the fact that, because of their subordinate position in British society, working-class British Bangladeshis are more likely to draw strength and pride from identification *as part of a group*, defined in terms of their common faith as well as in more general cultural terms.[70] It is not surprising, then, that the protesters read this rare representation of Tower Hamlets Bangladeshis as a distorted reflection of their own community, just as the majority reading public – including some Bangladeshis who claimed to identify with the novel's depiction of the community[71] – read it as an 'authentic' reflection.[72] My aim here is not to make a case for the protesters' right to substitute their representation of 'their' community for Ali's representation in her novel. Rather, it is to argue for a materialist reading of the protest as symptomatic of social inequalities. Access to discourse is not just about establishing the primacy of a particular representation; it is predicated on social position and can also impact on social position, potentially empowering a community by endowing it with a legitimate subjectivity.

Ian Jack alerts us to the uneasy contrast between the guests at the 'glorious' launch party for Ali's novel, which took place at the Truman's

Brewery buildings (a fashionable venue off Brick Lane), and the 'long-bearded men in long shirts selling okra just down the road'.[73] The limits of a liberal multiculturalism are materialised in the contiguity of poor street vendors to a venue, marketable because of its multicultural location, housing the launch of a book marketed through the multicultural label. Both venue and novel as product lie inside these limits, whereas the men selling okra lie outside. This division can also be applied to the reception of the novel: the discursive arena within which its legitimate critics are located is comfortably inside the limits of multiculturalism, while the community members are not considered to be legitimate participants in a discourse that is, at least to some extent, engaged with them – and with a space in Britain that they have carved out for themselves. It echoes the chasm Sarita Malik sketches in her astute reading of the *Behzti* controversy between Britain's ethnic minority communities and 'our' artistic spaces. Highlighting the context-bound nature of the response to the play, she notes the 'deep disconnection and disengagement between minority ethnic communities and "our" gallery, museum and theatre spaces' and, by contrast, the significance to British Sikhs of the space of the gurdwara, 'one of the few shared, community public spaces where Sikh communities do feel integrated'. In this context, it is not surprising that the representation – and perceived defilement – of the space of the gurdwara within an arts space from which members of the Sikh community feel excluded might trigger a 'rise in defensiveness, honour and communal pride'.[74] Similarly, in the *Brick Lane* affair, the space of literary fiction (which few working-class Bangladeshis can access) and that of the street Brick Lane and its environs (which a large community of working-class Bangladeshis have settled, shaped and made their home) are brought together with volatile effect.[75] Just as the community within the novel is detached from its context, so the novel as social fact occupies a middle-class liberal domain that must be kept discrete; the GSDWC and other protesters threatened that social exclusivity and in so doing threatened to expose the antagonistic relations of class that connect a working-class minority community to the liberal middle classes and literary establishment.[76]

Describing how its status has shifted from that of an intermediary (connecting places) to that of a place in itself, Lefebvre writes the following of the street: 'A site of coming and going, of intrusion, circulation and communication, in an astonishing reversal it turns into the mirror image of the things it connects, more alive than those things.' It is a site of the spectacle, where fetishisation is taken to an extreme. He goes on to contrast the site of consumption to the site of production and the site of the labourer's home life: 'Far away, in the factories (factories that produce the wonderful objects, or produce the means of producing them), everything is functional … Far away, in the workers' suburbs or on the working-class housing estates, everything is functional, a signal of the repetitive actions that maintain the workforce in its everyday life.'[77] The street Brick Lane is not just a site of commodification and consumption; the name itself is a commodity – a marketable multiculturalism that sells, and that sells a book. Another reason why writing a novel called *Brick Lane* is not the same as writing a novel called *Rosevale Gardens, N4 6UT* is that the former signifies not just a specific working-class minority community but also a specific consumer style ('multiculturalism'). The geographical distance that separates the site of consumption from the working-class residential district in Lefebvre's Paris does not always apply to London, where material divisions often function on a micro scale, but the distance between Lefebvre's factories and street can be seen in the distance between these two meanings of 'Brick Lane'. Brick Lane itself brings immigrant labour (or the site of production) and the street-as-commodity/image into the same space, and the image must repress the labour so that the social relations that connect image and labour remain concealed. This occlusion of the unevenness of the discursive arena can be traced in majoritarian liberal responses to the protests, including in Ali's own. For example, her assertion that those commentators who voiced support for the protesters against her novel because of a misguided 'respect for minorities' in fact 'silenced' other minority voices, such as those of Rushdie, Kaur Bhatti and herself, implies an uneasy equation between working-class British Bangladeshis and British Asian members of the literary establishment.[78]

To return finally to *Brick Lane* itself, the circularity of the protest that takes place within the novel – the riot, which is 'just about what it is', according to Karim – is broken beyond the novel in a corresponding act of territorialisation by the Bangladeshi protesters. This time, the commodified surface of Brick Lane the street and of *Brick Lane* the novel as product is disrupted by the rioters. Further, the challenge to the anthropological gaze of the filmmaker within the novel, which Nazneen averts rather than confronts, is enacted by the Bangladeshi protesters beyond the novel. But while the antagonism that is repressed within the novel emerges at the point of its reception, it is immediately contained through the ideology of the autonomous literary text which labels the protests as 'misguided', 'ill-informed' and not to be taken seriously. If the reaction of the Brick Lane protesters, like that of Salman Rushdie's British detractors, can be justifiably labelled 'extreme', this is in part a function of the *a priori* delegitimisation of their voice within the discursive arena.[79] In their highly critical response to the *Brick Lane* protests, PEN refer to the need for 'strong political leadership' in order to support writers and artists against threats of censorship: this, they say, will bring Britain nearer to 'building a genuinely pluralist society'. But such a project can only be achieved with a historicised, materialist awareness of the social inequalities that position Britain's Muslim minority at the bottom of its social scale and underpin protests against creative works.[80]

NOTES

1   Kenan Malik, *From Fatwa to Jihad: The Rushdie Affair and its Legacy* (London: Atlantic Books, 2009), p. 172.

2   Ralph Grillo, 'Artistic licence, free speech and religious sensibilities in a multicultural society', in Prakash Shah (ed.), *Law and Ethnic Plurality: Socio-Legal Perspectives* (Leiden: Koninklijke Brill, 2004), pp. 107–26, pp. 123–4.

3   See Pnina Werbner, *Imagined Diasporas among Manchester Muslims: The Public Performance of Pakistani Transnational Identity Politics* (Oxford: James Currey, 2002).

4   By December 2005, 892,163 copies of the novel had been sold in the UK alone (Mick Brown, 'Voice of experience', *Telegraph* (27 May 2006), www.telegraph.co.uk/culture/books/3652679/Voice-ofexperience.html, cited in Bethan Benwell, James Procter and Gemma Robinson, 'Not reading *Brick Lane*', *New Formations*, 73 (2011), 90–116, 100.

5   Matthew Taylor, 'Brickbats fly as community brands novel "despicable"', *Guardian* (3 December 2003), www.theguardian.com/uk/2003/dec/03/books.arts (last accessed 6 November 2014). See www.gscuk.org for more information on the Greater Sylhet Development and Welfare Council. Benwell *et al.* provide illuminating information about the content of the letter ('Not reading *Brick Lane*', 105–7).

6   Malik, *From Fatwa to Jihad*, p. 169.

7   Arifa Akbar, 'Brick Lane rises up against filming of Ali's novel', *Independent* (22 July 2006), www.independent.co.uk/news/uk/this-britain/brick-lane-rises-up-against-filming-of-alis-novel-408885.html (last accessed 6 November 2014); Richard Lea and Paul Lewis, '"Insulted" residents and traders threaten to halt filming of bestselling novel *Brick Lane*', *Guardian* (18 July 2006), www.theguardian.com/uk/2006/jul/18/film.media (last accessed 6 November 2014).

 8 For an illuminating reading of the *Behzti* controversy, see Grillo, 'Artistic licence'. For a considered appraisal of the Mohammed cartoons controversy, see Geoffrey Brahm Levey and Tariq Modood, 'Liberal democracy, multicultural citizenship and the Danish cartoon affair', in Levey and Modood (eds), *Secularism, Religion and Multicultural Citizenship* (Cambridge: Cambridge University Press, 2009), pp. 216–42. The controversial Racial and Religious Hatred Bill aimed to give equal protection to all faiths, bringing Muslims and other religious groups in line with Jews and Sikhs who were already covered by race hate laws. Opposition, largely on the grounds that the bill would curtail freedom of speech, was substantial. The bill was eventually passed but in modified and considerably weakened form after the House of Lords introduced amendments that the government failed to overturn ('Racial and Religious Hatred Act 2006', *Guardian* (19 January 2009), www.theguardian.com/commentisfree/libertycentral/2008/dec/16/racial-religious-hatred-act (last accessed 6 November 2014)). Artistic controversies in Britain that followed include, in 2007, the cancellation of an adaptation of Aristophanes' *Lysistrata* set in a Muslim heaven by the Royal Court Theatre, and the removal of artist Hans Bellmer's life-size nude dolls from an exhibition at Whitechapel Art Gallery, to avoid shocking Muslim residents (Malik, *From Fatwa to Jihad*, ch. 5).

 9 English PEN, 'The Brick Lane affair: English PEN warns of dangers of community censorship' (press release), English PEN (31 July 2006), www.englishpen.org/legacy/images/brick_lane/Brick%20Lane%20Press%20Release-30%20July%2006.pdf (last accessed 6 November 2014).

10 Lisa Appignanesi, 'PEN is concerned about protests over the filming of Monica Ali's Brick Lane', English PEN (19 July 2006), www.englishpen.org/pen-is-concerned-about-protests-over-the-filming-of-monica-alis-brick-lane/ (last accessed 6 November 2014).

11 Jonathan Heawood, 'The battle for Brick Lane', *Guardian* (27 July 2006), www.theguardian.com/commentisfree/2006/jul/27/noskatinginsaris (last accessed 6 November 2014).

12 Malik, *From Fatwa to Jihad*, pp. 169–70.

13 Sean O'Neill, 'Asian leaders warn of violence against Brick Lane film', *The Times* (22 July 2006), www.timesonline.co.uk/tol/news/uk/article690967.ece (last accessed 6 November 2014).

14 Natasha Walter, 'The book burners do not speak for all of Brick Lane', *Guardian* (1 August 2006), www.theguardian.com/commentisfree/2006/aug/01/comment.bookscomment (last accessed 6 November 2014).

15 See, for example, Madhav Sharma, 'A view from inside', in Lisa Appignanesi (ed.), *Free Expression is No Offence* (London: Penguin, 2005), pp. 32–8.

16 See Salil Tripathi, 'No offence', Special to the *Wall Street Journal* (11 August 2006), www.englishpen.org/legacy/images/brick_lane/No%20Offence%20by%20Salil%20Tripathi.pdf (last accessed 6 November 2014); Monica Ali,

'The outrage economy', *Guardian* (13 October 2007), www.guardian.co.uk/ books/2007/oct/13/fiction.film/ (last accessed 6 November 2014).

17 Akbar, 'Brick Lane rises up'.

18 Mario Cacciottolo, 'Brick Lane protesters hurt over "lies"', BBC News (31 July 2006), http://newsvote.bbc.co.uk/mpapps/pagetools/print/news.bbc. co.uk/1/hi/uk/5229872.stm (last accessed 6 November 2014).

19 Malik, *From Fatwa to Jihad*, p. 172; Monica Ali, 'Do we need laws on hatred?', in Appignanesi (ed.), *Free Expression is No Offence*, pp. 47–58, p. 58; Monica Ali, 'Outrage economy'.

20 Appignanesi, 'PEN is concerned'.

21 A report by the Commission on British Muslims and Islamophobia documents the social deprivation of Britain's Muslim minority: Pakistani and Bangladeshi people suffer from higher rates of poor health and experience higher levels of unemployment than national averages; and three-quarters of the communities' children 'live in households earning less than half the national average'. Further, Islamophobic anti-terrorism legislation has led to an increased experience of victimisation among Britain's Muslims: 'In 2002–03, there were 32,100 searches under the Anti-Terrorism Act, 21,900 more than in the previous year and more than 30,000 above 1999–2000 levels. Resulting from 32,100 searches, just 380 people were arrested' (see Richard Stone (chair), *Islamophobia: Issues, Challenges and Actions: A Report by the Commission on British Muslims and Islamophobia* (Stoke-on-Trent: Trentham Books, 2004), pp. 30, 38; for a discussion of British Asian masculinities, see Claire E. Alexander, *The Asian Gang: Ethnicity, Identity, Masculinity* (Oxford: Berg, 2000), especially pp. 235–6).

22 Walter, 'Book burners'.

23 See, for example, Jasdev Singh Rai, 'Behind Behzti', *Guardian* (17 January 2005), www.theguardian.com/stage/2005/jan/17/theatre.religion (last accessed 6 November 2014); see also Grillo, 'Artistic licence'.

24 Singh Rai, 'Behind Behzti'.

25 Ali, 'Do we need laws on hatred?', p. 49.

26 *Ibid.*, p. 50.

27 Polly Toynbee, 'My right to offend a fool', *Guardian* (10 June 2005), p. 27.

28 See also Tariq Modood, *Multiculturalism: A Civic Idea* (Cambridge: Polity, 2007), pp. 70–1.

29 Monica Ali, *Brick Lane* (London, Doubleday, 2003), p. 210. All subsequent citations are given within the body of the chapter and are to this edition of the text. Constraints of space have meant that I have been able to include only occasional references to the film adaptation of the novel. However, it was mainly the filming of the novel in the Brick Lane area rather than the film itself which sparked the protests.

30 Henri Lefebvre, *The Production of Space*, trans. Donald Nicholson-Smith (Oxford: Blackwell, 1991), p. 97.

31 Sara Upstone, 'Representation and realism: Monica Ali's *Brick Lane*', in
    Rehana Ahmed, Peter Morey and Amina Yaqin (eds), *Culture, Diaspora, and
    Modernity in Muslim Writing* (Abingdon and New York: Routledge, 2012),
    pp. 164–79, pp. 165–8. See also Ali's own account of the different expec-
    tations that she was burdened with by her readership ('Where I'm coming
    from', *Guardian* (17 June 2003), pp. 4–5). While one camp (mainly white)
    positioned her as an authentic spokesperson for the Bangladeshi community,
    the other (Bangladeshi) declared her insufficiently authentic to represent it.
    Her frustration with this '"two-camp" split', and the problematic notion of
    authenticity ascribed to by each camp, is understandable. Yet, in her account,
    her self-positioning as peripheral (disaffiliated as she is from both camps by
    virtue of her mixed-race identity) works to occlude her own privileged class
    status which surely places her closer to the centre than to the margins.

32 Sukhdev Sandhu, 'Come hungry, leave edgy' (review of *Brick Lane*), *London
    Review of Books*, 25:19 (9 October 2003), 10–13.

33 Lefebvre, *Production of Space*, p. 27.

34 Sandhu, 'Come hungry'.

35 M. K. Chakrabarti, 'Marketplace multiculturalism' (review of US edition
    of *Brick Lane*), *Boston Review: A Political and Literary Forum* (December 2003–
    January 2004), http://new.bostonreview.net/BR28.6/chakrabarti.html (last
    accessed 6 November 2014).

36 Naila Kabeer, *The Power to Choose: Bangladeshi Women and Labour Market Deci-
    sions in London and Dhaka* (London and New York: Verso, 2000), especially
    ch. 7.

37 Lefebvre, *Production of Space*, p. 97.

38 Sarfraz Manzoor, 'We've ditched race for religion', *Guardian* (11 January
    2005), www.theguardian.com/world/2005/jan/11/race.religion (last accessed
    6 November 2014); Sarfraz Manzoor, *Don't Call Me Asian*, BBC Radio 4 (11
    January 2005).

39 On the need to erode the liberal public/private division for the accommoda-
    tion of assertive Muslim identities, see Tariq Modood, 'Muslims, religious
    equality and secularism', in Levey and Modood (eds), *Secularism, Religion
    and Multicultural Citizenship*, pp. 164–85, pp. 168–75; on the importance of
    distinguishing between the mobilisation of Muslims *as Muslim* and 'religious
    fundamentalism', see Modood, *Multiculturalism*, p. 135.

40 Halima Begum and John Eade, 'All quiet on the eastern front? Bangladeshi
    reactions in Tower Hamlets', in Tahir Abbas (ed.), *Muslim Britain: Communi-
    ties under Pressure* (London and New York: Zed Books, 2005), pp. 179–93, p.
    187. See also a comment by a local social worker cited in Fareena Alam, 'The
    burden of representation', *Guardian* (17 January 2005), www.theguardian.
    com/books/2003/jul/13/fiction.features (last accessed 6 November 2014):
    'Bengali women in Tower Hamlets are excelling far more than their male
    counterparts. Sadly, the local government isn't equipped with what it takes

to facilitate their growth. Self-development is seen in secular liberal terms, and therefore, ignores the religious and ethnic peculiarities of different communities.'

41 Gurchathen Sanghera and Suruchi Thapar-Bjorkert, '"Because I am Pakistani ... and I am Muslim ... I am political" – gendering political radicalism: young femininities in Bradford', in Tahir Abbas (ed.), *Islamic Political Radicalism: A European Perspective* (Edinburgh: Edinburgh University Press, 2007), pp. 173–91, pp. 186–7.

42 While the Islamic politics espoused by Karim is implicitly dismissed in the film as well, here the viewer is not presented with a secularised alternative. As in the novel, however, there is a strong inference that Islam belongs in the private domain.

43 Lefebvre, *Production of Space*, p. 55.

44 *Ibid.*, p. 81.

45 Nazneen's gaze frequently rests on the footwear of Razia, Mrs Islam, Karim, the Questioner and Chanu (20, 30, 45, 200, 284). In these instances, feet become detached from the whole person, or disembodied. Other instances of disembodiment also occur: Nazneen's neighbour becomes a 'bobb[ing]' head, 'bald and red with unknown rage' (42); a juggler that she watches in Covent Garden disappears into his smile and the waitress who serves her disappears into her ringed fingers (377, 379); Razia's husband makes dolls and brings home the fragmented, broken bodies of the rejects (39, 76). The dismembered objects are re-membered not through contextualisation but through self-referral.

46 Graffiti, too, is an act of territorialisation involving the inscription of (lack of) ownership onto space. Typically, in Nazneen's gaze, the graffiti on the community centre is aestheticised: the claims and counter-claims of the white working class and their Muslim antagonists '[kaleidoscope] into a dense pattern of silver and green and peacock blue, wounded here and there with vermilion, the colour of mehindi on a bride's feet' (230; see also 197).

47 Paul Bagguley and Yasmin Hussain, 'Flying the flag for England? Citizenship, religion and cultural identity among British Pakistani Muslims', in Abbas (ed.), *Muslim Britain*, pp. 208–21, pp. 210–12.

48 See, for example, Tahir Abbas, '"After 7/7": challenging the dominant hegemony', in Richard Phillips (ed.), *Muslim Spaces of Hope: Geographies of Possibility in Britain and the West* (London: Zed Books, 2009), pp. 252–62, p. 255; Arun Kundnani, *The End of Tolerance: Racism in 21st Century Britain* (London: Pluto, 2007), ch. 8, especially p. 126; Madeleine Bunting, 'The muscular liberals are marching into a dead end', *Guardian* (12 September 2005), www.guardian.co.uk/politics/2005/sep/12/politicalcolumnists.comment/ (last accessed 6 November 2014).

49 Sandhu, 'Come hungry'; Natasha Walter, 'Citrus scent of inexorable desire', *Guardian* (14 June 2003), p. 26.

50 Monica Ali, Laura Jones and Abi Morgan (writers) and Sarah Gavron (director), *Brick Lane* (2006).

51 Upstone, 'Representation and realism', especially pp. 173–7.

52 Modood, 'Muslims, religious equality and secularism', pp. 168–9.

53 Kabeer, *Power to Choose*; Alam, 'Burden of representation'.

54 Upstone, 'Representation and realism', p. 176.

55 Pierre Macherey, *A Theory of Literary Production*, trans. Geoffrey Wall (New York and London: Routledge, 1996 [1978; French original 1966]), pp. 77–9.

56 Robert Eaglestone, '"The age of reason is over … an age of fury was dawning": contemporary Anglo-American fiction and terror', *Wasafiri*, 22:2 (2007), 19–22, 21.

57 Diran Adebayo, 'Interview: Monica Ali with Diran Adebayo', in Susheila Nasta (ed.), *Writing across Worlds: Contemporary Writers Talk* (Abingdon: Routledge, 2004), pp. 340–51, pp. 350–1.

58 Doreen Massey, *Space, Place and Gender* (Cambridge: Polity, 1994), pp. 148–51.

59 See, for example, the posting of an *Evening Standard* article on the Islamophobia Watch website: www.islamophobia-watch.com/islamophobia-watch/2010/1/12/evening-standard-says-dont-give-publicity-to-choudary.html (last accessed 6 November 2014); at the bottom of the article, links to various Islamophobic *Standard* articles are given.

60 Geraldine Bedell, 'Full of East End promise', *Observer* (15 June 2003), www.theguardian.com/books/2003/jun/15/fiction.features1 (last accessed 6 November 2014).

61 Graham Huggan, *The Postcolonial Exotic: Marketing the Margins* (London: Routledge, 2001), pp. 157–8.

62 *Ibid.*, p. 159 and Introduction.

63 Adebayo, 'Interview', pp. 349, 351.

64 Lefebvre, *Production of Space*, p. 98. Adebayo claims that much of the fiction produced in Britain by successful non-white writers is 'once removed' from contemporary black Britain either in space or in time, arguing that it is 'far easier for a reader to feel pity for a slave than to be moved by the story of twenty-first-century young black British males when it's these same males she fears when she walks out on to the street'. He asks whether a novel without 'white lines of entry' can have universal appeal ('Diaspora chic', *Index on Censorship*, 32:2 (2003), 214–18, 215, 217). The success of Ali's novel despite its immersion in a non-white community and absence of obvious 'white lines of entry' would suggest an affirmative answer. But while *Brick Lane* is not 'once removed', its portrayal of Britain's Bangladeshi inhabitants as discrete or 'a world apart' enables the reader to enter into another culture without feeling disorientated, displaced or implicated, and therefore to feel comfortably 'moved'.

65 See, for example, Malik, *From Fatwa to Jihad*, pp. 168–9.

66 Ian Jack, 'It's only a novel …', *Guardian* (20 December 2003), www. theguardian.com/books/2003/dec/20/featuresreviews.guardianreview3 (last accessed 6 November 2014).

67 *Ibid.*

68 Reader's posting in response to Germaine Greer, 'Reality can bite back', *Guardian* (5 August 2006), www.theguardian.com/commentisfree/2006/ aug/05/bookscomment (last accessed 6 November 2014). It is worth noting that there were dissenting opinions, expressing sympathy for the protesters. Notable among these is a comment by 'Queensreader' (7 August 2006): 'censorship is about power. Who has the power in this situation – the marginalized ethnic group or the Booker-nominated writer?'

69 Edward Said, *The World, the Text and the Critic* (Cambridge, MA: Harvard University Press, 1983), pp. 34–5.

70 Modood, *Multiculturalism*, pp. 39–40, 61, 106.

71 Reader's posting in response to Greer, 'Reality can bite back' ('Starlight', 5 August 2006).

72 Citing the GSDWC's letter, authored by Kalam Choudhury, Benwell *et al.* demonstrate that for Choudhury 'there is no contradiction between the fictional status of the text and its responsibility to portray a real community based in historically accurate facts'. They read Choudhury's letter, therefore, as 'a challenge to the way in which text-centred literary criticism traditionally neglects readers' and argue for a re-centring of 'real readers' and non-readers. Elucidating the different values attached to reading and non-reading (close-mindedness and intolerance, where Muslim non-readers are concerned), they argue that non-reading is in fact 'a fertile and contested site of meaning production that still has much to teach us about the significance of recent book controversies'. Thus, in a different way, they too legitimise the Bangladeshi protesters' response to the novel (Benwell *et al.*, 'Not reading *Brick Lane*', 107, 110).

73 Jack, 'It's only a novel'.

74 Sarita Malik, 'Censorship – life after Behzti', *Arts Professional*, 101 (4 July 2005), www.artsprofessional.co.uk/magazine/article/censorship-life-after-behzti (last accessed 6 November 2014). See also 'The trouble with Brick Lane' (leader), *Guardian* (27 October 2007), www.theguardian.com/ commentisfree/2007/oct/27/books.immigration (last accessed 6 November 2014).

75 In an article on the Brick Lane area's gentrification, Sarah Brouillette also represents the protest as a struggle for ownership of space, arguing that the local Bangladeshi community's reception of the novel was shaped partly by a concern that their claim to the area would be undermined by 'those newly arriving with more elite forms of cultural and economic capital' ('Literature and gentrification on *Brick Lane*', *Criticism*, 51:3 (2009), 425–49, 443).

76 Maya Jaggi's account of Transworld's refusal to grant her an interview on the

grounds of her race, and her suggestion that, to attain 'universal' interest, a novel must be anointed by a white (preferably male) reviewer highlights the hierarchies of race, class and gender that shape literary publishing (see 'Colour bind', *Guardian* (7 February), www.theguardian.com/books/2003/feb/07/fiction.race (last accessed 6 November 2014)).

77 Henri Lefebvre, *Key Writings*, ed. Stuart Elden, Elizabeth Lebas and Eleonore Kofman (London and New York: Continuum, 2003), p. 92.
78 Malik, *From Fatwa to Jihad*, p. 170.
79 Slavoj Žižek, 'A leftist plea for "Eurocentrism"', in *The Universal Exception: Selected Writings*, vol. 2 (London and New York: Continuum, 2006), p. 205.
80 Appignanesi, 'PEN is concerned'.

5

Creative freedom and community constraint in Nadeem Aslam's *Maps for Lost Lovers*

'I am sorry if you are offended but I can't paint with handcuffs on.' (*Maps for Lost Lovers*[1])

The fact is that we are a society which, almost without noticing it, is becoming more divided by race and religion ... some districts are on their way to becoming fully fledged ghettoes – black holes into which no-one goes without fear and trepidation, and from which no-one ever escapes undamaged ... we are sleepwalking our way to segregation. We are becoming strangers to each other, and we are leaving communities to be marooned outside the mainstream. (Trevor Phillips[2])

THE 'FAILURE' OF MULTICULTURALISM

Situated in a working-class, enclaved British Asian neighbourhood in a fictional English town named Dasht-e-Tanhaii, Nadeem Aslam's 2004 novel *Maps for Lost Lovers* revolves around the 'honour killing' of a pair of lovers, exploring both the events that led to the crime and its repercussions for the families involved. With its focus on an immigrant Muslim family and written using some of the conventions of the social realist novel, it bears comparison with *Brick Lane*. However, while Monica Ali's novel is concerned primarily with the protagonist's personal journey of self-development from Bangladeshi immigrant to British citizen, Aslam's exploration of the Aks family immerses itself in a glut of patriarchal crimes and forms of abuse within the community, including child sex attacks, female foeticide, forced marriage and, most centrally, 'honour crime'. This violence is often captured in bald statements which scream from the page, bringing to mind the Islamophobic headlines which periodically adorn the pages of the *Daily Mail* or the *Sun*. 'Semen was found on the mosque floor late last evening' are the provocative words that open one of the chapters, while just a few pages earlier the central character, Shamas Aks, declares: 'Pakistan is not just a wife-beating country, it's a wife-murdering one' (234, 226). In the light of this, it might seem surprising that it was Ali's novel rather than Aslam's that sparked a controversy.[3] Indeed, some reviews of the latter pointed to its potential for provocation, with the *Economist* declaring it 'so anti-clerical that it would be no surprise if the author were to become the subject of a fatwa',[4] and Ron Charles for the *Washington Post* pronouncing it 'anti-Islamic'. Charles also alludes to the rhetorical power of this 'insider' account of a British Pakistani community: 'the frontal attack by a prejudiced outsider is relatively easy to repel; even blows from a bitter apostate often inspire only a sense of sanctified victimization. But Aslam ... speaks in the quiet, sympathetic voice of an insider as he portrays the physical and psychological violence committed in the name of God.'[5]

While much of the writing of the novel, which took eleven years, preceded 9/11 and the summer 2001 race riots in the north of England, its emergence at a particularly fraught moment in British multicultural politics heightened the risk of offence. In the wake of 9/11 and the race riots, political and media spokespeople on the left of the spectrum began to expound the supposed failure of multiculturalism, focusing overwhelmingly on Muslims.[6] After the 7/7 bombings on London Transport, this discourse hardened: Trevor Phillips, for example, declared to the Manchester Council for Community Relations that 'we are sleepwalking our way to segregation', blaming the 'black holes' of Britain's 'ghettoes' on a tolerance of diversity and advocating instead an assertion of the core values of 'our' 'Britishness'. Underpinned by an 'us' and 'them' differentiation, as M. A. Kevin Brice points out, Phillips's speech also implies that while 'we' are barely conscious of the path that we are forging towards segregation, 'they', by contrast, *are* – and are therefore to blame.[7] Just a couple of years before Phillips's speech, many of the young Muslims involved in the 2001 race riots experienced this blame in the form of substantial custodial sentencing: the Institute of Race Relations has shown the significant discrepancy between the sentences imposed on the British Pakistani rioters of Bradford's Manningham district and those resulting from other, similar disturbances in the UK, including on a mostly white neighbouring estate the following day.[8] As discussed in Chapter 4, official reports and media responses to the 2001 riots used essentialising narratives which constructed South Asian Muslim cultures as 'the problem' and their communities as 'in crisis', obscuring external factors such as 'white flight', racism and class inequality.[9] This is an example of what Mahmood Mamdani describes as 'Culture Talk', an assumption 'that every culture has a tangible essence that defines it' and an explanation of 'politics as a consequence of that essence'.[10] In this construction, Muslim culture is rendered singular and static, closed to a heterogeneity of influences and removed from progress and history. The move towards 'a more regulated and pedagogic pursuit of universalist liberal goals and acculturation' that followed the events of 2001 and 2005 also resulted in initiatives around 'citizenship' and 'integration' that undermined the legitimacy of Muslim concerns – about religious legislation, the building of mosques, veil controversies, the English Defence League and, of course, foreign policy – and pushed Muslims further towards the margins of the nation.[11]

The presence of gender and sexuality in discourses about the 2001 riots is also revealing. David Blunkett's interview for the *Independent on Sunday* just two days before the official reports on the riots were released referred to forced child marriage as well as genital mutilation, apparently linking these criminal practices to Muslim communities in the north of England and their role in the riots.[12] In their critique of the reports on the riots, Paul Bagguley and Yasmin Hussain point to their focus on gender oppression and the silencing of women's viewpoints within the Muslim community. While acknowledging the presence of gender inequality in the community, they argue that the reports 'construct these questions in a racialised way, glossing over the diversity, change and forms of resistance to gender inequality that are found among British Muslim women'. The implication is that gender inequality and the spectre of the passive Muslim woman were deployed as a means of corroborating culturalist constructions of the men and their role in the riots, as in Blunkett's disjunctive assertions.[13] As Claire Alexander says, in homogenising representations of Muslims in Britain, gender is often 'cast as the only salient division' within a reductive categorisation which conceals other diversifying factors such as class, nation of origin, location in Britain, not to mention different forms and lived practices of Islam.[14]

Like forced marriage, honour-related violence can readily feed culturalist discourses, and it was in the early years of the new millennium that honour-related violence, the focus of Aslam's novel, assumed a more prominent presence in the media. The crime which is said to have led to the coining of the term 'honour killing' took place in October 2002: a sixteen-year-old British Iraqi-Kurdish woman Heshu Yones was murdered by her father Abdulla Yones when he discovered her relationship with a man from outside their Kurdish Muslim culture.[15] Just a few years before, in 1998, a British Pakistani woman, Rukhsana Naz, was murdered by her mother and brother because she had refused to stay married to an older man in Pakistan and was pregnant by her Pakistani lover in Britain, while in early 2003 Sahjda Bibi, also a young British Pakistani, was killed by her cousin for refusing to marry a blood relative.[16] As Amina Yaqin states, 'There is certainly nothing to be gained by whitewashing or ignoring the appalling practices in which women especially are victimized, brutalized and murdered.' However, as she demonstrates, an awareness of this cannot ignore the Islamophobic context in which they are discussed, the prurience they engender in the media and the ways in which they can be constructed to corroborate neo-Orientalist stereotypes about Muslim communities.[17]

In this context, Aslam's portrayal of a segregated Muslim community riven by honour crime is precariously poised on a faultline of twenty-first-century British multiculturalism. The novel ventures onto this politically sensitive terrain with apparent fearlessness. Its refusal to shoulder the 'brown man's burden' is voiced in the novel itself. Charag, a young artist, shows his parents a nude self-portrait which depicts him uncircumcised. Witnessing their dismay, he tells them: 'I am sorry if you are offended but I can't paint with handcuffs on' (321).[18] Indeed, *Maps for Lost Lovers* thematises the politics of minority offence and the binary of individual freedom versus cultural oppression that has framed responses to controversies surrounding artistic representations of Islam and Muslim cultures, including the *Satanic Verses* and *Brick Lane* affairs. The chapter first considers the novel's negotiation of the relationship between creative freedom and the sacred before exploring the extent to which it can be read as a critical artistic intervention in discourses surrounding honour crime and, more broadly, British Muslims and multiculturalism.

CREATIVITY, THE SECULAR AND THE SACRED

Nadeem Aslam's third novel, *The Wasted Vigil* (2008), opens with a striking scene: a Russian woman Lara places a circular mirror on the floor to examine the reflection of a ceiling covered in books, 'each held in place by an iron nail hammered through it. A spike driven through the pages of history, a spike through the pages of love, a spike through the sacred'.[19] This unusual library belongs to a house situated near the Tora Bora mountain range of Afghanistan, and to its English owner, Marcus

Caldwell. The books, we later learn, were fixed there by Qatrina, his Afghan wife, as a form of protest against the Taliban, who had banned them. The image is suggestive of the valorisation of the literary, and of artistic creativity more generally, in opposition to the dogma, censorship and repression that is associated with the Taliban, but also much more broadly with religious, and especially Muslim, groups and cultures. Similar imagery in the novel echoes this polarity: the murals which adorn the walls of the house have been daubed with mud to conceal them from the Taliban and are painstakingly cleaned by Marcus; and Lara attempts to reassemble painted plaster fragments of the smashed walls of the uppermost room which had illustrated the theme of love.

In his review of the novel, Amit Chaudhuri foregrounds the image of books nailed to the ceiling and goes on to describe the talismanic status that the book, and especially the novel, assumed after the protests against Salman Rushdie's *The Satanic Verses*. The novel, Chaudhuri points out, became 'a fetish of humanism, an incarnation of history, not only a receptacle of human wisdom, but a living thing with its own precarious career in the contemporary world'.[20] But in *The Wasted Vigil*, Chaudhuri argues, Qatrina's insanity when she fixed the books to the ceiling, and the fact that she is dead even before the novel begins, undermines a straightforward interpretation of this dominant image as endorsing the liberal fetishisation of the literary or creative. Once viewed in the light of Qatrina's madness and absence, the image signifies rather differently:

> The Taliban are mad, but they represent a utopian idea of order; Qatrina's madness was a protest against utopia. But it was also a melancholy surrender of herself. The mad attack books; but the urge to fix books, to sacralise them by making them static, or to make them static by rendering them physically or metaphorically immovable, is also mad. It's an instance of the kind of liberal utopianism about culture that sounded very loudly after the fatwa. Aslam's novel, and the little fable in it about Qatrina and the books, reminds us that the liberal romanticism that appeared in the 1990s was, in its own way, problematic, one of the reasons being its soaring transcendentalism.[21]

Indeed, while Qatrina is depicted as an admirable character, deeply mourned by Marcus and, according to their daughter Zameen's former lover David Town, 'endlessly kind in her personal conduct', her non-belief tends towards a secularist intolerance of faith (77). Her set of ninety-nine paintings depicting humans 'doing all the things that Allah is supposed to do', described by Marcus as 'Her comment on the non-existence of

God' (202), is redolent of some of the artworks that have caused offence to Muslims in the contemporary West; and she believed the destruction of Afghanistan was caused by 'the character and society of the Afghans, of Islam', and by their resistance to change (77). By contrast, it is Marcus, a non-believer who seeks to respect belief, who, with the exception of the departed Lara, is the sole survivor of the mansion's inhabitants by the end of the novel; and it is his doubt, rather than the precarious certainties of David or of the radicalised young Afghan Casa, that has the potential to give clarity (355).[22]

Chaudhuri represents the 'liberal utopianism about culture' exemplified by Qatrina's books as a phenomenon of the 1990s, which Aslam, writing in a post-9/11 context, eschews. But, as discussed, a liberal secularist endorsement of culture and creativity above and against religious belief or culture, read as inherently dogmatic and repressive, remains prevalent in contemporary representations of controversies surrounding freedom of expression and minority rights. Indeed, in the context of the New Atheism that has emerged in the 2000s in response to fundamentalist interpretations of Islam as well as of Christianity in North America, we are witnessing 'a new and intensely polemicized phase in the relation between fiction and non-belief'.[23] For writers including Martin Amis, Ian McEwan and Salman Rushdie, all influenced by the New Atheist movement, 'the novel apparently stands for everything – free speech, individuality, rationality and even a secular experience of the transcendental – that religion [according to them] seeks to overthrow'.[24] Paradoxically, the religious transcendentalism and dogmatism they critique is echoed by these writers' own secular transcendentalism and 'aesthetic-political dogmatism – about science, about reason, about religion and, in many cases, about Islam'.[25] While Amis in particular may be a straw target when it comes to critiquing Islamophobic discourses, as the Pakistani writer Kamila Shamsie pointed out in her *Guardian* riposte to particularly pernicious remarks by Amis in the *Times Magazine* (publicly supported by both McEwan and Rushdie), he is recognised as a highly significant writer who has 'the moral authority which comes with that recognition' and is 'given generous space in serious newspapers to air his views via fiction, interviews, articles'.[26] Amis's overt Islamophobia should not be conflated with the vociferous opposition by writers to the 2005 proposals for religious incitement legislation by English PEN, or with normative constructions of the *Behzti* and *Brick Lane* protesters, discussed in Chapter 4. However, they share a liberal valorisation of freedom of expression that obscures the social and political context of Muslim minority offence or protest, simultaneously diminishing religion to a set of (false) ideas which should be privatised *and* inflating it until it figures as the primary cause of repressive practices. The effect of this is to patronise and stigmatise Muslims.[27]

Shamas and Kaukab Aks, the central couple of *Maps for Lost Lovers*, can be said to personify the dichotomy of secular freedom versus religious repression. Shamas is a socialist, atheist and former poet, an important figure in the community of Dasht-e-Tanhaii ('Wilderness of Solitude' or 'Desert of Loneliness'), frequently representing their interests in the world beyond and serving as the director of the Community Relations Council. His wife Kaukab, by contrast, is deeply pious; her worldview is shaped by a literalist interpretation of the Quran and steeped in a patriarchal culture of superstition and dogma which she equates with Islam. In the view of her adult daughter Mah-Jabin, she is 'trapped within the cage of permitted thinking ... the most dangerous animal she'll ever have to confront' (110–11). Uneducated, with a poor grasp of English and afraid of the racism and licentious culture that, she believes, will assault her beyond the relative sanctuary of Dasht-e-Tanhaii, she is also physically trapped within her neighbourhood and home. Shamas's younger and much loved lepidopterist brother, Jugnu – also a non-believer whose rationalism, atheism and love of freedom is captured in the name of his boat, *The Darwin* (63) – is already dead when the novel opens, murdered with his lover Chanda, the twice-divorced daughter of the local shopkeepers. Killed by Chanda's two brothers, known as Barra and Chotta ('Big' and 'Small'), for living together outside of marriage, despite the fact that Chotta is having a sexual relationship with an older Sikh woman, Kiran, the dead lovers haunt the novel – but this central narrative of a so-called honour killing is overlain and interwoven with several other stories of thwarted love or freedom of choice where attempts to transgress religious, cultural, communal or racial codes or boundaries exact devastating penalties. A relationship between a Hindu boy and a Muslim girl, who remain nameless and cipher-like, ends in the girl being beaten to death by a cleric who claims she has been possessed by djinn (185–6). A young woman, Suraya, is separated from her son because her inebriated husband divorced her for the shame she brought to her family by attempting to speak up for a rape victim (131–2). All three of the couple's children have left the town: the eldest, Charag, is an artist in London, separated from the white English mother of his young son; Mah-Jabin escaped an abusive marriage to a cousin in Pakistan and is living and studying in London; Ujala, the younger son, has suffered the most at the hands of his misguided mother – dosed with bromide as a child, on the direction of a cleric, to control his strong will, his severance from family, community, culture and religion is near absolute (304).

Further, this dichotomy of individual freedom versus religious or cultural dogma frequently emerges in the novel in the form of an aesthetic freedom in opposition to the censure and censorship that is normatively identified with the South Asian Muslim community in Britain. Shamas is encouraged to write poetry again by his lover Suraya whom he meets regularly at the lakeside bookshop, the Safeena. Notably, the name of the bookshop means 'boat' as well as 'notebook', aligning physical freedom with literature as well as with Jugnu's boat and so the rationalism captured by its name (136). For this she brings him a gift of a box of gold-leaf Koh-i-noor pencils which contains inside it a positive pregnancy test, revealing that she is carrying his child (240). Fertility – life – and an illicit relationship are mapped onto artistic creativity and counterposed to the sterility of Shamas's relationship with his wife Kaukab who obliterated the only remaining copy of the poems of his youth when she burnt her wedding dress, onto which they were embroidered. In the period before their marriage, in Pakistan, Kaukab had cut a sewing pattern, and so the contours of her young body, out of the pages of the literary supplement of a newspaper, not knowing that Shamas would ask to borrow it. Shamas's response is to write love poems to her in the margins of the borrowed newspaper before he returns it to Kaukab – poems which she then sews onto her wedding dress (66–9). She burns the dress, many years later, after Shamas hits her for making the tiny infant Ujala observe Ramadan because she believes that he, born without a foreskin, is a holy child (139–42). Romantic love and the literary are aligned and the desecration of the latter is associated with religious superstition. Charag's self-portrait depicts him as uncircumcised, devastating his mother; his freedom to paint 'without handcuffs on' is identified with his liberation from the oppressive cultural and religious practices of the Pakistani community (320). Unlike Qatrina's books, those of the Safeena bookshop are accessible, but the bookshop is under threat, its owner missing and probably murdered by jealous relatives on a return visit to Pakistan (152). The books in five languages that adorn Shamas's shelves at home are contrasted to the single Book that Kaukab is able to understand (56, 70).

This symbolism, at times heavy-handed, suggests a fetishisation of creativity. However, while the identification of the transgression of

boundaries with freedom may seem redolent of the individualist liberalism
that is dominant in Kureishi's work, *Maps for Lost Lovers* takes care to contex-
tualise the community's segregation, its members' adherence to cultural
and religious codes, and the patriarchal abuses enacted on its women and
children in the racism, poverty and disenfranchisement they experience
in Britain.[28] In an early chapter of the lives of Shamas and Kaukab, before
their move to England, familial, cultural and religious duty meshes with
love, deconstructing the dichotomy that is evident elsewhere: the mysterious man who writes Kaukab poems in the margin of the newspaper,
and with whom she has fallen in love, turns out to be the man her parents
have chosen for her to marry, Shamas (69). Thus, it is implied that it is the
impact of immigration and the material realities of their lives in England
that have entrenched patriarchal cultural traditions for the first generation
and especially for the uneducated, vulnerable and deeply pious Kaukab,
whose retreat into a literalist interpretation of her faith pushes away the
people that she loves. Further, while Kaukab might at first bring to mind
the monstrous character of Hind, proprietor of the Shaandaar Café in
Rushdie's *The Satanic Verses*, with Shamas echoing Hind's literature-loving,
socialist husband Sufyan, both emerge as much more complex figures.[29]
Kaukab is constantly struggling to reconcile her interpretation of her faith
and the opprobrium of Jugnu and Chanda that it dictates, with her love for
Jugnu, her brother-in-law, and her devastation at his death, which has left
her feeling 'utterly empty almost all the time, as though she has outlived
herself, as if she has stayed on the train one stop past her destination' (270;
see also 146–7). Her dismay at the pregnancy of Stella, Charag's girlfriend,
is overcome by her desire to be with the mother of her future grandchild
and she determines to travel to London, only to realise that she cannot find
her way there (313). Shamas, and the reader, are frequently left wondering
'which of the two Kaukabs is the real one' (316). When Mah-Jabin turns
to her mother in anger for encouraging her to go to Pakistan to marry
a cousin she did not know at the age of sixteen, Kaukab's response is to
tell her: 'I did not have the freedom to give you that freedom, don't you
see?' (115). Freedom is configured as an effect of privilege, and racism is a
palpable presence in the novel, with violent physical attacks, abusive insults
such as the deposit of a pig's head on the steps of the mosque, and name-
calling alienating and at times devastating the lives of its protagonists (11,
14, 160, 178–9). In this respect, the novel contrasts starkly with Ali's *Brick
Lane* in which the Bangladeshi community of Tower Hamlets is largely
isolated from its wider social context.

A fetishisation of creativity might also be suggested by the highly aestheticised, simile- and metaphor-laden language of the novel and the pastoral imagery that dominates. Dasht-e-Tanhaii is a place of butterflies and peacocks, orchids and parakeets, a lake with a jetty and cherry trees laden with blossom. At times, the effect is one of stasis as the repeated imagery becomes self-referential and the density of the language obscures the narrative trajectory. This sense of stasis recalls the immobility of Qatrina's books, fixed to the ceiling. Neel Mukherjee claims similarly that 'the social heart of the novel remains occluded' beneath its excessive, dense language. But Mukherjee goes further to argue that the language has an exoticising effect: 'the relentlessness of all this florid excess', writes Mukherjee, 'shows up the dishonest core of the book: it is heaving and straining for ethnic exoticism. It's the perfect book for the insidious, patronising neo-colonial lobby who are still looking for the mysterious magic of the Subcontinent, of the smell of spice bazaars and the colours of gorgeous handwoven textiles in their retarded idea of the Subcontinental novel.'[30] Yet, against Mukherjee's reading, the novel seems rather to be ironising notions of the 'mysterious magic of the Subcontinent', revealing the realities that the exoticising iconography that Mukherjee lists so often conceals. The rolls of sequinned, glittering cloth in Chanda's family's shop carry an insidious sense of threat: 'Two scissors hang from strings like a pair of dead birds, upside-down, drained of blood. Rolls of cloth ... lean against the counter, the loose edges of the materials trailing, like a queue of very thin and very tolerant women wearing saris' (212). This last image recalls an illegal all-night quail fight and the box of 'dying blood-soaked birds' that Jugnu helps the barber with on the morning of his death (337), as well as the passive acquiescence to patriarchal abuses of power on the part of the community's women. Similarly, the scented geraniums in the house of the 1960s immigrant workers are not merely decorative; rather their scent of 'rosehips and ripening limes' acts as a night-time warning to the men of white racist intruders brushing against the flowers after breaking in (11). Nirmal Puwar writes critically of the 'ability of whiteness to celebrate versions of marketed difference, alongside a historical amnesia of the violence endured by South Asian women'. Illuminating the rage that this evokes in South Asian women, she unsettles exoticising practices of dress.[31] The imagery in *Maps for Lost Lovers* similarly unsettles the exoticising celebrations of cultural otherness that Mukherjee describes. While the language and imagery orientalises the landscape, its beauty is broken or fractured by the harsh realities of the lives of the inhabitants of Dasht-e-Tanhaii. Thus the gaze belongs to the Pakistani immigrant, not to the exoticising outsider.

In *Maps for Lost Lovers*, there is a trope of failed art or writing: Shamas's poems are destroyed and he will die before he has a chance to write more; Charag's painting, while successful in metropolitan London, fails to communicate with Shamas and offends Kaukab; the Hindu boy's love letter to his dead lover, a desperate attempt to communicate with her beyond the grave, is removed from her shroud, torn into fragments and thrown into the lake (193–4, 204).[32] On the one hand, it would seem to be Islam, or its interpretation, that is fragmenting the aesthetic and restricting its critical and communicative potential, censuring and censoring. In this respect, it might seem that, as in McEwan's *Saturday*, an Arnoldian vision of culture provides the civilisational yardstick of Aslam's novels, against which Kaukab's and the community's dogmatism, are measured.[33] But, on the other hand, the novel brings art down from its pedestal – or the ceiling – reattaching it to its moorings in the social: its failure (to be complete, to communicate universally, to connect across humankind) is rooted in the material so that the liberal ideology of the aesthetic is undermined.[34] Kaukab's offence is contextualised in her dislocation, disenfranchisement and deprivation. If art is shown to be a privileged domain, predicated on social status, it loses the naturalised transcendental status as the new religion with which the New Atheist novelists, among others, have endowed it. Art, then, does not 'mark the difference between humans and non-humans' (read secular Europeans and Muslims, respectively), as in the 'aesthetic discourse' that Pierre Bourdieu critiques or the secularist or 'worldly' criticism that Talal Asad dethrones.[35]

The presence of an Islamic aesthetic in *Maps for Lost Lovers* also works to dislocate the dichotomy between creativity – identified with free speech, individuality, rationality – and religious culture. Poet Faiz Ahmed Faiz and artist Abdur Rahman Chughtai are two of the dedicatees of *Maps for Lost Lovers*; the town of Dasht-e-Tanhaii takes its name from a Faiz poem and Chughtai's illustrations preface each of the chapters, with the titles of two of them echoing those of paintings by Pakistani artists Anwar Saeed and Bhupen Khakar, both of whom have dealt critically in their work with oppressive aspects of Pakistani culture, focused around sexuality in particular.[36] Lindsey Moore also suggests the possible influence on the novel of the *dastan* – a long Urdu poem structured from a loosely connected series of episodes and, like the novel, featuring winged creatures – and compares the trajectory of Shamas's life to the structure of the *ghazal*.[37] Perhaps most significant is the concert given by Qawwali singer Nusrat Fateh Ali Khan, which represents a critical, communal Islamic aesthetic with the potential to bring the inhabitants of Dasht-e-Tanhaii together in a shared appreciation of the music and outrage at the oppressive practices and abuse of power to which Nusrat gives voice. Significantly, Nusrat sings, as the fabled female character Heer, of the 'honour crime' she awaits:

> She would condemn [her murderers] with her last breaths, the poet-saints of Islam expressing their loathing of power and injustice always through female protagonists in their verse romances … And always always it was the vulnerability of women that was used by the poet-saints to portray the intolerance and oppression of their times: in their verses the women rebel and try bravely to face all opposition. (191–2)

Terry Eagleton describes the clash between 'civilization and culture', where civilisation means 'universality, autonomy, prosperity, plurality, individuality, rational speculation, and ironic self-doubt' and culture means 'the customary, collective, passionate, spontaneous, unreflective, unironic, and a-rational'. As he observes, this clash is 'increasingly mapped onto a West/East axis', and, I would add, a secularism/religion axis.[38] Here, both sides of the polarity of 'civilization' and 'culture' are located within the community as the description of Nusrat's performance, focalised through Shamas, is interwoven by stories of the devastation wrought by religio-cultural prescriptions on members of the audience, which are in turn grounded in the material (189–94). The clash is deconstructed, and patriarchy and Islam are seen as in tension rather than conflated.

Yet it is perhaps not insignificant that the progressive, critical version of Islam presented in the Qawwali performance is one that draws on Sufism, a branch of Islam characterised by an 'ascetical other-worldly orientation' and a 'concern with the esoteric dimensions of the faith' which tends to remain detached from the public, political domain.[39] It is, in its modern form, the brand of Islam advocated by Tony Blair's Labour government-endorsed Quilliam Foundation which urges Muslims to become integrated as British citizens and not as a community of faith.[40] Thus, in the novel a rare representation of Islam as critical and self-critical is identified with a politically quietist, individualised understanding of religious faith and culture and consigned to stories of the past.[41] The history of female agency and resistance articulated in Nusrat's song lacks a trajectory into the present. Puwar argues that, alongside the rage triggered by the consumption of ethnic otherness by the white majority, there exists among British Asian women 'another sense of aesthetics, one that cannot be strangled by the revulsion of the racialized or the celebratory anthropological lens ... a sensuousness of touch, fabric, shapes, colours and dreams'.[42] Not unlike Nusrat's song, clothing in Aslam's novel figures as an alternative aesthetic associated with a Pakistani female collectivism. But, while the mother–daughter bond between Kaukab and Mah-Jabin and the circulation of a shared culture among the neighbourhood's women are a vivid presence in the novel, they fracture as soon as they announce themselves. A gift of butterfly print fabric from Mah-Jabin to Kaukab is undermined by the fact that Kaukab cannot wear it 'because she would not be able to say her prayers in it: ... Islam forbids depictions of living things' (92); the rolls of fabric and array of colourful cosmetics and perfumes in the neighbourhood store are a gathering point for the community's women, causing Suraya to reflect on how much she misses the company of women that she had in Pakistan, but they also carry a sense of menace and oppression, as described above (215–16). The alternative sense of aesthetics that Puwar describes is stymied. Mahmood Mamdani's two definitions of culture – as 'creativity' and 'being human', and as 'habit' and rule-bound archaic practices – meet, but in each case the potential for a resistive minority collectivism of the former is quashed by the oppressive potential of the latter.[43]

Significantly, towards the end of the novel Charag is embarking on a new artistic direction. His next project will be based on a collection of photographs of the community, rescued from a local studio which has closed down.[44] When he announces this to his parents, Shamas is delighted that his son is turning from the personal or individual to the social in his art:

> He hasn't known how to read Charag's paintings in the past – they seem too personal to the boy to hold any interest for Shamas – but now, now that he has mentioned that he might do something with the photographs of immigrants, Shamas knows he is maturing as an artist, becoming aware of his responsibilities as an artist ... Good artists know that society is worth representing too. (319)

Here, too, there is the suggestion of a communicative aesthetic that can break down, and even perhaps bridge, the boundaries between the individual and the communal, the secular and the sacred. Art, for Charag, has provided an escape route from the community. His life in London, moreover, defined by his individual craft, threatens his relationship with his family: he is separated from his wife, has hit his son through frustration at the disruption that children cause to work, and has had a vasectomy (57–8). In this respect, he can be seen as the obverse of his mother whose literalist brand of worship (arguably the antithesis of Charag's secular individualism) similarly drives away her family. But Charag now plans to use his artistic practice to engage with the community. His creative plans, triggered by his lakeside meeting with the desperate Suraya – specifically, her challenge to him to paint her pain (133) – can be read as a self-reflexive comment on the novel itself, foregrounding the question of whether it bridges or entrenches these boundaries. Is it a site of productive intercultural encounter between secularism and Islam, where universalist narratives of each are similarly critiqued? Does the polyphony of voices enabled by the novelistic form contribute towards a productively conflictual negotiation between the competing demands of a secular liberalism and religious communalism, opening up a space for a 'politics of recognition'?[45] To what extent does the novel intervene in normative discourses about South Asian Muslims, multiculturalism and gender?

HONOUR CRIME, GENDER AND MULTICULTURALISM

Veena Meetoo and Heidi Safia Mirza argue that it is not the contextualisation of honour crime in Islamophobia and social and cultural hierarchies that leads to a tacit tolerance of it, but rather the 'ethnicisation' of it, or attributing it to the culture or religion of its perpetrators and victims. It is precisely by constructing honour crimes as 'ethnicised phenomena' rather than as a human rights issue that media reports can 'contribute to putting women at risk through sensationalising these crimes in their style and content of reporting, which results in voyeuristic spectacle (cries of "how dreadful") followed by multicultural paralysis and inaction ("nothing to do with us! It is part of their culture")'.[46] In fact, it is a 'cultural defence', a defence predicated on the idea that the culture of the accused has made it more difficult for him (or her) to refrain from committing the act of violence, that has been used in trials to obtain leniency for the accused, thereby diminishing the seriousness of the crime and simultaneously branding a culture and community as guilty of criminal practices. In the case of Heshu Yones, this is precisely what happened: the judge accepted Abdulla Yones's argument that his culture meant that he was provoked by his daughter's dress and choice of boyfriend as mitigation, and reduced the tariff by seven years.[47] The battle against honour crime, it is argued, should not be understood as a battle against culture but rather as a battle for human rights.[48] A highly problematic dichotomisation of feminism and multiculturalism, which an ethnicised, or culturalist, approach could engender, moreover, can lead to a reductive valorisation of the values of western liberalism in opposition to minority culture, and to a reduction of the Muslim woman to the double-sided stereotype of the cultural victim versus the liberated cultural escapee. As Muslim women are made visible, so they are simultaneously contained within a frame that casts them – and pathologises them – as victim.[49]

In *Maps for Lost Lovers*, Barra and Chotta, the perpetrators of Jugnu and Chanda's murder, conform to the stereotypes of young male Muslims that have circulated widely since the Rushdie affair and have gained momentum since the events of 2001.[50] Reformed drug dealers who have relinquished the rebellious crimes of their youth only to commit a crime in the name of family and community 'honour' (181), the two brothers also fit Claire Alexander's description of the boundaried, bifurcating representation of British Muslim men 'either as the heirs of … cultural disadvantage or the victims of a doomed "between two cultures" bid for freedom'. Alexander continues: 'To be inside "community" is to become an emblem of all the perceived ills of that cultural community; to be outside is to be without identity and on a course for social and cultural anomie: a lose-lose situation.'[51] Yet, Barra and Chotta are not depicted as the henchmen of an evil religious culture; rather, their crime can be traced in part to their own subordination and emasculation which has led to their violent rage. Barra is already angered by the 'crude' and 'demeaning' gossip surrounding their sister for living with a man outside of wedlock, as well as the taunt of a neighbour who had previously accused his wife of not being a virgin on their wedding night (350, 343–4). Desperate for a son after five daughters, he then learns that his wife had mistakenly had a male foetus aborted (349). Chotta finds his lover Kiran in bed with another man (284–5). Incensed and inebriated, he seeks out his sister's lover Jugnu and beats him to death. Joined by Barra, he searches for the injured Jugnu in the lovers' home where he finds Chanda and pushes her down the stairs, accidentally breaking her neck (350–69). 'We are men,' the brothers say to a friend in Pakistan, 'but she [Chanda] reduced us to eunuch bystanders by not paying attention to our wishes' (342). Thus the brothers' crime is configured as an extreme form of compensation for a failed masculine identity through the aggressive assertion of (limited) power.[52] While a culturalist understanding of this process would attribute it to an oppressively patriarchal Islamic culture located within a liberal Britain that challenges and erodes it, thereby triggering the assertion of a 'hyper-masculinity', Aslam's novel, despite its excoriation of their offence, eschews this easy narrative, grounding the brothers' behaviour in a more complex material context.

The judge's verdict in the murder trial of Barra and Chotta echoes that of the judge in the case of Heshu Yones. Neil Denison, QC, pronounced the case 'a tragic story of irreconcilable cultural differences ... between traditional Kurdish values and the values of Western society';[53] Aslam's judge, summarising the case, tells the court that 'the killers had found a cure to their problem through an immoral, indefensible act; a cure, a remedy – and *their religion and background* took care of the bitter aftertaste. *Their religion and background* assured them that, yes, they were murderers but that they had murdered only sinners' (278; emphases mine). The repetition of the words 'religion and background' serves to emphasise the judge's rooting of the crime in Islam. Barra and Chotta, the accused, react immediately: 'As for the murderers themselves, after the verdict had been announced they would begin to shout in the court, the litanies including words like "racism" and "prejudice". The judge's remarks would be deemed to have "insulted our culture and our religion". They'd said England was a country of "prostitutes and homosexuals"' (348). The word 'litanies', combined with the use of the past continuous tense, configures their response as scripted, the recitation of a formula that has lost its meaning through repetition and one that is, moreover, identified with religious doctrine. Thus the novel appears to simultaneously show an awareness of the culturalist discourses that surround such crimes *and* foreclose any legitimate critique of such discourses by attributing the only objection to the murderers themselves, whose misogyny and homophobia serve almost to parody their position. A similar move can be seen in an allusion to the media sensationalism surrounding honour killings which is often tinged with Islamophobia. A neighbour and friend of Kaukab, known as 'the matchmaker', says to Kaukab of the police's investigation of Jugnu and Chanda's deaths: 'the white police are interested in us Pakistanis only when there is a chance to prove that we are savages who slaughter our sons and daughters, brothers and sisters' (41); but she is an odious character, who pronounces Chanda 'a shameless girl ... so brazen' and accuses her, the victim, of getting Jugnu killed and ruining the lives of her brothers (41–2). Indeed, it would seem that the novel anticipates objections to negative representations of the community and dismisses them by underlining the potential complicity of such an attitude with criminal behaviour which targets women and children. For example, when the men who worship at the local mosque attempt to cover up the sex abuse there, they claim they are doing so because it 'would give Islam and Pakistan a bad name … and the Hindus and the Jews and the Christians would rejoice at seeing Islam being dragged through the mud' (235). Even an allusion by a neighbour to the abuse suffered by a veiled Muslim woman at the hands of the police in America is deflated by Mah-Jabin's suggestion that the police officers 'could've mistaken her face-veil for the hood of a Ku Klux Klan member', while the subsequent invasion of her body by the police search becomes, again through the focalisation of Mah-Jabin, a reflection on the community's refusal to allow their daughters gynaecological examination through fear of doctors damaging the hymen (107). Any criticism of the stereotyping of Islam or Muslims becomes a sanctioning of crime. Thus, there is a stasis or circularity to the novel whereby the potential for a meaningful multicultural critique is constantly deflected or stymied, often through a focus on the oppression of women.

The novel does on occasion point to the shortcomings of a secular liberal feminism that occludes both class and faith, especially in its portrayal of Kaukab. In response to Ujala's condemnation of the role that he believes Islam gives to women, she says: 'Why when you spend your time talking about women's rights, don't you ever think of me? What about my rights, my feelings? Am I not a woman, am I a eunuch?' (322). Notably, no one responds to her questions. Instead, Ujala continues his critique of Islam, trapping Kaukab into increasingly defensive and self-condemnatory statements until she is forced to concede that she believes Jugnu and Chanda were 'dirty, unclean sinners' (323). Mah-Jabin's defence of her mother only highlights the older woman's vulnerability, thereby tracing her lack of fit in liberal feminist discourses to her position as a working-class, uneducated migrant, rather than to a viable alternative discourse that might challenge an understanding of Muslim cultures as antithetical to women's rights and complicate the dichotomy of feminism versus multiculturalism. Further, leaving the community entails a relinquishment of the rigid gender roles that it prescribes and an assertion of individual subjectivity against communitarian prescriptions, so that gender equality and Muslim culture – and feminism and multiculturalism

– are again polarised: Barra and Chotta's aggressive, compensatory hyper-masculinity contrasts with the cultural 'escapee' Charag's purposeful 'unmanning' of himself in the form of a vasectomy, which in turn brings to mind his sister Mah-Jabin's 'defeminising' of herself by cutting off her hair (92, 104, 249). This polarisation can only lead to a reductive stereotyping of the Muslim woman as victim.

Consistent with this, in the end the novel appears to present just three positions for the community's women: victimhood (experienced by Kaukab, as well as the majority of the women in the community), complicity with the oppressive misogynistic practices of the community (primarily the older generation of women), or individual withdrawal and dissent from community, culture and faith (enacted by Maj-Jabin). Suraya, Shamas's lover, combines a feminist spirit with piety but the two remain polarised, with piety and patriarchy quashing her spirit ultimately (157–60). The ghostly Chanda, arguably, constitutes the trace of a disjunctive presence in the novel, in so far as she asserts her individual will to choose Jugnu while remaining within the community, living with him outside of wedlock because her husband cannot be located to request a divorce. But, just as in life her brothers tried to erase her after her failed marriages – first by asking her, unsuccessfully, to wear a burqa, then by painting over her name on the front of their store (342) – so her spectral presence in the novel suggests an inability to conceive of the possibility of a British Muslim female subjecthood that complicates and defies the totalising categories of the liberated cultural escapee who has delivered herself into enlightenment and progress, and the oppressed victim at the mercy of husbands, brothers and fathers who enforce a code of 'purity' and 'honour'. The limited roles prescribed for the community's women undermine the possibility of an agential – or indeed any meaningful – female collectivity. There is little space for the idea of Muslim culture as a force of community coherence, strength and resistance in the face of racism and other types of inequality. The novel eschews culturalism through its materialism but returns to it, almost, through its apparent inability to conceptualise a cultural communitarianism that is not oppressive.

SPACE, TIME AND BRITISH MUSLIM MODERNITIES

Nadeem Aslam has remarked that, on visiting Ground Zero, 'I asked myself whether in my personal life and as a writer I had been rigorous enough to condemn the small scale September 11s that go on every day

… Jugnu and Chanda are the September 11 of this book.'[54] Thus, he appears to equate two very different crimes – a terror attack and an honour killing – via their association with Islam, obscuring the heterogeneity of factors that contribute to each and potentially feeding reductive, culturalist discourses surrounding the religion. Yet, at a reading at the Royal Festival Hall on 8 July 2004, Aslam explained the novel's relation to September 11 in rather different terms: he pointed to the fact that, just as the initial appearance of 9/11 concealed a complexity that denied easy explanations, so in his novel the reader does not know what the characters' motivations are and assumptions are frequently disturbed. Indeed, Jugnu and Chanda are described in the novel as 'a bloody Rorschach blot: different people see different things in what happened' (137). The fact that the crime has occurred and the perpetrators have been identified before the narrative even begins means that its focus is not on *who* but rather on the mesh of stories that lead to and from, and circle around, the crime. These stories, moreover, are focalised through several different characters, giving a multiplicity of perspectives. This, together with the contradictory nature of Kaukab in particular, and the fact that narrative strands are left hanging and questions unanswered, destabilises reductive explanations of the central events.[55] The two contrasting interpretations of his analogy of 9/11 with honour crime point to the central ambivalence in the novel: while it digs beneath stigmatising narratives about Islam to a degree, offering multiple perspectives, humanising the adherents of this faith and materialising their failings, it also struggles to get beyond these conflicting discourses to conceive of an alternative notion of Muslim culture with a legitimate purchase on contemporary multicultural Britain.

The discovery of Jugnu and Chanda in bed together by five young boys who had climbed a tree to spy on them is likened to the King of Samarkand's discovery of his wife embracing a kitchen boy: just as the latter set in motion *A Thousand and One Nights*, so the boys' shocking find had become 'the starting point of another set of tales' (61). These 'tales' – the trails of gossip that spread through the community – impact on a range of inhabitants of Dasht-e-Tanhaii, precipitating more narrative strands, which creates a digressive structure to the novel and a sense of entrapment within it, not unlike Scheherazade's storytelling which must, of necessity, stop time by creating a never-ending web of stories. Indeed, the reader's somewhat claustrophobic entrapment within a maze of stories echoes the characters' own entrapment within the prescriptions of community and culture which prevent them from following their individual desire. This is explicitly articulated when Shamas, haunted by a chance meeting with the Hindu boy whose Muslim lover was killed, makes his way desperately to his own lover Suraya: 'He speeds up madly to make a way out of the cemetery … getting lost, needing a map of this labyrinth, a flaw in the net to burst through, this net made up of almost a thousand knots' (197). The image of a labyrinth without a map recalls the title of the novel which suggests the significance of cartography. In his 'Encyclopaedia Pakistanica' series for the magazine *The First Children on the Moon* Shamas's father invites readers to write the histories of their towns, villages and neighbourhoods which are then published alongside maps (76, 81). Thus, they lay claim to the history and geography of a new nation. In England, too, the South Asian immigrants rename the streets of their neighbourhood in an attempt to make it their own (28–9, 156). But there they lack the coordinates to find a sense of belonging or self-empowerment. This lack is evident also in the opening and closing scenes of the novel which take place in thick snow. The disorienting effect of the snow in the first scene, where Shamas stands at his front door watching a tiny indiscernible figure in the distance making her way through the falling flakes, is announced: 'Perspective tricks the eyes and makes the snowflakes falling in the far distance appear as though they are falling slower than those nearby' (5). Even the glimpses of the structure of the town connote a labyrinthine circularity, with streets forming tiers around the curve of hillside. In Shamas's final scene, having lost his way in the snow, he again finds the lost Hindu lover whom he escorts home before he dies. His last thoughts repeat with near-precision those that the novel opens with: 'He stretches out an arm to receive the small light snowflakes on his hand. A habit as old as his arrival in this country, he has always greeted the season's first snow in this manner' (367). This repetition – reinforced by the near-repetition or mirroring of numerous images and scenes throughout[56] – in turn reinforces the cyclical structure of the novel, its movement through the seasons, which suggests a circling of time rather than a forward movement. The fact that the novel's climactic event, the murder of Jugnu and Chanda, has already happened before it begins, also works against a sense of temporal progression, effecting instead a series of revolutions around and responses to a crime which has already been solved.

Just as the falling snow plays tricks with Shamas's sense of perspective, so the novel's metaphor- and simile-laden prose and fragmented form play with the reader's perspective, making it difficult to see beyond the over-loaded language to the events that are taking place. Aslam describes his intention when writing the novel as a creation of 'the literary equivalent of a Persian miniature, in which there is a remarkable density of detail'.[57] Indeed, with its intricate imagery and digressive, layered form, the novel does seem akin to a series of Persian miniatures where the even lighting, overlaying of different elements of the image, and intercutting or juxta-position of different views disturb conventional perspective to defamil-iarising effect. Aslam has said that the density of the language purposely obscures the story to reflect the characters' own myopia, their inability to see what is happening in their lives because they are missing Pakistan so much (Royal Festival Hall, 8 July 2004). I would add that it suggests their sense of entrapment in the community, as well as their detach-ment from majoritarian Britain and exclusion from liberal discourses and policies of multiculturalism that fail to account for the effects of social deprivation and cannot accommodate faith-based identities. The fact that Chanda's eyes change colour with the seasons links her to the cyclical structure of the novel, its revolutions that result only in stasis (54, 359). This, together with her and Jugnu's absence or spectral presence in the narrative, implies the impossibility of their evasion of the moral boundaries of their community. Yet it also suggests the impossibility of the transgression of the boundary between a cultural communitarianism and subjective desire that they attempt to enact. Indeed, the silencing of Jugnu and Chanda, as well as the silences that pervade the neighbourhood (45), point to another, ideological novelistic silence,[58] namely that of a British Muslim collectivism that is not antithetical to individual rights and gender equality and that exists beyond stereotyping discourses.

The circularity of the structure and language of the novel, and the sense of stasis it creates, can be seen to feed the othering of the Muslim community, its particularisation against 'our' universal. On entering Dasht-e-Tanhaii, the reader is drawn into a secret, hidden space. The impression given is that of the penetration of an unknown and forbidden enclave redolent of Phillips's description of Britain's 'black holes into which no-one goes without fear and trepidation'. As Yaqin points out in an article on BBC Radio 4 programmes, highlighting the use of the word 'inside' in two of the programme titles, 'Inside the harem' and 'Inside a Muslim school', this is a dominant representational trope with clear ideological effects.[59] Further, the sheer quantity and range of the prob-lems which affect the inhabitants of Dasht-e-Tanhaii, as well as the rather contrived nature of some passages in the novel, where the characters' voices appear to disappear into an account of these problems and 'issues', give an ethnographic character to the narrative. Ujala's anti-Islamic tirade at the family dinner that takes place towards the end of the novel provides just one example of this (321–2).[60] In this sense, Aslam's portrayal of this segregated Muslim community riven by the all too familiar narratives of forced marriage and honour crimes *is* on occasion suggestive of the exoticisation of the cultural Other, a process that relays the alien through recognisable paradigms, rendering it ripe for eventual conversion to 'our' sameness – a process that could, moreover, corroborate a neo-Orientalist legitimisation of the policing of Muslim culture and of British Muslims themselves.[61]

This threatened exoticism is in contradistinction to – and ultimately disenabled by – the defamiliarising effect of the novel's formal character- istics which works against an easy consumption. Yet, these same char- acteristics, together with the anonymity of the location, also create a quality of abstraction which serves to place the neighbourhood outside of 'our' modern space and time. This abstraction of the neighbourhood is in curious tension with the materialist leanings of the narrative, its repre- sentation of the space of Dasht-e-Tanhaii as a product of its profoundly unequal interrelations with the outside world. Similarly, the effect of circularity and non-progression is at odds with the strong sense of history in the novel. But, while the histories of imperialism and migration in which the inhabitants of Dasht-e-Tanhaii and their host country are rooted are a strong presence in the novel – captured most forcefully in the story of Deepak and Aarti, Shamas's father and lost aunt, who were hit during the 1919 bombing of Gujranwala, just days after the Amritsar massacre (48–53) – the present is stripped almost bare of allusions to its historical moment. Doreen Massey describes how, in neoliberal narra- tives of globalisation, certain regions of the world are attributed to an early stage of a singular narrative that 'obliterates the multiplicities, the contemporaneous heterogeneities of space' and 'reduces simultaneous coexistence to place in the historical queue'.[62] This process also takes place in relation to Muslim communities in Western Europe who are relegated to premodernity by secular liberal discourses which, as Salman Sayyid has shown, also works to consign them to the private, non-political domain.[63] Redolent of this, the abstraction or despatialisation of the neighbourhood in *Maps for Lost Lovers* works to detach it from contemporary time, or, put differently, to turn space into time – so that Dasht-e-Tanhaii could become identifiable with an earlier place 'in the historical queue' and its inhabitants with an earlier point in the trajectory towards 'true humanity' that Asad describes.[64] There is little sense of Islam or Muslim culture as a positive part of modernity, as a progressive, transformative and transforming narrative or force. In this sense, the Manichean geographies of 'us' and 'them' underpinning dominant understandings of the post-9/11 world are largely undisturbed.

The circularity or stasis conveyed in the novel also comes from a sense of entrapment in conflicting discourses that remain locked into a polarity and non-communicative – whether at the acrimonious family dinner after the trial of Jugnu and Chanda's killers, or in the court where the culturalist prejudice of the judge clashes with the killers' illegitimate accusations of racism. Yaqin describes the novel's polyphony as a 'cacophony of voices [that] is not truly dialogic as nobody is prepared to listen to one another'.[65] The conflicting discourses are suggestive of the fissures and contradictions of multiculturalism in Britain, the difficulties of reconciling the need to protect Muslims from Islamophobia and negative representation with the need to highlight gendered violence within Muslim communities, or of reconciling a multiculturalism that recognises collective minority rights with a commitment to gender equality. Significantly, in Aslam's novel the gaps between the discourses cannot be bridged so that there is an ideological stalemate. Pierre Macherey writes:

> The book is ... generated from the incompatibility of several meanings, the strongest bond by which it is attached to reality, in a tense and ever-renewed confrontation ... it unites in a single text several different lines which cannot be apportioned ... What the work says is not one or the other of these lines, but their difference, their contrast, the hollow which separates and unites them ... This is why we always find gaps and contradictions in the fabric of the work.[66]

In *Maps for Lost Lovers* it is the gap or difference between its materialism – its grounding of the behaviour and practices of these British Muslims in their disenfranchisement, poverty, race and religion, and consequent eschewal of a liberal culturalism – and its contradictory valorisation of individualism against communalism that is perhaps what it most importantly says. This conflict of discourses is also traceable in the novel's form. *Maps for Lost Lovers* adheres to the form of the social realist novel in many ways, and yet it also departs from it in its circular trajectory and lack of narrative development, as well as its pastoral imagery, aestheticised language and elements of surreality. The combination of social realism with a more self-consciously aestheticised form suggests the tension between the novel's materialist grounding and the liberalism that pervades it. It gets beneath reductive discourses that align Muslim culture with patriarchal crime and gives voice powerfully to the inhabitants of a working-class Muslim neighbourhood, suggesting a commitment to this minority community, and yet it is simultaneously hampered by an inability to think its way out of the polarity of minority communitarianism against individual freedom, ultimately adhering to an individualist liberalism. The novel is premised by a quote from Octavio Paz: 'A human being is never what he is but the self he seeks.' The emphasis here is on becoming, yet there is little space in *Maps for Lost Lovers* for the notion of a faith-based British Muslim becoming.

NOTES

1 Nadeem Aslam, *Maps for Lost Lovers* (London: Faber, 2004), p. 321. All subsequent citations are given within the body of the chapter and are to this edition of the text.

2 Trevor Phillips, 'After 7/7: sleepwalking to segregation', speech given at the Manchester Council for Community Relations (22 September 2005).

3 The fictional status of the location of *Maps for Lost Lovers* may have minimised its potential for causing offence. This in turn underlines the significance of the specificity of place to the *Brick Lane* controversy.

4 'A travesty of honour' (review of *Maps for Lost Lovers*), *Economist* (1 July 2004), www.economist.com/node/2876737/ (last accessed 6 November 2014).

5 Ron Charles, 'Holy terrors' (review of *Maps for Lost Lovers*), *Washington Post* (18 May 2005), www.washingtonpost.com/wp-dyn/articles/A1856–2005May18.html (last accessed 6 November 2014).

6 See Introduction, pp. 8–9.

7 Phillips, 'After 7/7'; M. A. Kevin Brice, 'Sleepwalking to segregation or wide-awake separation: investigation of distribution of white English Muslims and the factors influencing their choices of location', *Global Built Environment Review*, 6:2 (2007), 18–27, 18–19.

8 Richard Stone (chair), *Islamophobia: Issues, Challenges and Action: A Report by the Commission on British Muslims and Islamophobia* (Stoke-on-Trent: Trentham Books, 2004), p. 38.

9 Paul Bagguley and Yasmin Hussain, 'Flying the flag for England? Citizenship, religion and cultural identity among British Pakistani Muslims', in Tahir Abbas (ed.), *Muslim Britain: Communities under Pressure* (London and New York: Zed Books, 2005), pp. 208–21, pp. 210–12.

10 Mahmood Mamdani, *Good Muslim, Bad Muslim: America, the Cold War, and the Roots of Terror* (New York: Three Leaves Press/Doubleday, 2005 [2004]), p. 17.

11 Claire Alexander, 'Imagining the Asian gang: ethnicity, masculinity and youth after "the riots"', *Critical Social Policy*, 24:4 (2004), 526–49, 540. That David Cameron has more recently echoed this discourse, pronouncing 'state multiculturalism' a failure, responsible for promoting segregation, and, as Madeleine Bunting points out, confusing and conflating counter-terrorism and community cohesion, serves to emphasise the narrowing of the gap between left and right where Muslims are concerned ('Blame consumer capitalism, not multiculturalism', *Guardian* (6 February 2011), www.theguardian.com/commentisfree/2011/feb/06/capitalism-multiculturalism-cameron-flawed-analysis (last accessed 6 November 2014)).

12 Colin Brown, 'If we want social cohesion we need a sense of identity' (David Blunkett interviewed by Colin Brown), *Independent on Sunday* (9 December 2001), p. 4; Stone, *Islamophobia*, pp. 57–8.

13 Bagguley and Hussain, 'Flying the flag for England?', p. 212.

14 Alexander, 'Imagining the Asian gang', p. 533. As shown in Chapter 4, gender works in a similar way in mainstream responses to literary controversies: the fact that the *Brick Lane* and *Behzti* protesters were mainly men became a means of delegitimising these protests – by locating them within patriarchal culture and, in the process, obscuring the protesters' own vulnerabilities.

15 See Joanne Payton, 'Collective crimes, collective victims: a case study of the murder of Banaz Mahod', in Mohammad Mazher Idriss and Tahir Abbas (eds), *'Honour', Violence, Women and Islam* (Abingdon: Routledge, 2011), pp. 66–79, pp. 72–5; Hannana Siddiqui, '"There is no 'honour' in domestic violence, only shame!": women's struggles against "honour" crimes in the UK', in Lynn Welchman and Sara Hossain (eds), *'Honour': Crimes, Paradigms, and Violence against Women* (London: Zed Books, 2005), pp. 263–81, p. 263.

16 Siddiqui, 'There is no "honour"', p. 269. In response to these crimes and others, in 1999 the Labour government established the Home Office Working Group on Forced Marriage; in 2001 the London Metropolitan Police initiated the campaign 'Enough is enough – domestic violence strategy', which focused on honour-related violence; and in 2005 the Foreign and Commonwealth Office, together with the Home Office, launched the Forced Marriage Unit.

17 Amina Yaqin, 'Muslims as multicultural misfits in Nadeem Aslam's *Maps for Lost Lovers*', in Rehana Ahmed, Peter Morey and Amina Yaqin (eds), *Culture, Diaspora, and Modernity in Muslim Writing* (Abingdon and New York: Routledge, 2012), pp. 101–16, p. 103. Yaqin provides an excellent discussion of honour killings and the way in which they are identified with Islam and sensationalised by the media. See also Tahir Abbas, 'Honour-related violence towards South Asian Muslim women in the UK: a crisis of masculinity and cultural relativism in the context of Islamophobia and the "war on terror"', in Idriss and Abbas (eds), *'Honour', Violence, Women and Islam*, pp. 16–28, p. 18.

18 Hanif Kureishi, *The Black Album* (London: Faber, 1995). When questioned by an audience member at a reading at the Royal Festival Hall (8 July 2004) about his thoughts on the reaction to the novel by the Pakistani community, Aslam asserted, 'That is something that doesn't concern me.' In an interview, he points out that when he began to write the novel, in the early 1990s, honour crime was not a hot topic (Claire Chambers, 'Nadeem Aslam', in *British Muslim Fictions: Interviews with Contemporary Writers* (Basingstoke: Palgrave Macmillan, 2012), pp. 134–57, p. 155). And, of course, he could not have anticipated the increase in tensions surrounding Muslims and multiculturalism at the time the novel emerged.

19 Nadeem Aslam, *The Wasted Vigil* (London: Faber, 2008), p. 5. All subsequent citations are given within the body of the chapter and are to this edition of the text.

20 Amit Chaudhuri, 'Qatrina and her books' (review of *The Wasted Vigil*), *London Review of Books*, 31:16 (27 August 2009), 3 and 5–7, 5.

21 *Ibid.*

22 Despite its critique of a hardline secularism, the Muslims in the novel are the less developed characters, lacking in complexity and nuance in comparison to their white counterparts, which undermines the novel's articulation of a secularism that recognises religiosity (see Chambers, 'Nadeem Aslam', p. 139).

23 Arthur Bradley and Andrew Tate, *The New Atheist Novel: Fiction, Philosophy and Polemic after 9/11* (London: Continuum, 2011), pp. 10–11.

24 *Ibid.*, p. 11.

25 *Ibid.*, p. 12.

26 Kamila Shamsie, 'Martin Amis's views demand a response', *Guardian* (19 November 2007), www.theguardian.com/books/booksblog/2007/nov/19/martinamissviewsdemandare (last accessed 6 November 2014). Shamsie is referring to the interview Amis gave to Ginny Dougary for the *Times Magazine*: 'Martin Amis interviewed by Ginny Dougary', *Times Magazine* (9 September 2006).

27 Talal Asad, 'Free speech, blasphemy and secular criticism', in Talal Asad, Wendy Brown, Judith Butler and Saba Mahmood, *Is Critique Secular? Blasphemy, Injury and Free Speech* (Berkeley, CA: Townsend Center for the Humanities, 2009), pp. 20–63, p. 56.

28 The valorisation of creative freedom (Shamas) against religion and community (Kaukab) is also undermined by the representation of Shamas as deeply flawed, as discussed by Dave Gunning (*Race and Antiracism in Black British and British Asian Literature* (Liverpool: Liverpool University Press, 2010), pp. 88–90).

29 Salman Rushdie, *The Satanic Verses* (London: Random House, 1999 [1988]).

30 Neel Mukherjee, '*Maps for Lost Lovers* by Nadeem Aslam' (review) (26 June 2004), www.neelmukherjee.com/articles/maps-for-lost-lovers-by-nadeem-aslam/ (last accessed 6 November 2014).

31 Nirmal Puwar, 'Multicultural fashion … stirrings of another sense of aesthetics and memory', *Feminist Review*, 71 (2002), 63–87, 64.

32 In *The Wasted Vigil* the art object is literally deconstructed: the books nailed to the ceilings are left with holes through all of their pages, and the fractured paintings can never be adequately reassembled or restored. The trope of failed writing in *Maps for Lost Lovers* resonates with the repeated image of writing that fails to make a mark on the page in *The Wasted Vigil* (264, 320–1, 355). In Aslam's first novel, *Season of the Rainbirds* (London: Bloomsbury, 1993), there is also a trope of failed writing or communication: a bag of post that had been lost in a train crash twenty years earlier is found.

33 Ian McEwan, *Saturday* (London: Vintage, 2006). For readings of *Saturday* that make this point, see Robert Eaglestone, '"The age of reason is over … an age of fury was dawning": contemporary Anglo-American fiction and terror', *Wasafiri*, 22:2 (2007), 19–22; and Stephen Morton, 'Writing Muslims and the global state of exception', in Ahmed *et al.* (eds), *Culture, Diaspora, and Modernity*, pp. 18–33.

34 Terry Eagleton, *Reason, Faith, and Revolution: Reflections on the God Debate* (New Haven and London: Yale University Press, 2009), p. 155.

35 Pierre Bourdieu, *Distinction: A Social Critique of the Judgement of Taste*, trans. Richard Nice (London: Routledge, 1984), especially p. 491.

36 Allusions to and quotations from other Pakistani/Urdu poets recur in the novel; for example, Chanda's mother sings a poem by Punjabi poet Abid Tamimi (271).

37 Lindsey Moore, 'British Muslim identities and spectres of terror in Nadeem Aslam's *Maps for Lost Lovers*', *Postcolonial Text*, 5:2 (2009), 1–19, 8.

38 Eagleton, *Reason, Faith, and Revolution*, p. 155.

39 Malise Ruthven, *Islam: A Very Short Introduction* (Oxford: Oxford University Press, 1997), p. 17.

40 See Anshuman A. Mondal's 'Bad faith: the construction of Muslim extremism in Ed Husain's *The Islamist*', which makes a similar point in relation to the memoir's endorsement of Sufi-influenced brands of Islam (in Ahmed et al. (eds), *Culture, Diaspora, and Modernity in Muslim Writing*, pp. 37–51). See also the Quilliam Foundation website which Mondal references: www.quilliamfoundation.org (last accessed 6 November 2014).

41 It is perhaps not insignificant that shortly after his performance, Nusrat dies and the community mourns (238).

42 Puwar, 'Multicultural fashion', p. 64.

43 Mahmood Mamdani, 'Good Muslim, bad Muslim – an African perspective', 10 Years after September 11 (October 2001), http://essays.ssrc.org/10yearsafter911/good-muslim-bad-muslim-an-african-perspective/ (last accessed 6 November 2014); reprinted with revisions as 'Good Muslim, bad Muslim: a political perspective on culture and terrorism', in Eric Hershberg and Kevin Moore (eds), *Critical Views of September 11: Analyses from Around*

the World (New York: New Press, 2002), pp. 44–60, cited in Derek Gregory, *The Colonial Present* (Oxford: Blackwell, 2004), p. 22. In the novel cooking also offers an alternative sense of aesthetics, but similarly the potential for this frequently disintegrates: Kaukab's intricate preparation of dishes for the family dinner after the trial deteriorates into an acrimonious dispute leading to Kaukab's attempt to poison herself.

44 'The cache of photographs that will form the subject matter of Charag's next project is a reference to Tony Walker's Belle Vue portrait studio in Bradford which had taken photographs of immigrant families in the city from 1926 to 1975 (see Chambers, 'Nadeem Aslam', p. 153).

45 See Tariq Modood, 'Muslims, religious equality and secularism', in Geoffrey Brahm Levey and Tariq Modood (eds), *Secularism, Religion and Multicultural Citizenship* (Cambridge: Cambridge University Press, 2009), pp. 164–85, pp. 168–9.

46 Veena Meetoo and Heidi Safia Mirza, '"There is nothing 'honourable' about honour killings": gender, violence and the limits of multiculturalism', in Idriss and Abbas (eds), *'Honour', Violence, Women and Islam*, pp. 42–66, pp. 55–6.

47 Payton, 'Collective crimes', p. 75.

48 Arun Kundnani, *The End of Tolerance: Racism in 21st Century Britain* (London: Pluto, 2007), p. 138.

49 Meetoo and Mirza, 'Nothing "honourable"', p. 44.

50 Tariq Modood, *Multicultural Politics: Racism, Ethnicity and Muslims in Britain* (Edinburgh: Edinburgh University Press, 2005), p. 14; Claire Alexander, *The Asian Gang: Ethnicity, Identity, Masculinity* (Oxford: Berg, 2000), p. 7.

51 Alexander, *Asian Gang*, p. 231. See also Rehana Ahmed, 'British Muslim masculinities and cultural resistance: Kenny Glenaan and Simon Beaufoy's *Yasmin*', *Journal of Postcolonial Writing*, 45:3 (2009), 285–96.

52 Mairtin Mac an Ghaill and Chris Haywood, *Gender, Culture and Society: Contemporary Femininities and Masculinities* (Basingstoke: Palgrave Macmillan, 2007), p. 218; Alexander, *Asian Gang*, pp. 235–6.

53 Suruchi Thapar-Bjorkert, 'Conversations across borders: men and honour-related violence in the UK and Sweden', in Idriss and Abbas (eds), *'Honour', Violence, Women and Islam*, p. 185.

54 Marianne Brace, 'Nadeem Aslam: a question of honour', *Independent* (11 June 2004), www. independent.co.uk/arts-entertainment/books/features/nadeem-aslam-a-question-of-honour-731732.html (last accessed 6 November 2014).

55 For example, we never know whether Chanda's father was complicit in the crime or a victim of it, grieving for the loss of his daughter (138–9, 176).

56 Examples of repeated images/scenes include the image of the initials of lovers carved in Hindi, Urdu, Bengali and English on the jetty of the lake (17, 149); the image of Jugnu's face reflected in the back of a scarab beetle (279, 323); and, of course, the butterflies, parakeets and orchids.

57 Chambers, 'Nadeem Aslam', p. 143.
58 Macherey, *A Theory of Literary Production*, trans. Geoffrey Wall (New York and London: Routledge, 1996 [1978; French original 1966]), p. 79.
59 Amina Yaqin, 'Inside the harem, outside the nation: framing Muslims in radio journalism', *Interventions*, 12:2 (2010), 226–38, 235.
60 Other examples are the somewhat overplayed account of the characters' lack of contact with and perception of white people and the 'textbook' accounts of their experience of racism (see 262, 297).
61 Graham Huggan, *The Postcolonial Exotic: Marketing the Margins* (London: Routledge, 2001), pp. 13–28.
62 Doreen Massey, *For Space* (London: Sage, 2005), p. 5.
63 Salman Sayyid, 'Contemporary politics of secularism', in Levey and Modood (eds), *Secularism, Religion and Multicultural Citizenship*, pp. 186–99, p. 199.
64 Asad, 'Free speech', p. 56.
65 Yaqin, 'Muslims as multicultural misfits', p. 113.
66 Macherey, *Literary Production*, pp. 99–100.

6

Reason to believe?
Five British Muslim memoirs

[A]lthough virtual, the 'I' of autobiography can pack a punch in the material world, and life narratives have a distinctive role to play in the struggle to shape dialogues across cultures. (Gillian Whitlock[1])

Those who remain faceless or whose faces are presented to us as so many symbols of evil, authorize us to become senseless before those lives we have eradicated, and whose grievability is indefinitely postponed. Certain faces must be admitted into public view, must be seen and heard for some keener sense of the value of life, all life, to take hold. (Judith Butler[2])

MEMOIR, MUSLIMS AND THE MARKET

In the wake of 9/11 and the 'war on terror', the 'Muslim' has become an object of curiosity and at times fearful fascination for a western reading public. The demands of the market are evidenced in the proliferation of autobiographical memoirs by writers of Muslim heritage on both sides of the Atlantic. In North America, Iranian-American Azar Nafisi's *Reading Lolita in Tehran: A Memoir in Books* (2003) has achieved both commercial success and critical acclaim, while memoirs by journalists reporting on the 'war on terror' such as Anne Garrels's *Naked in Baghdad* (2003) have assumed increasing prominence. The 'veiled best-seller' – romantic biographies of Muslim women – as well as Norma Khouri's highly successful hoax testimony, *Honor Lost: Love and Death in Modern-Day Jordan* (2003), affirm the public hunger for greater 'knowledge' of its Muslim Other.[3] American (formerly Dutch) Somali Ayaan Hirsi Ali's ghost-written *Infidel: My Life* (2007) was a *New York Times* bestseller as well as a commercial success in the Netherlands, where it was launched.[4] In Britain, especially following 7/7 when the reality of 'home-grown' terrorism shone the spotlight on the heterogeneous Muslim youth of the nation, memoirs by young writers of Muslim heritage have secured a spot in the marketplace. This chapter focuses on five recent examples of popular autobiographical memoir to explore the ways in which they intervene in Muslim–majority relations and mediate cross-cultural understanding in multicultural Britain: Ed Husain's *The Islamist* (2007), Sarfraz Manzoor's *Greetings from Bury Park: Race, Religion and Rock 'n' Roll* (2007), Yasmin Hai's *The Making of Mr Hai's Daughter: Becoming British* (2008), Zaiba Malik's *We are a Muslim, Please* (2010) and Shelina Zahra Janmahomed's *Love in a Headscarf* (2009).[5] These autobiographical works are important examples of British Muslims 'transform[ing] themselves from objects of representation to Subjects of self-representation', asserting their subjectivities in the context of the homogenising neo-colonial discourses that surround Muslims.[6] They also inevitably carry a weighty burden of representation in a climate of fear and perceived threat – a burden that they shoulder knowingly and by choice, in order to make an intervention in representations that circulate about British Muslims.[7] Their designated status as 'insider' accounts that are representative of 'Muslim experience' endows them with a particular potency to challenge but also, alternatively, to reproduce and confirm such discourses. The chapter considers the 'double agency' of the memoirs; their ability to 'work in very different interests and constituencies at one and the same time', to facilitate dialogue across cultures while also, at times, obscuring the power relations that underpin that dialogue and, potentially, serving to exclude from it those who are too 'different'.[8]

The penultimate chapter of Sarfraz Manzoor's *Greetings from Bury Park* is titled 'Reason to believe', a reference to a song by Bruce Springsteen, whose lyrics underpin the narrative throughout, providing chapter titles and epigraphs, as well as the title of the book itself (an allusion to Springsteen's first studio album, *Greetings from Asbury Park, NJ*, released in 1973, shortly before two-year-old Manzoor's arrival in Bury Park, Luton). The song 'Reason to believe' suggests the tenacious faith of humankind in the face of adversity, a 'universal' story that transcends 'geography, race [and] religion' (102). In Manzoor's memoir, it is also used to denote the narrator's own conflicted relationship with his inherited religion, Islam; his unsuccessful struggle to find a 'reason to believe'. Thus, the phrase, with its dual meaning, encapsulates the layering of and tension between a universalising and individualising narrative that could relate to 'anyone', and a culturally specific memoir that is rooted in and conveys the experience of being an Asian Muslim Briton. This duality in turn maps onto the intersection of the private and the public evident in all of the memoirs. Each is punctuated by private events which have universal resonance (most significantly, in the narratives of Manzoor, Hai and Malik, the death of their fathers) and public events with particular significance for Muslims, notably the 9/11 and 7/7 attacks. Indeed, each memoir can be read in both private/universal and public/culturally specific terms. Husain's narrative is one of a confused adolescent's quest for belonging *as well as* a journey into 'radical Islam'; Manzoor, Hai and Malik tell stories of the loss of a beloved father *as well as* of an originary, stable sense of home and self through migration, and explore the conflict between youthful desire and parental expectation *as well as* between the competing demands of secular individualism and religious community; while Janmohamed articulates the obstacles 'everywoman' encounters in her search for romantic love *as well as* the vicissitudes of the arranged marriage system that she negotiates.

This duality, integral to much postcolonial autobiography, underlines the powerful potential of these personal, and at times highly emotive narratives to enable but also, conversely, to circumscribe a critical engagement with public discourses about Islam. Gillian Whitlock describes the ability of autobiography, or the more capacious genre of 'life narrative', to elicit empathy from a reader. It is the personal nature of the genre, its reference to 'lived experience', as well as its 'gestures of sincerity, authenticity, and trust', which facilitate identification with the autobiographical subject.[9] The 'I' is the universal subject. Blake Morrison writes of the anti-hierarchical and 'democratising' nature of 'life-writing'; it eschews the grand narratives and high-profile protagonists of traditional biographies or memoirs of the past, enabling anyone to relate to the experiences narrated.[10] In the context of 'Muslim life narratives' marketed to and consumed by non-Muslim western readers, this affective dimension can work to 'personalize and humanize categories of people whose experiences are frequently unseen and unheard' and facilitate crucial cross-cultural dialogue, reshaping the way those in the West understand their relationship to Others.[11] However, as Whitlock points out, it is the rhetorical power of the genre that simultaneously makes it amenable to deployment as a subtly manipulating form of propaganda – not as 'the violent and coercive imposition of ideas' but rather as 'a careful manipulation of opinion and emotion in the public sphere'. For Whitlock, life narrative's capacity to give form and feature to the faceless Afghan or Iraqi subjects of media reportage on the 'war on terror' and so make connections across boundaries of nation, race and culture is blunted or 'softened' because of its susceptibility to co-option into constructions of the Muslim woman as victim of an oppressive misogynistic Islamic culture and assumptions of the status of liberal western culture as civilisational benchmark.[12]

In the context of post-9/11 multicultural Britain, where a rise in Islamophobia and a hardening of an anti-religious secularism among the liberal left underline the need to build and strengthen Muslim–majority relations, life narratives have an important role to play. At the same time, their potential for consolidating the pervasive stereotype of the Muslim woman as victim, as well as discourses that align political Islam with terrorism, must be considered. The emergence in the 2000s of a range of popular memoirs written by British Asian victims of forced marriage and its close cousin, 'honour crime' – including Jasvinder Sanghera's trilogy of books *Shame, Daughters of Shame* and *Shame Travels: A Family Lost, A Family Found* (2006, 2009, 2012) and Saira Ahmed's *Disgraced* (Headline Review, 2009) – bears witness to the marketability of 'misery memoirs' focusing on religious South Asian cultures in Britain, further suggesting the hegemony of reductive discourses among a majoritarian readership.[13] The memoirs examined here have been received by critics with epithets that suggest their ability to elicit empathy. Husain's *The Islamist* contains 'moving family vignettes and lyrical passages', while Manzoor's *Greetings from Bury Park* is 'tender', 'sad and lyrical' and 'richly humane', and Hai's *The Making of Mr Hai's Daughter* is 'affectionate, sometimes sad' and 'touching'.[14] But how is their emotive impact mobilised? Can it be co-opted into a confirmation of stereotyping constructions? Or do these narratives, rather, deconstruct and resist such constructions, in the vein of the 'autoethnographic' or counter-ethnographic accounts that Mary Louise Pratt explores, appropriating the 'idioms' of hegemonic discourses surrounding Muslims in order to challenge them?[15] Are these more nuanced narratives that facilitate a critical and counter-hegemonic cross-cultural engagement with a frequently subordinated and denigrated minority group?

The words 'reason to believe' also evoke the secularist dichotomy of Enlightenment reason versus blind faith. Manzoor gestures towards this dichotomy in his account of the role of Islam in his life: he alludes to Islam as indecipherable, inaccessible and remote, as rituals to be followed blindly and unquestioningly, while also acknowledging that this interpretation of Islam is shaped by his parents' adherence to certain cultural, as opposed to doctrinal, rules (215–17, 226–7). And yet the phrase also hints at a possibility of bridging, and therefore deconstructing, that dichotomy; the word 'to' is a linking word, a bridge rather than a barrier. It posits 'belief' as potentially stemming from 'reason' and so having some basis in the material and historical. It also sketches a connection between belief and individual choice, again destabilising normative associations of Islam with the suppression of individuation and free will. Charles Taylor has described how the othering of the British Muslim by secular westerners is fed not just by conflicts of liberal states with religion, but also by 'a specifically epistemic distinction: religiously informed thought is somehow less rational than purely "secular" reasoning. The attitude has a political ground (religion as threat), but also an epistemological one (religion as a faulty mode of reason).'[16] Taylor, along with Talal Asad, emphasises the importance of breaking down this distinction in order to attain an equality that extends to and encompasses religious, including Muslim, communities.[17] In the light of this, I ask how far these memoirs deconstruct the binary of reason versus belief that so frequently fixes Muslims as Britain's cultural Other.

With the exception of *The Islamist*, these memoirs are not commercial successes like several of the life narratives Whitlock discusses, or Sanghera's *Shame* trilogy. Their publishers – Bloomsbury (Manzoor), Virago (Hai), Random House's literary paperback imprint Windmill (Malik) and independent non-fiction press Aurum (Janmahomed) – suggest that their primary target is not a mass market but rather a middle-class liberal readership, one that considers itself receptive to and informed about cultural difference. This is corroborated by the serialisation of both Hai's and Malik's memoirs on the middle-class radio station Radio 4, while the fact that Manzoor wrote columns regularly for the liberal left broadsheet the *Guardian*, prior to publishing his memoir, implies the latter was aimed at a similar reader. All of the autobiographical 'I's, moreover, exist on the privileged peripheries of the British Muslim communities with which they engage. From a fairly humble background as the son of Bangladeshi immigrants who ran a takeaway restaurant in London's East End, Husain is a senior fellow at New York's Council on Foreign Relations and co-founder of the counter-extremism think tank endorsed by New Labour, the Quilliam Foundation. Janmahomed, belonging to the East African Asian diaspora in Britain, is a professional, middle-class Oxford University alumnus who contributes to *emel*, the Muslim lifestyle magazine, as well as the *Guardian* and *The Times*.[18] Manzoor, Hai and Malik are all successful journalists. While Hai is from a more privileged background than Malik or Manzoor (whose memoir is particularly moving in its evocation of the impoverishment of his family's early years in Britain and the impact this had on their futures), all three exist similarly between social categories and are socially and spatially mobile, ultimately moving away from their class as well as cultural backgrounds.

Whitlock draws a distinction between 'memoir', which for her is 'the prerogative of the literate elite', and 'testimony' as 'the means by which the disempowered experience enters the record ... not necessarily under conditions of their choosing'.[19] Here, I privilege the term 'memoir', yet all of the authors can be located on the borderline between these two categories. They are certainly 'authorized and accredited witnesses' of the British Muslim communities and cultures they represent, their class status arguably delimiting their ability to identify with the latter; but they are also 'marginal' and potentially 'resistant' subjects who are affiliated to those same communities.[20] Their borderline status is significant in so far as it means that they are able to cross between inside and outside, community and context. This has the potential to facilitate cross-cultural translation and also to an extent disable an easy consumption of their narratives of cultural difference. Kay Schaffer and Sidonie Smith describe how, in the last decade of the twentieth century, events such as South Africa's Truth and Reconciliation Commission and Australia's Stolen Generation reparations validated narratives of personal experience as vehicles towards social justice, paving the way for the popularity of life narratives. While this has helped to generate understanding and empathy for the cultural Other, however, privileged western readers of these narratives can too easily assume the role of enlightened, benevolent agents, potentially falling into an exoticist consumption.[21] By contrast, the borderline position of these five authors works against such an exoticisation, as well as problematising the idea of a singular authentic Muslim subject. However, their peripheral position in relation to the Muslim communities that they portray also has the potential to entrench divisions between the 'good Muslim', who has largely 'escaped' his or her cultural and religious background or for whom faith remains uniquely personal and spiritual; and the 'bad Muslim', who is immersed in culture and community and asserts his or her 'Muslimness' and right to being a Muslim in the public sphere.[22]

These memoirs are significant in so far as they write legitimate British Muslim subjectivities into local spaces (including the much maligned 'Muslim ghetto' towns of Bradford and Luton) and the national space.

By using a form that prioritises a liberal humanist notion of individual subjectivity, they are countering the tendency to represent Muslims as a homogeneous and indistinguishable collective. But are they, in the process, valorising certain subjectivities at the expense of others? Graham Huggan's work is useful here, specifically his appraisal of the tensions between the oppositional potential of 'ethnic autobiography' and the constraints placed upon it by the demands of a 'white-liberal elite' that it is expected to meet.[23] In the case of British Muslim autobiography, in order to cater to those demands, the autobiographical 'I' might distance itself from the aspects of Muslim culture that do not sit so easily with the central tenets of a liberal multiculturalism, and, in so doing, testify to the good character of some assimilated British Muslims. To what extent, then, do the narrators align themselves with and interpellate an 'outsider' liberal western reader who can, in turn, identify the autobiographical 'I's as enlightened 'escapees' from the perceived constraints of Muslim culture and valorise his or her own preconceptions in the process?[24]

ED HUSAIN'S *THE ISLAMIST*

The paratextual elements of a book influence the reader's expectations of what is to come and thus their approach to the text.[25] The front cover of Ed Husain's *The Islamist* leaves little room for doubt about the message it intends to convey. A British Asian youth sporting a short, neat beard and a hoodie surveys a busy London scene. The image of the youth is foregrounded and darkened, a semi-silhouette. In the slightly blurred background, people, many of whom appear to be Asian, queue to board a London bus, while two hijab-clad women shop at a market stall and a salesman dressed in a shalwar kameez awaits customers. The sense of threat connoted by the youth is aimed at multicultural London. This, combined with the iconic London bus, brings to mind the 7/7 bombings, when commentators, including Trevor Phillips, repeatedly cited the cultural diversity of the victims to legitimise the viewpoint that the bombings were an attack on 'our' plurality by 'their' singularity.[26] The darkened image of the youth, who is turned away from the camera so that his expression is barely visible, contrasts starkly with the author's photograph which appears on the back cover. A clean-shaven Husain, dressed in a casual suit jacket and open-necked shirt, looks directly at the camera, with a minimal smile denoting a combination of affability and gravitas. Dichotomies of closed versus open, dark versus light, and separatist versus integrated are conveyed by this imagery and emphasised by the book's tabloid headline style subtitle – 'Why I joined radical Islam in Britain, what I saw inside and why I left' – which indicates its structure of a central point of enlightenment sandwiched between a before and an after.

Indeed, the plaudits garlanding the back cover and preliminary pages of the book overwhelmingly depict the narrative as an uncovering of the 'truth' about Islamism. It 'takes you into the mind of young fundamentalists', provides 'penetrating insight of a former insider' and a 'uniquely well-informed guide to the netherworld of British Islamism', and 'reveals important warnings about the future of Islam'. Its discussion is 'open', 'frank' and full of 'insight'. Moreover, it is 'captivating', 'gripping', 'arresting', 'riveting' and 'shocking'; in short, a compelling read akin to a thriller, carrying a comparable sense of threat leading to revelation and resolution. The use of the first person for the subtitle and the back-cover blurb emphasises the narrative's 'authenticity'; the direct address from author to reader establishes a bond of trust that works against readerly scepticism. The fact that the commendatory publicity quotations are taken from a cross-section of Britain's broadsheet and tabloid newspapers, with the right-wing *Daily Telegraph* and *Mail on Sunday* brushing shoulders with the liberal left *Guardian* and the *Asian Leader*, suggests a universal appeal and positions the book as non-partisan. This positioning is enhanced by the preface. Opening in the first-person plural and representing Husain's journey into radical Islam as a story of human fallibility, it underlines the apparently universal resonance of his narrative, both enhancing its attraction to non-Muslim readers and deflecting the focus away from the political to the ethical. This is further corroborated when Husain presents his narrative as the result of his *'human duty* to speak out against what I see masquerading in Britain as "Islam"', and promises the reader a journey not just 'inside Britain's Muslim communities', but also 'inside my own heart' (Preface, n.p.; emphasis mine). The educational value and emotional intimacy offered by this humanist tale of failure and redemption confers on the reader the status of empathic confidante, enabling a cross-cultural identification with the autobiographical subject. This is not, however, a case of an exoticist consumption of the cultural Other by the western consumer which obfuscates asymmetries of power between the two; rather, the paratext and the narrative that follows set up an exclusionary universalism that aligns Muslim narrator with politically correct reader to exclude the 'Islamist', or political Muslim, who becomes the exception.[27]

Indeed, in its first year of publication, more than fifty thousand copies of the book were sold, underlining its widespread appeal.[28]

In *The Islamist*, then, the dichotomy of 'good Muslim'/'bad Muslim', which shapes the narrative, maps onto that of the pious Muslim who confines his faith to the private domain and the political Muslim who asserts his faith in the public domain. Islamism is implicitly conflated with any form of faith-based political mobilisation or activism by a repeated contrast between the spiritual Islam of Husain's father, his first spiritual leader 'Grandpa' and the influential American Islamic scholar Hamza Yusuf Hanson, and the political Islam of the two main groups that he is involved with, Jamat-e-Islami and Hizb ut-Tahrir, leaving little space for anything that fails to conform to either pole, or bridges the divide between them (22, 174, 177). Reason and belief are similarly polarised; while the latter is by no means dismissed by the pious narrator, it occupies an entirely different sphere from the reason that shapes the public and political world. Indeed, Husain returns repeatedly to the lack of religiosity among members of Hizb ut-Tahrir in particular, who often cannot recall the words of prayer. And the more actively involved in the organisation he himself becomes, the more he withdraws from God (146–7; see also 198). Husain's Muslim, like that of the Islamophobic secularism that Salman Sayyid describes, is 'the permanently transgressive subject, whose "religious essence" is constantly being undermined by temptations of the political'. For Husain, as for the secularism Sayyid critiques, 'The proper Muslim is religious … It follows that the Muslim who is political is not properly a Muslim.'[29] The 'good' or non-transgressive Muslim can only occupy the modern public sphere legitimately if his or her 'Muslimness' remains solely spiritual and internal.

The location of *The Islamist* in east London suggests an engagement with British multiculturalism on the part of the narrative. Indeed, Husain builds his narrative around his upbringing in Limehouse, his attendance of the Brick Lane and East London mosques, and his years at Tower Hamlets College, taking in some of the landmarks of this iconic multicultural space. Yet, despite this, the location emerges only vaguely, resonating with the blurriness of the cover image. Like the contrastingly sharp outline of 'the Islamist' that dominates the book's cover, Islamism subsumes the narrative, as it subsumes the narrator, reducing its local context to little more than a recruiting ground for extremism. Of course the blurred context underlines the autobiographical subject's near-total immersion in Islamist groups, which narrows his focus and blinds him to other aspects of his environment. But the effect of this is twofold. First, Islamism is decontextualised, or detached from hierarchical structures of class, race and religion. Thus, the space of the East End becomes a passive receptacle for extremism which functions as a transcendental signifier, grounded in nothing but itself.[30] So, for example, Husain asserts that 'Home-grown British suicide bombers are a direct result of Hizb ut-Tahrir disseminating ideas of jihad, martyrdom, confrontation, and anti-Americanism, and nurturing a sense of separation among British Muslims' (119). With this statement, not only does he flatten the complex array of factors that contributed to the 7/7 bombings, but he connects British Muslims' 'sense of separation' to the bombings and roots this in Hizb ut-Tahrir's propaganda machine, rather than in social and cultural conditions. Similarly, while the assertion that the bombers 'were symptomatic of a deeper problem' suggests a materialist explanation might follow, this 'deeper problem' turns out to be nothing more than 'unbridled Islamist ideology gaining a stronger hold in Britain's Muslim communities' (278). That, apparently, is as deep as it goes. Foreign policy is mentioned on occasion as a motivating factor for extremism and disenfranchisement among British Muslims, but this viewpoint is simultaneously dismissed by its attribution to extremists, so that it comes to appear as little more than an excuse (125, 277–8). The reduction of any criticism of neo-colonial practices and discourses to extremism and, ultimately, terrorism, undermines the legitimacy of such criticism on ethical grounds (278). The self-presence of Islamism is emphasised by the prophetic, doom-laden tone of the narrative, which constructs it as a bogeyman. As early as the second page of the book, we are told that 'lurking in the background [of Limehouse] were forces that were preparing to seize the hearts and minds of British Muslim children' (2), while by the penultimate chapter we are warned of the threat of 'the unleashing of a firestorm of violence by home-grown Wahhabi jihadists, inflamed by Islamist rhetoric, on the major cities of America and Britain' (265). This ominous tone is itself facilitated by the autobiographical form which creates a dual time-frame: the narrator knows what is in store for his vulnerable, naive former self – as well as for Britain – and can give us glimpses of the horrors waiting in the wings (86, 115, 215).

The second implication of the obscured social context of the events that unfold is that the Muslims and Muslim cultures of London's East End that are *not* reducible to Islamists and Islamism are pushed to the margins of the narrative. Either they remain enclosed in the private domain and confined to an older generation (Husain's parents), or they emerge hazily and en masse as political pawns at permanent risk of being lured into one or other of the fundamentalist groups that, according to Husain, prey on the area's Muslim youth. In a chapter entitled 'Targeting communities', members of Hizb ut-Tahrir, including Husain, disperse across Whitechapel in an attempt 'to move the masses', and strike up friendships with gangs of Muslim youths on street corners (112, 114), while Muslim children are 'targets' of the Young Muslims Organisation, who – by organising youth camps, football matches and fund-raising events for the mosque – maintain 'a tight grip on the lives of its members' (39). Public space, too, is barely visible except as 'Islamized' or as vulnerable to 'Islamization' (62–3).[31] The sinister edge to this depiction of the YMO is symptomatic of a general antipathy towards organisations, groups and any form of communitarianism, as Anshuman A. Mondal elucidates.[32] Organised religion had 'belittled' God and is opposed to piety (185, 27); by contrast, Hamza Yusuf Hanson, a figure whom Husain comes to revere during his period of 'recovery', understands Islam as 'empowering individuals rather than activist groups' (174). Indeed, as all Muslim organisation is, in Husain's narrative, associated – at the very least – with Islamism, there cannot be any legitimate Muslim mobilisation or activism. Muslims must choose between Islamism or 'non-political, individual pietism'.[33] Tariq Modood warns of this conflation: 'Religious fundamentalism, like all fundamentalisms and ideology, is a potential threat to democratic civic life but it cannot be equated with the participation of religious groups in multicultural citizenship.'[34] Such an equation, it is implied, will disable Muslim participation in British citizenship – and, indeed, Husain's attitude towards multiculturalism is consistent with a liberal individualism that presupposes an equal public sphere and so must, of necessity, marginalise and privatise Muslim cultural practices. The narrative opens with a nostalgic recollection of the 'colour-blind humanity' of the teachers at his primary school in the late 1970s and 1980s (2). This is contrasted favourably with the 'multiculturalism fostered by the Labour government', which has, according to Husain, 'created mono-cultural outposts in which the politics of race and religion were now being played out before my eyes' (282). This in turn resonates with the criticisms of multiculturalism as responsible for segregation that emerged among the liberal left in the wake of the 9/11 and 7/7 attacks.[35]

The reduction of Muslims to pawns is redolent of representations of Rushdie's working-class detractors, as well as precursory imperial constructions of South Asian Muslim lascars and pedlars in Britain.[36] Interestingly, there is a glimpse of the long history of Muslim settlement in east London with a cameo appearance by the elderly Haji Taslim Ali, Britain's first Muslim undertaker, discussed in Chapter 1:[37] 'under Islamist influences', Husain writes, 'I was too arrogant to respect him. In the eyes of an Islamist, he was not part of the Islamic movement and therefore not worthy of deference' (45). Thus, at the edge of his life as of the narrative, Taslim Ali exits. Husain's rationale for his exit is that, as an 'ordinary Muslim', the undertaker failed to fit the narrative that defined him at the time. However, there is another way in which he fails to fit Husain's narrative. The figure of Taslim Ali, who helped to imprint Muslim culture on British soil, hints at an assertive practice of Islam in Britain that is reducible neither to Islamism nor to a politically quietist, spiritual Islam. The establishment of Islamic burial rites, the foundation of mosques, mobilisation for halal meat in schools or for the right to veil in public places – all of these practices awkwardly straddle the binary division of 'good Muslim' and 'bad Muslim' that structures the narrative.[38] Thus, just as the wearing of the hijab (described as 'a pinned-down-tight, face-grabbing style') must be portrayed as a consequence of male Islamist indoctrination and identified with 'a rejection of the West' (67), so too Taslim Ali must be evacuated for consistency with the memoir's ideological narrative as well as its surface story.

In contradistinction to much postcolonial autobiography that is characterised by a fragmentary form to convey the loss of a coherent self and the lack of fit between the self and available discourses,[39] *The Islamist*, notwithstanding its declared awareness of the constructedness of history (154, 159, 160), presents itself as a seamless and authoritative narrative. The 'insider' perspective of the former Islamist, combined with the split time-frame, which underlines the narrator's experience, knowledge and self-reflection, further endows his account with authority, blunting sceptical readings. Husain identifies his journey from Islamism to enlightenment as one of maturity, a shedding of adolescent naivety and confusion that enables his return to his father and family (146, 196). Further, his discovery of 'true' or 'authentic' Islam is represented as the product of hard work and study which lends it added credibility (200–1, 214). Thus he frames his account in a personal and emotive narrative with a strong teleology that offers the reader a comfortable resolution – not just to his own life (his emergence as the clean-shaven, open Briton depicted in his photograph) but also to the contradictions of British multiculturalism:

the confinement of Islam in Britain to the private sphere, 'a spiritual rather than political Islam' (265).

SARFRAZ MANZOOR'S *GREETINGS FROM BURY PARK*, YASMIN HAI'S *THE MAKING OF MR HAI'S DAUGHTER* AND ZAIBA MALIK'S *WE ARE A MUSLIM, PLEASE*

Already evident on the cover of Sarfraz Manzoor's *Greetings from Bury Park* is a tension between 'universality' and cultural specificity. It comprises juxtaposed images of prayer beads, sunglasses, a Bruce Springsteen record and concert ticket, and childhood photographs of the author with his younger sister and father. The main paragraphs of the back-cover blurb, which describe the content of the narrative in broad brushstrokes, mapping its trajectory from 'Lahore to Luton to Ladbroke Grove' and clearly alluding to the protagonist's race and religion, are sandwiched between two summative comments which, echoing the title itself, emphasise its 'universal' themes, marginalising race and religion. So reviewer Andrew Collins says of *Greetings* that 'you don't have to be a Muslim ... to get into [it]', and just below it is described as 'an inspiring tribute to the power of music to transcend race and religion' and 'a touching salute of thanks from one working-class Pakistani Muslim boy to the father who died too soon for his son to make him proud'. This last comment simultaneously particularises (with the words 'Pakistani Muslim') and universalises (through emphasis on the father–son relationship and the overcoming of hardship). While the singularity of the word 'one' contests the racialising reduction of 'Pakistani Muslim boys' to a homogeneous collective, the individualisation it implies also connotes a distancing of the author from the group identity to which he is affiliated. Thus it suggests a refutation on the part of the singular autobiographical subject of both the homogenising tendencies of mainstream representations of Muslims and the collectivist demands of a minority Pakistani Muslim family and community.[40]

Greetings is in many ways a 'triumph-over-adversity' narrative,[41] about overcoming barriers – of class and poverty, traceable in part to the author's family's migration from Pakistan and their minority status in Britain, but also of (religious) culture and community which are often configured as constraining. In Manzoor's exploration of the marriage practices of his Pakistani family and community, the arranged marriage emerges as the antithesis to individual love (178–211). When, under maternal pressure, he agrees to be open to approaches from potential brides, his verdict is that 'everyone seemed a little too into religion; none sounded like they might actually be a laugh'. And on discovery that one of them wears a hijab, he runs scared (208–9). The 'God-fearing, super-Muslim' anonymous *hijabi* contrasts with the rebellious, foul-mouthed, dyed-haired Laila, the first focus of Manzoor's 'suppressed yearnings' (194–8). Whereas Laila liberates him from his own sense of cultural responsibility and comes to represent individual freedom, the *hijabi*, with her indifference to pop music and her disapproval of swearing, suggests conformity and obedience.[42] Traceable here is a dichotomy between religious observance and Enlightenment values such as autonomous subjectivity and freedom. It is, as is typical of *Greetings*, elliptical rather than overt, emerging here and there in glimpses, which suggests an uneasiness with an assertive Islamic identity on the part of Manzoor. As Reina Lewis has shown, it is, in fact, especially in contemporary British Muslim veiling practices that the binary of individual subjectivity versus religio-cultural prescription can be deconstructed. The rhetoric British Muslim women use to explain their decision to veil, Lewis demonstrates, frequently 'combines the secular-Enlightenment-derived notion of conscious choice with an allegiance to a universalizing revivalist politics that decrees veiling to be a divine requirement ... The exponent of veiling is presented as a self-directed sovereign subject – a riposte to the presumption of many ... that veiling is always and only a sign of female subordination and lack of individuation.'[43] Moreover, the co-existence of religious communitarianism with subjectivity, agency and argumentation becomes particularly evident if we consider the relationship between Muslim practices, such as veiling, and the unequal and frequently hostile context in which they are enacted. Especially for British Muslim youth, such practices can work as a form of agential self-empowerment within a predominantly secular liberal public sphere, as well as against the authority of their parents.[44]

Indeed, Manzoor does show an awareness of the possibility of a more critical Islam which does not prescribe obedience and the surrender of doubt, drawing a distinction between religion and the 'cultural values' of his parents' generation.[45] And yet his stated awareness remains truncated, failing to develop into a consideration of the forms this version of Islam might take. In a revealingly elliptical passage where he contemplates his religion of heritage, Manzoor asserts:

> The biggest lie that I was told when I was growing up was that there was only one way to be a Muslim. That way was to be obedient, deferential

and unquestioning; it was to reject pleasure and embrace duty, to renounce sensuality and to never ever ask why … I kept believing in an Islam which was more tolerant, which did not take itself so seriously that it burnt the books of those it did not approve of. I wanted to be a Muslim like Philip Roth was a Jew or Bruce Springsteen was Catholic. When I was young, that did not seem possible, and so I ran away from my religion. But, eventually, it caught up with me. I still hope to find my reason to believe. (238–9)

The certainty of the word 'lie' is not contrasted with any correction or enlightenment; on the contrary, as the narrative past cedes to the narrative present, where one might expect some illumination of the discovered 'truth', we learn that Manzoor has still not found an alternative mode of being Muslim. Indeed, the assertion that his religion has now 'caught up with' him repeats a claim just a few pages earlier that 'on 9/11 my religion caught up with me', thereby substituting the bafflement that dominates his response to the attacks of 9/11 for the greater understanding of Islam that the reader is set up to expect (235). Manzoor's reaction to 9/11, 7/7 and the much earlier protests against *The Satanic Verses* is characterised by 'alienation', 'confusion' and fear (228, 264); he cannot understand Rushdie's dissenters' anger or, in the case of the 7/7 bombers, 'why … they hate[d] this country so much' (264). Echoing the limits of understanding articulated in the responses of a range of liberal Anglo-American writers and commentators to the attacks on the Twin Towers, his bafflement forecloses explanation and engagement, severing these events from history, economics and politics.[46]

Revealingly, a more tolerant, open and enabling version of Islam emerges in the narrative only where it remains firmly in the private sphere and associated with an older generation. It is as a consequence of renewed interest in his faith, evidenced by frequent visits to the local mosque and plans to visit Mecca, that Manzoor's father takes his younger, fashion-crazy sister Uzma to purchase a pair of knee-high boots (43). Normatively counterposed, religiosity and an overtly sexy fashion item associated with secular permissiveness are brought together. In another incident, Manzoor's mother's religious blessing before a job interview that will give him independence from his family and cultural expectations is portrayed, in emotive terms, as profoundly enabling (174–5). It is in this individual, private and purely spiritual relationship with religious faith that the dichotomy between religious strictures and western freedoms breaks down. When religion is private, it is potentially enabling and breeds tolerance; conversely, when it asserts itself in the public domain, it is at best

humourless and at worst murderous. That the hijab remains virtual in
Manzoor's narrative, its wearer just a voice on the end of the telephone,
is suggestive of a general invisibility or absence of an assertive political
Muslim identity that is not extremist or violent, as in Husain's memoir.[47]
The other mention of the hijab in Manzoor's memoir occurs in passing
in a discussion of the 7/7 bombings. Here, Manzoor contrasts the legal
right to wear the hijab enjoyed by a younger generation of British Muslim
students with his elder sister Navela's pioneering battle to wear trousers
instead of the stipulated skirt to her local Luton school. This contrast
immediately follows one between the 'extremism' of the bombers, which
is construed as a form of ungrateful rejection of the secure Britishness
that they enjoyed, and Manzoor's own earlier struggle for acceptance as
British (267). Through this juxtaposition, the contemporary integration
of Muslim practices into Britishness, exemplified by the hijab, is implicitly aligned with a rejection of Britishness, or with separatism. There is an
uncomfortable hint in this somewhat disjointed passage of a continuum
from assertive Muslimness to separatism to extremism. This echoes the
implicit linking of the working-class men who protested against Rushdie's novel in the context of decades of social deprivation and hostility
towards local Pakistani communities with the perpetrators of violent
attacks such as those of 9/11 and 7/7: 'If they were prepared to get this
upset about a book', Manzoor asks of Rushdie's dissenters, 'what else
might they get angry about? What else might they be prepared to do?'
(228). In stark contrast to the uneasy presence of the hijab in Manzoor's
narrative, other forms of clothing (whether Uzma's boots, his brother
Sohail's stonewashed jacket and jeans, or the shalwar kameez his mother
and sisters design when they are not making dresses for British Home
Stores) are constructed as a means of asserting an individual identity
against the constraints of cultural conformity and poverty – the latter
signified by the family's women's exploited labour sewing clothes (174–5,
62, 66–7). The hijab is, then, an uncomfortable fit in the individualist
'triumph-against-adversity' narrative that dominates Manzoor's memoir.

Manzoor's reversion to his own and his sister's youth when considering twenty-first-century 'Islamic' extremism can also be seen as a sort
of narrative evasion or ellipsis. A more pronounced immersion in the
past dominates the final pages of the memoir. Curiously, in place of any
considered engagement with the London Transport bombings on the part
of the narrating autobiographical subject, we are offered the responses of
each of his parents – imagined, in the case of his deceased father:

'And if we had known that they would spit in the face of our labour and
our dreams, bring shame to the community, blacken the name of Pakistan
... and all for what? And they say they're Muslims, and they say it's about
politics.' ... 'Politics is what you talk about before you have families, isn't
that right Manzoor sahib' one of the others might say. (268)

Manzoor's father's imagined reaction is to perceive the bombers as
ungrateful for a previous generation's labour – a reaction associated with
the first generation of immigrants, grateful for a livelihood and lacking
the confidence to assert their religious culture or identity in the public
sphere. His father's friends abjure the political for the personal and prag-
matic, while Manzoor's mother sees 'the human tragedy rather than the
political context' of the bombings, contemplating the emotional fallout
for the families of the perpetrators (267). In her response, too – and
so, effectively, in Manzoor's – the personal obscures or privatises the
political. As in Hanif Kureishi's My Ear at his Heart, it is as if the autobiographical subject is taking refuge in an earlier generational perspective to compensate for his own lack of answers – for the breakdown of
his narration of the place of Islam in his own life and in contemporary
multicultural Britain. The split time-frame of the autobiographical form
enables a further degree of ellipsis: while we are told what the narrated
subject thinks and feels at various points in his life, the narrating subject
frequently remains silent. Greetings, then, through its expression of
bafflement and its strategies of evasion, could be said to 'perform [its]
own failure and collapse of voice' in the face of these events with British
Muslims at their centre.[48]

Yasmin Hai's The Making of Mr Hai's Daughter, is, like Greetings, a
coming-of-age memoir structured around a process of self-formation
and, to an extent, class mobility. Whereas Hai is from a more privileged
background than Manzoor, she too 'progresses', from the lower-middle-
class milieu of her north London suburb through Camden School for
Girls and Manchester University to the left-liberal, high-flying and
predominantly secular world of television journalism. For Hai, however,
the trajectory of 'progression' is complex and contradictory: her movement away from mahalla to 'mainstream' Britain is one that is facilitated
rather than impeded by her father, as is suggested by the memoir's title;
and yet it takes her beyond her father's broadly assimilationist attitude
to Britishness towards a more nuanced and critical engagement with her
culture and religion of heritage. If Manzoor's Greetings is characterised
by narrative occlusions and evasions, Hai's self-consciously addresses the

tensions and contradictions between her father's quest for 'Britishness', the collectivism and communitarianism of the *mahalla*, and the individual freedoms offered by liberal secular middle-class Britain. Indeed, in conjunction with its autobiographical focus on private lives, it engages explicitly with being Muslim in Britain, a focus triggered in part by Hai's experience as a journalist of Muslim heritage in the context of 9/11, 7/7 and their aftermaths.

In Hai's narrative, in contrast to Manzoor's, the hijab, and its fuller, more pious (or more militant) versions, is an explicit focal point for exploring the tensions between secularism and faith, individual and community. After describing the bafflement of her colleagues on the BBC programme *Newsnight* at Muslim women's turn to religion, Hai ventures her own opinion on the subject:

> And I must admit that I found it baffling, too. Who were these women who considered themselves secondary to men, shrouded themselves in black cloth to hide their female shame, allowed their husbands to have other wives, walked several steps behind them and happily gave up their careers to be the primary carer at home? Truly baffling – until I remembered that my colleagues were talking about the kind of women I had grown up with. And I didn't know one who usefully fitted their description. (244)

Hai's repetition of the word 'baffling' is redolent of Manzoor's response to Muslim extremism. Yet, here, bafflement yields to a qualification and illuminating contradiction. In a characteristic narrative move, Hai builds a stereotype, vocalising – almost ventriloquising – normative readings of veiled Muslim women, only to dislodge the stereotype, swiftly moving from a homogenising position to a deconstructive one. A similar move can be seen in her negotiation of the two social spheres of her teenage years, the 'Bhajis' (her British Pakistani friends from suburban Wembley) and the white, middle-class Camden girls. When her stories of the liberal and privileged lifestyle of her Camden friends are not met with admiration and envy by the Bhajis, she remarks: 'The Bhajis equated these Camden freedoms with burdens. I tried to tell them that this wasn't the case, but they never seemed convinced – though frankly, neither was I' (166). Hai occupies a borderline position; not only does she straddle cultural boundaries but she is apparently able to bridge the dividing line between a secular individualism and a religious communalism, between reason and belief, recognising that the concept of freedom does not have universal application. Similarly, while Hai, like Manzoor, is clearly troubled by the entry of religion into the public or political sphere – something that her father was passionately opposed to – her rejection of this combination paradoxically includes a tentative admission of its importance:

> Of course, I agree with my father. Religion doesn't have a role to play in politics or in our public lives. And yet ... my father's disapproval of religion extended to a disapproval of our old culture and ethnic loyalties. He couldn't accept such ideas having any bearing on our modern British selves. And yet, that was what provided me with an invaluable sense of who I was in later life. (332)

Here, as when she experiences the importance of an Islamic cultural identity to her sense of self in the wake of her father's death, religion can, arguably, remain in the private domain; her grief for her father, certainly, is private and enacted within the home or *mahalla*. Nevertheless, the potential for an overlapping between religion as private and religion as political emerges here in this characteristic self-contradictory moment in the text, marked by the repeated 'And yet ...'.

Hai is explicit in her aim to debunk Muslim stereotypes, describing, for example, her anger at 'hearing another politician bang on about Muslim segregation and Islamic head-dress' in the wake of 9/11 (317). But this anger, and her subtle disturbance of normative discourses surrounding Muslims, is at odds with her own discomfort at her childhood friends' increasing leanings towards religiosity, particularly the decision some of them, including her closest friend Afshan, take to wear the hijab. Despite her apparent understanding of this gesture as individual choice, for Hai her *mahalla* friends have nevertheless 'compromised their individuality': they 'are ready to go along with every diktat or folly of tribal politics in their desperate need to belong' (333). Echoing her father's burning of her mother's headscarves on her arrival in England from Pakistan decades earlier (25), Hai, with her use of the word 'tribal', implicitly aligns the hijab with the premodern, evoking Orientalist conceptions of Islam as incompatible with modernity;[49] and elsewhere, she articulates her difficulty in accepting Afshan's reinterpretation of Islam as feminist, egalitarian and just, as a means of integrating faith and belonging within modernity (230–9). For her, Afshan's self-identification as a 'proper Muslim' smacks of the moral absolutism that is opposed to modernity (236). Further, the belonging that the *mahalla* girls seek, while explicitly rooted in their outsider status, is aligned with the certainties of assimilation that Hai's father sought and ultimately contrasted with her own

ability 'to resist the easy answers', to doubt, to question and to criticise
(333). In fact, just as Hai's 'associational' identity as Muslim,[50] her borderline position, entails instability and doubt, so too the choice to embrace
and combine the ostensibly conflicting ideologies of religious faith and
an individuated post-Enlightenment sense of self arguably carries with it
contradiction and conflict that precisely 'resist the easy answers', as well as
a considerable degree of agency necessary for the visible adoption of faith
in a predominantly secular public sphere. Despite Hai's clear affection for
her childhood friends, a sense of complexity is lacking in her sketches
of Afshan and the other Bhajis. The choice to assume an overtly Islamic
identity is framed in Hai's narrative primarily in terms of conformity,
immersion and even submission rather than as an assertion of difference,
a form of resistance and a potential means to self-empowerment. The
headscarved woman is visibilised or made flesh – in contrast to in *Greetings* – but her voice remains peripheral, leaving the reader wondering:
'How would the Bhajis tell their story?'

The moments of contradiction in Hai's narrative can be traced in
part to the structural limitations of the individuating, humanistic autobiographical form for accommodating a communitarian cultural identity. But, unlike in Manzoor's memoir, in Hai's the narrator's trajectory
towards the formation of an individual subjectivity is complicated by
a partial, attenuated gesture towards a Muslim collectivity near the
end. Whereas Manzoor asserts a patriotic Britishness at the close of
his memoir, one that silences or occludes the religious culture of his
heritage, Hai positions herself as a *British Muslim* in the final sentences
of hers, asking: 'if I don't write and others don't either, how will we
Asian Muslims ever contribute to the debate – mostly being conducted
by others – about our Britishness? After all, this is our country too'
(334).[51] Hai's final self-identification as Muslim is an important gesture
of claiming a voice for British Muslims, which expresses solidarity and
opens out the category of 'Muslim' beyond stereotype, reversing the
conventional misery-memoir trajectory that sees the protagonist finally
reject Islam in favour of western freedoms. However, it could also feed
into the 'good Muslim'/'bad Muslim' dichotomy that structures western
understanding of this minority British group. Interestingly, it is a review
quote by Muslim journalist Yasmin Alibhai-Brown, reproduced on the
paperback edition of the book, that exposes how Hai's memoir could
be read along these lines: 'At long last we have a young British Muslim
woman writing about her life ... This book is a gem, from a Briton who

needs no lessons on Britishness.' The description is revealingly para-doxical. It endows Hai with a representative status (a status which she clearly does not have but which it is hard not to burden her with); and, with its allusion to 'lessons on Britishness' evoking discourses that have positioned assertive Muslims outside this spurious identity category,[52] it simultaneously suggests another, less savoury 'type' of Muslim that contrasts with the autobiographical subject. In similar vein, a quote from a reviewer for the British Asian magazine *Eastern Eye*, also on the cover of the paperback edition, states that Hai's portrait 'convinces me that it is entirely possible to be Muslim and British'.[53] However, the compatibility of the autobiographical subject's mode of being Muslim with 'Britishness' conceals the many other British Muslim subjectivities that are sketched in her memoir and are not so consistent with a normative conception of a 'British' identity. Whitlock asks: 'which bodies are breathed into life ... by autobiography?' and 'What does this product do to the community of origin?'[54] These questions highlight the ways in which memoirs that give voice to British Muslim subjects could nevertheless be co-opted into an exclusionary narrative that peripheralises or even stigmatises alterna-tive modes of being Muslim. Articulated from the powerful position of 'native informant', Hai's bafflement at her friends' decision to don the hijab, and Manzoor's denunciation of the 7/7 bombers' anger and hatred as simply unintelligible, are all the more compelling, combining with the universalist and emotive address of their autobiographies to potent effect.

In Zaiba Malik's *We are a Muslim, Please*, situated in Bradford, the Islamic section of a cemetery lovingly tended by a white Bradfordian serves as a disruptive presence both in associations of this town with racial antagonism and self-segregation and, more significantly, in post-9/11 critical appraisals of multiculturalism. Gravedigger Graham Swain has learnt Urdu and studied 'the Islamic way', his sentences are 'peppered with Urdu words' as he explains the minutiae of Muslim burial conven-tions to his British Pakistani interlocutor, and he considers it his zakat (charitable obligation) to be available during the night to accommodate the practice of burying as soon after death as possible (240–1). Brad-ford's first Muslim interment, of a Somalian woman, dates back to 1904, while the most recent was of a young man named Qasim whose funeral attracted some five thousand mourners (242–3). Online tributes to him are written 'in a language that was part religion, part street': 'studio on a Friday/Saturday isn't d same u used to get sum sik haircuts rip cant get over it we will meet again jannat inshallah' (244). These examples

– the gravedigger's attachment to the community he serves and immersion in their culture, the material presence of a Muslim burial ground, a
youth culture that incorporates faith – defy notions of integration that
consign Islam to the private sphere. Instead, the receptivity of majority
to minority and the peaceful imprint of a minority religion on British
soil and language offer a glimpse of a hybridisation of culture that has the
potential to unsettle the exclusivity of secularism but cannot readily be
recuperated into stereotypes of separatism and fundamentalism. Unlike
in *The Islamist*, where the potentially disruptive presence of undertaker
Taslim Ali is swiftly removed, here there is a productive complication
of hegemonic discourses surrounding working-class British Muslim
cultures and communities.

Qasim serves as a counterpoint to 7/7 bomber Shehzad Tanweer,
another Bradford Muslim, whose crime frames Malik's narrative (244).
We are a Muslim, Please is structured around the narrator's identification
and disidentification with Tanweer who was born in the hospital just
behind the house she grew up in and, she discovers, prepared the explo-
sives for the terror attacks in the house in Leeds where she was born
(122, 275). Most chapters close with the narrator directly addressing
Tanweer, while the book itself ends with a long letter from Malik to
him. His presence in the narrative functions as a means of disarticu-
lating British Muslim culture and scriptural Islam from acts of terror: by
juxtaposing her own and her family's understanding of Islam and being
Muslim as well as quotations from Quranic surahs with Tanweer's act of
terror (66, 260–4), Malik powerfully debunks this association, which has
littered public pronouncements on Islam since 9/11, and asserts a legitimate British Muslim subjecthood from within a town that has become
almost synonymous with Muslim segregation and rioting. Thus, while
Malik's memoir is shaped by a somewhat stereotypical clash-of-cultures
narrative, signposted by the hackneyed strap-line on the front cover –
'One girl, two lives'[55] – and captured in a range of metaphors (32, 100,
123–5), the duality that emerges does not finally congeal into one of
reason versus belief, or freedom versus constraint. Further, the boundary
between the narrated self of the past and the narrating self of the present
is, at times, blurred, undermining a comforting reading of the narrative
as one of progress, from blind faith to lucid rationality. The significance
of Quranic stories to the narrator in her early life, for example, is not
discredited or contrasted to an enlightened present (53). Similarly, Malik's
negative representation of her experience of a local Bradford nightclub

and Manchester's famed Hacienda eschews the conventional gendered trajectory of cultural constraint to emancipation (182–94). Echoing the contradiction and ambivalence of Hai's narrative, Malik writes of her nightclubbing peers: 'I couldn't tell the girls that my life was so different to theirs. I couldn't tell them that I wanted to be nothing like them. I couldn't tell them that actually I wanted to be just like them' (188).

Like Manzoor and Hai, Malik exists on the periphery of the northern Muslim community that she depicts. Her education in an almost uniquely white grammar school, and the university education and journalist career that this led to, position her on the boundary line that separates the working-class Pakistani 'community' in which she grew up, 'with its overcrowded grey terraced houses, the fused smell of frying onions, chilli, and garlic and ginger, the Nissans double-parked on the streets', from affluent 'White Bradford' and professional Britain beyond (175–6). Indeed, while the portrayal of her community is at times profoundly empathic, the narrative is shaped by a clear disjunction between the individual autobiographical subject and the developing Muslim collectivism around her. In the mid-1980s, as 'the right to be different' and 'for communities to have their own identity and values' became validated by race relations policies (145), and an inclusive 'black' identity began to give way to more culturally specific identities, the community finds its voice and Malik loses hers: 'I retreated into myself and it marched forward, demanding to be recognised' (148). The growth of a multiculturalism that recognises and seeks to enable cultural and religious groups signals Malik's retreat from the community and, for a long period, her faith (146). The newfound pride and confidence of the Pakistani protesters against Ray Honeyford contrasts starkly with her own confusion and ambivalence (151), and a few years later, when the community 'state[s] its identity' in the form of protests against Rushdie's novel, Malik leaves home to find hers (205). Thus, as in the memoirs of Hai and Manzoor, as well as Husain, a discomfort with public – and so political – Muslim identities is evident, as is a nostalgia for the acquiescence of the first generation of immigrants (224). Malik withdraws from overt criticism of politicised Muslim identities, expressing an understanding of their provenance in British foreign policy as well as poverty, racism and cultural displacement, and makes clear the relationship between her class position and her distance from such identities. Nevertheless, her distance potentially others such identities for the reader (144–52, 204–5). Her depiction of Bradford as a shadowy place, harbouring secrets relating to drug

smuggling, money laundering or terror 'behind closed doors', potentially
feeds normative discourses surrounding Muslim 'ghettoes' (216, 222, 269),
while her final comparison of the contemporary moment, marked by
'suicide bombers', 'inflammatory clerics', 'war on terror', 'Islamism' and
'Islamophobia', to her childhood, when 'there was just my father and his
four children sat at the kitchen table quietly reading the Koran', serves
to entrench the public/private division that is traceable throughout the
narrative (277).

Malik's loss of voice in the face of her community's development of
an assertive Muslim public voice is a literal one. The observational, non-
participatory role that she assumes both at school and at home takes an
extreme form as, unable to reconcile her 'two lives', she retreats into a
private mental space and becomes silent for a year of her adolescence
(123–53). Malik cannot speak because she falls between legitimate subjectivities; her identity is literally unspeakable. Indeed, the adolescent
Malik's literal silence could be read as signifying an autobiographical
subjectivity that is resistant to categories. Ill at ease with both an assertive, communitarian Muslim identity and a liberal secular identity, the
autobiographical 'I' cannot readily be recuperated into conventional
discourses surrounding British Muslims. While the narrating subject
appeals frequently to the reader's ability to identify across cultures – for
example, by a direct, second-person address, or more explicitly still with
the phrase 'If you're like me' (35, 111, 116, 126) – a 'comforting narcissistic
recognition' on the part of the reader, one that 'denies difference across
cultures', is, at times, productively disabled.[56] Malik's borderline identity,
then, does not congeal into the self-assured in-betweenness or hybridity
of many of Hanif Kureishi's protagonists, but remains disjunctive with a
secular liberalism and not quite consumable. And yet, at the same time,
it is, arguably, more palatable to the 'market reader' than a more assertive Muslim identity from within the community.[57] While Qasim and
the Muslim youth who mourn for him might offer a glimpse of such an
identity, not unlike the Bhajis in *The Making of Mr Hai's Daughter* they
remain absent or shadowy figures. Qasim's death or absence, then, can be
read also as an ideological silence marking the limits of the writeable: if
Shezhad Tanweer's crime defies the narrator's comprehension, his counterpoint Qasim's very subjectivity arguably strains at the representational
possibilities of the memoir form.

SHELINA ZAHRA JANMOHAMED'S *LOVE IN A HEADSCARF:*
MUSLIM WOMAN SEEKS THE ONE

In contrast to the covers of the three memoirs authored by journalists, that of Shelina Zahra Janmohamed's *Love in a Headscarf* eschews the
nostalgic focus on the past implied by childhood photographs. Instead,
there is a sense of the present and a hint of the future, with the young,
glamorous hijab-clad woman shown driving a convertible through the
capital denoted by a skyline featuring Regent's Park Mosque alongside
the 'Gherkin', the Millennium Wheel and St Paul's Cathedral. The title
deconstructs the opposition between individual desire and religion that
so often configures the Muslim woman as hapless victim of an arranged
marriage, while the subtitle endows the female subject with agency and
choice, further countering such stereotyping. The front-cover image of
a glamorous, independent woman, combined with its purple and pink
colour scheme and the heart-shaped 'v' of the word 'Love', and the
subtitle's resonance with the title of a women's lifestyle magazine article
connote a post-feminist 'chick-lit' narrative that jars provocatively with
the primary focus on a Muslim woman.[58] Thus, the paratext suggests a
desire to appeal to a majoritarian female reader without relinquishing or
compromising the cultural specificity that is signified so starkly by the
headscarf.[59]

Janmohamed clearly signals her desire to challenge preconceptions
about female British Muslim subjecthood in both her introduction and
her prologue. 'Stories like mine have remained unheard, as they do not
fit neatly with prevailing stereotypes which tell tales of Islam's oppression', she writes, and, addressing the reader directly, asks: 'Do you ever
wonder what really goes on in the life of the Muslim women who
you walk past in the street?' (xiii, 1).[60] The memoir was published just
a few years after a range of significant veiling controversies in Britain,
including Luton schoolgirl Shabina Begum's protracted (and ultimately
unsuccessful) court battle for the right to wear the head-to-toe jilbab to
her school (2002–5), former Labour Member of Parliament Jack Straw's
expression of discomfort with the face-veiling practised by some of his
Blackburn constituents (2006) and Aisha Azmi's dismissal from her position as a classroom assistant at a west Yorkshire school for insisting on
wearing a niqab (2006).[61] Thus, it emerged into a context characterised by
images of veiled Muslim women perceived as 'submissive or dangerous,
deluded or transgressive, oppressed or threatening depending on whether

their covering is thought to have been forced or chosen', and unveiled women 'uncritically assumed to be progressive, liberated, secular and integrated into modern British or European society'.[62] *Love in a Headscarf* subverts these stereotypes by articulating an agential and assertive, yet non-threatening, veiled subjectivity and representing the practice of veiling as consistent with (rather than antithetical to) western feminist discourses (170). Indeed, throughout, the narrative overturns assumptions about Muslim culture and self-consciously undoes the opposition between western liberalism and Islam: the 'weight of tradition ... rested ... pleasantly' on Janmahomed's shoulders; matchmakers and communal advice are configured as important and enabling, and community leaders portrayed in a positive light; romantic love and poetry are located within the Quran; the practising Muslim is represented as inquisitive rather than as blindly accepting; and Muslim women are shown to be proactive in seeking relationships in contrast to the female passivity which often characterises traditional western notions of romantic love (5, 23, 30, 106, 223–4, 75, 29, 67, 60–1).

By recounting her own rejection by a potential suitor because she wears a headscarf, Janmahomed gives voice to the cipher-like *hijabi* rejected by *Greetings'* narrator-subject (164). The veiled woman is no longer 'spoken for', a mysterious essence awaiting explication.[63] Similarly, this memoir offers an assertive riposte to Hai's mystification at the voiceless Bhajis' decision to veil. In contrast to the tribalism and need for belonging that Hai attributes to her Wembley friends, Janmahomed's individuality is underscored by the very form of the autobiographical memoir. Yet, unlike Hai's Bhajis, Janmahomed, educated at a fee-paying school and Oxford University, is from a privileged social background (35, 17). This unsettles some of the assumptions about veiling traceable in Hai's narrative in particular, and prevalent in normative British culture – namely, the association of the practice with either a working-class cultural traditionalism or a subaltern resistance cum radicalism born of class- as well as race-marginalisation and disaffection. Indeed, Janmahomed explicitly eschews an oppositional political reading of her hijab: 'For me, wearing a headscarf was not a political decision, nor a form of public statement, it was just one part of my everyday clothing' (155). Despite her important recognition of the illogicality of confining faith to the private sphere (to leave her headscarf at home would be to leave her 'social values in the private sphere', and 'what was the point of a social value if it wasn't practised out in society?' (161)), she mainly retreats from an assertive political Muslim identity. This, combined with her comfortable middle-class background, and the memoir's preoccupation with romantic love and finding Mr Right, positions the autobiographical subject within a normative post-feminist narrative, arguably facilitating a mainstream identification with her.[64] Blind dates, women's magazine advice, 'girly' chats and cyber-dating all feature in this Muslim woman's search for 'the One' (225, 120–8, 228). Further, while the narrator frequently asserts the presence of independent, pioneering women both in the Quran (the Prophet Mohammed's first wife Khadijah, in particular) and in contemporary Islamic debate, she also appreciates 'the value that [Islam] placed on "womanly" things' (131–3, 122, 171). Her association of conventionally gendered notions of femininity and beauty with the Islamic faith further normativises the latter, while her use of the veil as a fashion accessory, as well as a means of signifying and practising her faith, links Islam with modernity and consumption, refuting Orientalist constructions of this religion as resistant to the modern (129–31).[65]

The insertion of a veiled Islamic subjectivity into a post-feminist, chick-lit femininity is an important political gesture, notwithstanding the concomitant dilution of an oppositional gender – and also class – politics. The narrative facilitates identification with the cultural Other while preventing the absorption of the (veiled) Other into the Self by making visible the former's significant difference. Arguably, then, *Love in a Headscarf* attains the asymmetrical identification that Whitlock describes.[66] In this sense, given its potential to unsettle rather than corroborate established frameworks for understanding British Muslims, it is perhaps unsurprising that this memoir, unlike the 'veiled best-sellers' that it can be seen to be challenging, was published by a small outfit, Aurum Press, and lacks the endorsements by broadsheet reviewers garnered by Husain's *The Islamist* and, to a lesser extent, Manzoor's and Hai's memoirs. Yet, the dominance of a self-consciously explanatory mode in Janmahomed's narrative, redolent of documentary journalism, at times works against the emotional appeal that characterises those of Manzoor, Hai and Malik in particular, undercutting its rhetorical power. For it is the personal appeal of these autobiographical narratives, the individualism of their form, which endows them with the potential to communicate across cultural barriers but also delimits that communication in ways. All five memoirs manifest a much more straightforward claim to authenticity than much postcolonial autobiography (for example, Hanif Kureishi's *My Ear at his Heart*), eschewing a concern with undoing the notion of autobiographical truth in order to prioritise the writing of their 'Muslim' selves squarely into contemporary British subjecthood. And yet, shaped by the limitations of the autobiographical form, as well as by the class position of the autobiographical subjects and the expectations of a mainstream readership eager to 'know' the Muslim Other, each memoir, to greater or lesser extent, pushes certain British Muslim subjectivities to the margins of the sphere of legitimacy that they carve out. Despite this, however, Hai's, Malik's and Janmahomed's perspectives in particular suggest a will to translate across cultures, to articulate a universalism that encompasses plurality,[67] and to negotiate between and complicate individualism and communitarianism, reason and belief.

NOTES

1 Gillian Whitlock, *Soft Weapons: Autobiography in Transit* (Chicago: University of Chicago Press, 2007), pp. 1–2.

2 Judith Butler, *Precarious Life: The Powers of Mourning and Violence* (London: Verso, 2006 [2004]), p. xviii.

3 Azar Nafisi, *Reading Lolita in Tehran: A Memoir in Books* (New York: Random House, 2003); Anne Garrels, *Naked in Baghdad* (New York: Farrar, Straus & Giroux, 2003); Norma Khouri, *Honor Lost: Love and Death in Modern-Day Jordan* (New York: Atria Books, 2003). For a critical discussion of these texts, their marketing and reception, and of the North American context, see Whitlock, *Soft Weapons*.

4 Ayaan Hirsi Ali, *Infidel: My Life* (London: Free Press, 2007).

5 Ed Husain, *The Islamist* (London: Penguin, 2007); Sarfraz Manzoor, *Greetings from Bury Park: Race, Religion and Rock 'n' Roll* (London: Bloomsbury, 2007); Yasmin Hai, *The Making of Mr Hai's Daughter: Becoming British: A Memoir* (London: Virago, 2008); Zaiba Malik, *We are a Muslim, Please* (London: Windmill, 2010); Shelina Zahra Janmahomed, *Love in a Headscarf: Muslim Woman Seeks the One* (London: Aurum, 2009). All subsequent citations are given within the body of the chapter and are to these editions of the texts.

6 Bart Moore-Gilbert, *Postcolonial Life-Writing: Culture, Politics and Self-Representation* (London and New York: Routledge, 2009), p. 112. Another example of an autobiographical account by a British Muslim is Moazzam Begg's *Enemy Combatant: A British Muslim's Journey to Guantánamo and Back* (with Victoria Brittain; London: Free Press, 2006).

7 Kobena Mercer, 'Black art and the burden of representation', *Third Text*, 10 (Spring 1994), 61–78, 62. Elizabeth Poole and John E. Richardson demonstrate the dominance of negative stories of Muslims in the British media and describe the climate in the last few years as one of 'threat, fear and misunderstanding' (Poole and Richardson (eds), *Muslims and the News Media* (London:

I. B. Tauris, 2010), p. 1).

8   Whitlock, *Soft Weapons*, p. 22.

9   *Ibid.*, p. 12.

10 Susheila Nasta, 'Writing a life: Hanif Kureishi and Blake Morrison in conversation', *Wasafiri*, 21:2 (2006), 19–26, 26.

11 Whitlock, *Soft Weapons*, p. 3.

12 *Ibid.*, pp. 17–18, ch. 2.

13 Jasvinder Sanghera, *Shame, Daughters of Shame* and *Shame Travels: A Family Lost, A Family Found* (London: Hodder, 2006, 2009, 2012); Saira Ahmed, *Disgraced* (London: Headline Review, 2009). Similar titles include Ferzanna Riley's *Unbroken Spirit* (London: Hodder, 2008) and Sameem Ali's *Belonging* (London: John Murray, 2008).

14 These comments appear on the book covers, with the exception of 'richly humane', which is from Danny Kelly, 'There's just one boss in this family', *Observer* (27 May 2007), www.guardian.co.uk/books/2007/may/27/biography. features (last accessed 6 November 2014).

15 Mary Louise Pratt, *Imperial Eyes: Travel Writing and Transculturation* (London and New York: Routledge, 1996), p. 7.

16 Charles Taylor, 'Why we need a radical redefinition of secularism', in Judith Butler, Jürgen Habermas, Charles Taylor and Cornel West, *The Power of Religion in the Public Sphere*, ed. Eduardo Mendieta and Jonathan Vanantwerpen (New York: Columbia University Press, 2011), pp. 34–59, p. 51.

17 *Ibid.*; Talal Asad, 'Free speech, blasphemy and secular criticism', in Talal Asad, Wendy Brown, Judith Butler and Saba Mahmood, *Is Critique Secular? Blasphemy, Injury, and Free Speech* (Berkeley: Townsend Center for the Humanities, 2009), pp. 20–63.

18 A glossy lifestyle magazine launched in 2003, *emel* has been part of an attempt to counter negative images of Muslims in the post-9/11 period (see www.emel.com).

19 Whitlock, *Soft Weapons*, p. 132.

20 *Ibid.*

21 Kay Schaffer and Sidonie Smith, *Human Rights and Narrated Lives: The Ethics of Recognition* (Basingstoke: Palgrave Macmillan, 2004), pp. 4–5, p. 12.

22 See Mahmood Mamdani, *Good Muslim, Bad Muslim: America, the Cold War, and the Roots of Terror* (New York: Three Leaves/Doubleday, 2005 [2004]).

23 Graham Huggan, *The Postcolonial Exotic: Marketing the Margins* (London: Routledge, 2001), pp. 155–76, especially p. 163. Huggan's focus here is on Aboriginal autobiography.

24 I recognise that this 'type' of reader is a construct and that readers do not form a singular homogeneous group. Readers, however, operate within certain 'regimes of value' formed by specific social relations. See Graham Huggan's discussion, via John Frow, of the readers of postcolonial writing, in *Postcolonial Exotic*, pp. 30–1.

25 Gerard Genette, *Paratexts: Thresholds of Interpretation* (Cambridge: Cambridge University Press, 1997).

26 Trevor Phillips, 'Let's show the world its future', *Observer* (10 July 2005), www.theguardian.com/uk/2005/jul/10/olympics2012.olympicgames   (last accessed 6 November 2014). See Introduction, pp. 2–3.

27 On the universal exception, see Slavoj Žižek's *The Universal Exception: Selected Writings*, vol. 2 (London and New York: Continuum, 2006), especially chs 9 and 10.

28 As Madeleine Bunting notes, its attraction lay in its implicit promise to answer two pressing questions, especially in the wake of Britain's longest-running terror trial, the Crevice trial: 'what is the appeal of violent jihadi Islam, and how can it be defeated?' ('We were the brothers', *Guardian* (12 May 2007), www.guardian.co.uk/books/2007/may/12/religion.news (last accessed 6 November 2014)). On the memoir's popularity and influence, see Anshuman A. Mondal, 'Bad faith: the construction of Muslim extremism in Ed Husain's *The Islamist*', in Rehana Ahmed, Peter Morey and Amina Yaqin (eds), *Culture, Diaspora, and Modernity in Muslim Writing* (Abingdon and New York: Routledge, 2012), pp. 37–51, p. 37.

29 Salman Sayyid, 'Contemporary politics of secularism', in Geoffrey Brahm Levey and Tariq Modood (eds), *Secularism, Religion and Multicultural Citizenship* (Cambridge: Cambridge University Press, 2009), pp. 186–99, p. 199.

30 Henri Lefebvre, *The Production of Space*, trans. Donald Nicholson-Smith (Oxford: Blackwell, 1991), p. 27.

31 Husain's description of the 'total Islamization of the public space' of Tower Hamlets College recalls alarmist responses to the plans to expand Abbey Mills Mosque in Stratford, east London. See the Introduction to this book, as well as Jamie Doward, 'Battle to block massive mosque', *Observer* (24 September 2006), www.guardian.co.uk/society/2006/sep/24/communities. religion (last accessed 6 November 2014).

32 Mondal, 'Bad faith', pp. 40–1. Mondal offers a highly perceptive reading of the narrative's antipathy towards any sort of Muslim organisation and failure to distinguish between moderate and extremist Muslim organisations.

33 *Ibid.*, p. 40.

34 Tariq Modood, *Multiculturalism: A Civic Idea* (Cambridge: Polity, 2007), p. 135.

35 See Kenan Malik, *From Fatwa to Jihad: The Rushdie Affair and its Legacy* (London: Atlantic Books, 2009), ch. 2. See also Bunting, 'We were the brothers', where Husain claims that government policies of multiculturalism 'encouraged separate communities' and that 'multiculturalism was the perfect cover … for his Hizb ut-Tahrir activities'.

36 See Chapters 1 and 2.

37 See Caroline Adams (ed.), *Across Seven Seas and Thirteen Rivers: Life Stories of Pioneer Settlers in Britain* (London: Eastside Books, 2nd edn, 1994 [1987]), pp. 53, 160–1.

38 See Mondal, 'Bad faith', p. 41, for further examples of a Muslim politics that is not reducible to extremism.

39 Examples include Edward W. Said's autobiography, *Out of Place* (London: Granta, 1999; see also Tobias Döring's reading of it, 'Edward Said and the fiction of autobiography', *Wasafiri*, 21:2 (July 2006), 71–8); Hanif Kureishi's *My Ear at his Heart: Reading my Father* (London: Faber, 2004); Assia Djebar's *Fantasia: An Algerian Cavalcade*, trans. Dorothy S. Blair (Portsmouth, NH: Heinemann, 1985).

40 On the postcolonial writer's embrace of autonomy for these two different reasons, see Moore-Gilbert, *Postcolonial Life-Writing*, p. 33.

41 Huggan, *Postcolonial Exotic*, p. 161.

42 See also Manzoor's autobiographical piece, 'White girls', in the 'Pakistan' edition of *Granta* (112 (2010), 243–54).

43 Reina Lewis, 'Veils and sales: Muslims and the spaces of post-colonial fashion retail', in Richard Phillips (ed.), *Muslim Spaces of Hope: Geographies of Possibility in Britain and the West* (London: Zed Books, 2009), pp. 69–84, p. 70.

44 On the quest for self-empowerment among British Muslims, see Anshuman A. Mondal, *Young British Muslim Voices* (Oxford: Greenwood, 2008), pp. 20–8.

45 *Ibid.*, pp. 25–6.

46 Robert Eaglestone, '"The age of reason is over … an age of fury was dawning": contemporary Anglo-American fiction and terror', *Wasafiri*, 22:2 (2007), 19–22.

47 The implied binary of political Islamism versus private faith also appears in Manzoor's BBC2 film *Luton, Actually*: 'political Islam' is equated with 'a ranting and raving Omar Bakhri' and kept distinct from religion as a 'personal, private faith' (broadcast 5 March 2005).

48 Eaglestone, '"The age of reason"', 20.

49 See Sayyid, 'Contemporary politics of secularism'.

50 Modood, *Multiculturalism*, p. 106.

51 This implicit difference in the final self-identifications of Manzoor and Hai could be traced in part to gender: it is perhaps understandable that Manzoor might feel a particular urgency to distance himself from the hyper-masculinised subjectivities that are so frequently attributed to male Muslim youth, aligning them with criminality and terror.

52 Ziauddin Sardar, 'Spaces of hope: interventions', in Phillips (ed.), *Muslim Spaces of Hope*, pp. 13–36, pp. 20–3; Hai herself criticises 'phoney definitions' of Britishness (329).

53 While these quotations are taken from longer reviews, which may qualify their implications, it is their selection for reproduction on the book itself, and the effect of this, that is of primary interest here.

54 Whitlock, *Soft Weapons*, pp. 9, 15.

55 This echoes the strap-line on the front of the DVD of Kenny Glenaan and Simon Beaufoy's *Yasmin*: 'One woman, two lives' (2004).

56 Whitlock, *Soft Weapons*, p. 15.

57 Wendy Waring, 'Is this your book? Wrapping postcolonial fiction for the global market', *Canadian Review of Comparative Literature*, 22:3/4 (1995), 455–65, 462, cited in Huggan, *Postcolonial Exotic*. p. 165. Useful in relation to degrees of cultural difference is Sara Ahmed's discussion of how the multi-cultural nation '*differentiat[es] between differences*', incorporating 'the other who *appears* as a stranger' and excluding 'the other who *is* a stranger' (*Strange Encounters: Embodied Others in Post-Coloniality* (London: Routledge, 2000), ch. 5, especially pp. 106–7).

58 Laura Barton describes the book as a 'chick-lit memoir' ('Hot dates and headscarves', *Guardian* (18 February 2009), www.theguardian.com/life-andstyle/2009/feb/18/shelina-zahra-janmahomed-arranged-marriage (last accessed 6 November 2014).

59 Claire Chambers, drawing on an interview with Janmahomed, reveals that the cover image was influenced by the author who rejected the austere and pious version proposed by the publisher in favour of a more 'light-hearted' and 'British' image. Further, while Aurum perceived the arranged marriage story as the most important aspect of the narrative, for Janmahomed its universal appeal was more significant ('Countering the "oppressed, kidnapped genre" of Muslim life writing: Yasmin Hai's *The Making of Mr Hai's Daughter* and Shelina Zahra Janmahomed's *Love in a Headscarf*, *Life Writing*, 10:1 (2013), 77–96, 84–6).

60 For Janmahomed's intentions, see also Barton, 'Hot dates'; and Chambers, 'Countering the "oppressed, kidnapped genre"', 84.

61 On the Shabina Begum and Jack Straw controversies, see Emma Tarlo, *Visibly Muslim: Fashion, Politics, Faith* (Oxford: Berg, 2010), ch. 5 and pp. 144–7.

62 *Ibid.*, p. 4.

63 Lewis, 'Veils and sales', p. 70.

64 For a critical discussion of post-feminism, see for example Angela McRobbie, 'Post-feminism and popular culture', *Feminist Media Studies*, 4:3 (2004), 255–64.

65 Lewis, 'Veils and sales', pp. 71–2.

66 Whitlock, *Soft Weapons*, p. 13.

67 For discussion of a notion of universalism that encompasses plurality, see Judith Butler, 'Is Judaism Zionism?', in Mendieta and Vanantwerpen (eds), *Power of Religion*, pp. 70–91, p. 85.

Conclusion

Salman Rushdie's use of the third person in his 2012 memoir *Joseph Anton* might suggest a desire on his part to draw a clear distinction between the narrator and the narrated subject, between his present self and the man who underwent the ordeals he describes. This in turn could imply that the passage of time has brought about a shift in perspective, perhaps added nuance to his views on the global controversy triggered by his 1988 novel and subsequent disputes concerning freedom of expression and religious or cultural offence. Yet, there is no evidence of this in *Joseph Anton*: towards the end of the book, the protagonist, now released from Khomeini's fatwa, expresses his determination to defend his fellow artists, as he had been defended, to 'try to do the same for others in need … others who pushed boundaries, transgressed and, yes, blasphemed; all those artists who did not allow men of power or the cloth to draw lines in the sand and order them not to cross'.[1] A typically reductive polarisation of art and religion – with the former under attack from the latter – stands in for the complexities of artistic controversies, their actual power dimensions and the interplay of contextual factors in shaping them, and there is no ironic detachment on the part of the narrative from its almost messianic protagonist. Significantly, the protagonist's story ends just after the 9/11 attacks, when the identification of Islam with repression and terror as well as the sacralisation of western 'freedoms' reached an apogee. Thus, the narrative leaves little space for considered reflection, and, by paralleling the *Satanic Verses* controversy and the terror attacks (its two climactic bookends), further divests the former of any nuance.

While Rushdie's hardline, myopic perspective may be shaped by harrowing personal experiences, the views of the liberal intelligentsia more generally do not seem to have progressed since the late 1980s. As this book has shown, the responses on the part of the cultural elite and the media to subsequent controversies, including those surrounding *Brick Lane, Behzti, The Jewel of Medina* and religious hatred legislation, suggest a kind of stasis, at best, in thinking about freedom of expression and religious minority offence in Britain. Reflections on the Rushdie affair by a number of writers and publishers on the eve of the publication of *Joseph Anton* reveal a similarly stubborn adherence to a blanket valorisation of free speech.[2] The terror attacks carried out in the name of Islam in Europe and North America, as well as the attribution of segregation, rioting and disaffection to Muslim culture in critiques of multiculturalism across the political spectrum, have reinforced the dichotomisation of Islam and secular freedoms over the last twenty-five years, while, in the cultural sphere, the rise of the New Atheist movement has hardened the construction of Islam as the enemy of art as well as of science and all rational thought. Anshuman A. Mondal demonstrates the link between a hardline liberal championing of freedom of speech and an Islamophobic cultural imperialism. That an 'absolutist position on freedom of speech can … be traced back to the repercussions of the *fatwa*', he writes, and that such a position 'has been invoked each time a subsequent Muslim-related freedom of expression controversy has ignited … but *not* during other freedom of expression controversies … underscores the point that this rhetoric … is still performing a gesture of cultural supremacy. Its purpose is to position "Islam" outside the frame of "freedom" and, therefore, of civilization.'[3] As this book has shown, moreover, this 'gesture of cultural supremacy' is also, in the context of Britain, a gesture of *class* supremacy. The framing of freedom of speech debates in terms of a courageous lone artistic voice fighting against reactionary forces of repression occludes the cultural supremacy that in fact underpins this discourse; similarly, such a construction plasters over the social chasm between the privileged advocates of freedom of expression and those members of Muslim communities who protest. While Islam is placed 'outside the frame of "freedom" and … civilization', class is rendered invisible. Equality of access to discourse can only be attained when material hierarchies are removed.

If, then, the Rushdie affair can be said to have established, or at least embedded, the normative terms of conceptualising freedom of expression controversies, its influence on perceptions of Islam and Muslims in Britain has been pervasive and persistent. Not only has Islamophobia reinforced an absolutist understanding of free speech, but the latter has infiltrated debates about citizenship and Muslims more generally. In his speech declaring Britain a society 'sleepwalking to segregation', delivered shortly after 7/7 (and in the wake of the *Brick Lane*, *Behzti* and religious hatred legislation disputes), Trevor Phillips cited 'freedom of speech' and 'a tradition of poking fun at politicians, priests and do-gooders' as key items in his list of qualities of 'Britishness'.[4] A lack of such qualities is implicitly located within the nation's 'fully-fledged ghettoes' – those, no doubt, that for Phillips harbour crypto-Islamists and would-be rioters. His double allusion to freedom of expression tacitly positions Muslims as its antithesis, as well as demonstrates the seepage of received understandings of the Rushdie affair into discourses on multiculturalism. Moreover, as this book has suggested, the impact of the Rushdie affair extends beyond the political and social domains into that of cultural, and more specifically literary, production. While Arthur Bradley and Andrew Tate investigate the influence of New Atheist thought on the work of four high-profile contemporary British novelists, including Rushdie himself,[5] the preceding chapters have suggested the influence of the Rushdie controversy on South Asian Muslim-authored British fiction. As Lindsey Moore points out, while religion has been neglected in critical studies of British Asian fiction, reflecting a secularist bias in Euro-American scholarship, in fact 'Black British and British Asian fiction also presents a paucity of texts privileging faith as primary and positive determinant of identity'. Moore cites Hanif Kureishi's early work as valorising other aspects of minority British identities and casting Islam in a negative light, and argues that in the 'counter-canonization' of writers such as Kureishi, 'internal hierarchies of minority experience become settled'.[6] In other words, certain (secular) minority experiences are privileged over others – arguably by the publishing industry as well as by aspiring writers themselves – so that positive or even nuanced or complex religious experiences are marginalised. Novels such as Monica Ali's *Brick Lane* and Nadeem Aslam's *Maps for Lost Lovers* have broken this mould in ways, yet, as I have shown, neither significantly transgresses the parameters of a secular liberalism in its representation of subjects and communities of faith.

For Bradley and Tate, in contrast to the New Atheist novel, 'post-atheist fiction … dramatizes … neither a return to some pre-rational religious dogmatism nor the fetishisation of liberal Enlightenment values but an attempt to move beyond the Manichean clash of religious and secular fundamentalisms epitomized by 9/11 and its aftermath'.[7] While the fiction of British writers of South Asian Muslim heritage explored here is, in different ways and to varying degrees, hamstrung by a secular liberalism, other recent works depicting British Muslim culture and communities move further beyond the Manichean clash described. British Syrian writer Robin Yassin-Kassab's 2008 novel *The Road from Damascus* explores the journey of young Londoner and struggling PhD student Sami as he moves from a secularist repudiation of Islam, the religion of his heritage, to what is described as a 'trembling, contingent faith', and from a rejection of his pious mother and betrayal of his headscarved wife to a tentative reunion and reconciliation.[8] His British Iraqi wife Muntaha, a secondary school teacher who decides to wear the hijab, defies stereotypes of the oppressed victim of patriarchal Islamic culture or the radicalised agent of 'political Islam'. While the path Sami takes reverses the conventional trajectory from religious obfuscation to secular enlightenment, his wife's also destabilises conventional routes to 'freedom'; not only does she don the veil, rather than have it lifted, but she rejects her artist colleague Gabor's romantic advances, thereby diverting the story away from the marketable terrain of boundary-crossing, multicultural infidelities (inhabited by much of Kureishi's fiction) towards that of commitment, faith and belonging: 'She said no, and so prevented the story from moving into the universal territory we can all relate to. She said no, choosing to remain in her particularity. In her own ethnic group, in her religio-cultural space, in what they call a "community". She said no, and made the story a local one. Limited the story's scope.'[9] Here the narrative is ironising Gabor's exoticising perception of Muntaha and the hybrid couple that he would like them to form. But it also gestures towards its own refusal of the polarity of hybridity versus separatism and zealotry, its transgression of secular liberalism's limits. In the novel, the sacralisation of literature against a monolithic and retrogressive Islam is ventriloquised by one Rashid Iqbal, a writer whose talk Sami attends and clearly a parody of Salman Rushdie.[10] By contrast, the novel itself breaks down this dichotomy. While Iqbal's groundbreaking novel is called *Taboo Buster* – a title that connotes the free speech that Rushdie claims to stand for – *The Road from Damascus* itself suggests there are secularist taboos that fiction needs to bust and goes some way towards doing this.

A rather different representation of British Muslim culture can be found in Sudanese writer Leila Aboulela's 2005 novel *Minaret*.[11] But here, too, faith is a positive component of identity and here, too, the protagonist Najwa journeys from a vague cultural identification with Islam to a profound and enabling piety. As for Muntaha, so for Najwa, the donning of the hijab marks a deepening of faith and becomes a source of strength. Further, in *Minaret*, Islam enables the formation of a supportive community of women around Regent's Park Mosque, where they worship, which contrasts sharply with the female community in *Maps for Lost Lovers* which fractures almost at the point of coming together, torn apart by the oppression inflicted from inside and outside its parameters. Thus there is in Aboulela's novel a sense of a religious collective as enabling rather than inherently oppressive. Significantly, however, while the novel gives voice to a normatively silenced subjectivity, Najwa's self-confessed political naivety combined with her modesty and vulnerability means that her religious identity remains largely within the private sphere. Faith, for her, is primarily a retreat from the material to the spiritual. Further, despite the female collective in the novel, there is little sense of a community that is grounded in a particular locale; the worshippers are brought together by a faith which is largely detached from class, race or place. In this respect, difference in the novel is contained and detached from normative Britishness.

Even in *The Road from Damascus*, the faith-based identities of the characters are enacted at considerable distance from Phillips's 'black-hole' ghettoes, despite the downward mobility some have endured, and, displaced for political reasons, they are, to some degree, rootless in London.[12] Thus – and notwithstanding Muntaha's younger brother Ammar's overtly (and misguidedly) political, 'street' Muslim identity, handled with sensitivity by Yassin-Kassab – they are at a relatively safe remove from the working-class, and largely South Asian, Muslim communities that are at the root of the phobia of multiculturalism which has gained prominence in the last decade. As Sami, initially reluctant to identify as Muslim, reflects, 'In Britain Muslims meant Pakis, which meant crumbling mills and corner shops ... Dismal northern towns where day never truly dawned. They had a proletarian role in the economy, and a bourgeois conservatism ... Badly dressed and poorly educated. Islam's cobwebs in their eyelashes, and its mould on their tongues.'[13] It is perhaps not too far-fetched to suggest that literary representations by writers of South Asian Muslim heritage and of South Asian Muslim culture in contemporary Britain are especially constrained by the conceptual framework entrenched by the Rushdie affair – one which occludes or contains class hierarchies and valorises the individual against the group to remain within the limits of liberalism.[14] Certainly, the texts discussed in this book reflect, expose and illuminate the uncomfortable fit of Muslims within a secular liberal

Britain that cannot tolerate communitarian faith-based identities. As new generations of Britons of South Asian Muslim heritage find their literary voices, it will be illuminating to see how far and in what ways their writing will exceed the paradigms of secular liberal thought, potentially facilitating intercultural understanding and trust in multicultural Britain.

NOTES

1 Salman Rushdie, *Joseph Anton* (London: Jonathan Cape, 2012), p. 628.
2 'Looking back at Salman Rushdie's *The Satanic Verses*', *Guardian* (14 September 2012), www.theguardian.com/books/2012/sep/14/looking-at-salman-rushdies-satanic-verses (last accessed 6 November 2014).
3 Anshuman A. Mondal, 'Revisiting *The Satanic Verses*: the *fatwa* and its legacies', in Robert Eaglestone and Martin McQuillan (eds), *Salman Rushdie* (London: Bloomsbury, 2013), pp. 59–71, pp. 61–2.
4 Trevor Phillips, 'After 7/7: sleepwalking to segregation', speech given at the Manchester Council for Community Relations (22 September 2005).
5 Arthur Bradley and Andrew Tate, *The New Atheist Novel: Fiction, Philosophy and Polemic after 9/11* (London: Continuum, 2010).
6 Lindsey Moore, 'British Muslim identities and spectres of terror in Nadeem Aslam's *Maps for Lost Lovers*', *Postcolonial Text*, 5:2 (2009), 1–19, 4.
7 Bradley and Tate, *New Atheist Novel*, p. 109.
8 Robin Yassin-Kassab, *The Road from Damascus* (London: Hamish Hamilton, 2008), p. 348.
9 *Ibid.*, p. 293.
10 *Ibid.*, p. 300.
11 Leila Aboulela, *Minaret* (London: Bloomsbury, 2005).
12 Phillips, 'After 7/7'.
13 Yassin-Kassab, *Road from Damascus*, p. 61.
14 I am grateful to Claire Chambers and Lindsey Moore, my fellow panellists at the British Association for South Asian Studies Annual Conference 2013 (University of Leeds), for a discussion that helped to crystallise my thoughts on this. One non-Muslim British Asian who has exceeded this framework is Sunjeev Sahota, whose 2011 novel *Ours are the Streets* deftly grounds the radicalisation of young Sheffield-born Pakistani Imtiaz Raina in his disenfranchisement as a British Muslim and the racism and poverty experienced by his immigrant parents, as well as in the global suffering of the *ummah* (London: Picador, 2011).

Bibliography

WORKS DISCUSSED

Ali, Monica, *Brick Lane* (London: Doubleday, 2003).

Aslam, Nadeem, *Maps for Lost Lovers* (London: Faber, 2004).

Hai, Yasmin, *The Making of Mr Hai's Daughter: Becoming British: A Memoir* (London: Virago, 2008).

Husain, Ed, *The Islamist* (London: Penguin, 2007).

Janmahomed, Shelina Zahra, *Love in a Headscarf: Muslim Woman Seeks the One* (London: Aurum, 2009).

Kureishi, Hanif, *The Black Album* (London: Faber, 1995).

Kureishi, Hanif, *Love in a Blue Time* (London: Faber, 1997).

Kureishi, Hanif, *Intimacy* (London: Faber, 1998).

Kureishi, Hanif, *Midnight All Day* (London: Faber, 1999).

Kureishi, Hanif, *The Body and Seven Stories* (London: Faber, 2002).

Kureishi, Hanif, *Collected Screenplays 1* (London: Faber, 2002).

Kureishi, Hanif, *My Ear at his Heart: Reading my Father* (London: Faber, 2004).

Kureishi, Hanif, *Something to Tell You* (London: Faber, 2008).

Kureishi, Hanif (writer) and Udayan Prasad (director), *My Son the Fanatic* (1997).

Malik, Zaiba, *We are a Muslim, Please* (London: Windmill, 2010).

Manzoor, Sarfraz, *Greetings from Bury Park: Race, Religion and Rock 'n' Roll* (London: Bloomsbury, 2007).

Rushdie, Salman, *The Satanic Verses* (London: Random House, 1999 [1988]).

ARCHIVAL SOURCES

British Library, St Pancras, India Office Collections: MSS Eur F143/80, 'Woking – arrangements with Imam of mosque at —', 2 February–12 October 1915.

British Library, St Pancras, India Office Collections: India Office Records, L/PJ/12/455, 'India League: reports on members and activities', 6 January 1943–27 July 1944.

British Library, St Pancras, India Office Collections: India Office Records, L/PJ/12/468, 'Aid for the establishment of the East London Mosque and Islamic

Culture Centre', July 1927–June 1946.

British Library, St Pancras, India Office Collections: India Office Records, L/I/1/599, 'Insults to Indians', 3 December 1935–7 June 1948.

British Library, St Pancras, India Office Collections: India Office Records, L/PJ/12/614, 'Muslim protest against references to the Prophet Muhammad in *A Short History of the World* by H. G. Wells', 16 August 1938–20 April 1939.

British Library, St Pancras, India Office Collections: India Office Records, L/PJ/12/630, 'Indian seamen: reports on unrest, welfare and union activities', November 1939–January 1945.

British Library, St Pancras, India Office Collections: India Office Records, L/PJ/12/645, 'Indian Workers' Union or Association: reports on members and activities', January 1942–July 1947.

British Library, St Pancras, India Office Collections: India Office Records, L/PJ/12/646, 'IPI notes on Indian organisations in UK', April 1942–June 1946.

British Library, St Pancras, India Office Collections: India Office Records, L/PJ/12/658, 'Swaraj House, London: activities of members and meetings', November 1942–July 1947.

British Library, St Pancras, India Office Collections: India Office Records, L/PJ/7/831, '"Lives of a Bengal lancer": protests at offensive incidents in film', 15 March–16 September 1935.

British Library, St Pancras, *Islamic Review*, 1913–67.

Institute of Race Relations, Black History Collections, Periodicals: *Anglo Asian Magazine, Asian Hackney, Asian Post, Asian Voice in Hackney, Asian Youth Association News, Asian Youth News, Bradford Black, Fowaad!, Free the Bradford 12, Indian Worker, Indian Workers Association GB Newsletter, Kala Tara, Liberation Mukti, Mukti, Newham Youth Movement, New Monitor, Newsletter of National Association of Muslim Youth UK, Northern Black, Paikaar*.

Institute of Race Relations, Black History Collection, 'Other racial violence campaigns': The Steering Committee of Asian Organisations newsletter (January 1981).

OTHER SOURCES CITED

Abbas, Tahir, 'British South Asian Muslims: before and after September 11', in Tahir Abbas (ed.), *Muslim Britain: Communities under Pressure* (London and New York: Zed, 2005), pp. 3–17.

Abbas, Tahir, '"After 7/7": challenging the dominant hegemony', in Richard Phillips (ed.), *Muslim Spaces of Hope: Geographies of Possibility in Britain and the West* (London: Zed Books, 2009), pp. 252–62.

Abbas, Tahir, 'Honour-related violence towards South Asian Muslim women in the UK: a crisis of masculinity and cultural relativism in the context of Islamophobia and the "war on terror"', in Mohammad Mazher Idriss and Tahir Abbas (eds), *'Honour', Violence, Women and Islam* (Abingdon: Routledge, 2011), pp. 16–28.

Aboulela, Leila, *Minaret* (London: Bloomsbury, 2005).

Adams, Caroline (ed.), *Across Seven Seas and Thirteen Rivers: Life Stories of Pioneer Settlers in Britain* (London: Eastside Books, 2nd edn, 1994 [1987]).

Adebayo, Diran, 'Diaspora chic', *Index on Censorship*, 32:2 (2003), 214–18.

Adebayo, Diran, 'Interview: Monica Ali with Diran Adebayo', in Susheila Nasta (ed.), *Writing across Worlds: Contemporary Writers Talk* (Abingdon: Routledge, 2004), pp. 340–51.

Ahmad, Aijaz, *In Theory* (London and New York: Verso, 1992).

Ahmed, Rehana, 'British Muslim masculinities and cultural resistance: Kenny Glenaan and Simon Beaufoy's *Yasmin*', *Journal of Postcolonial Literature*, 45:3 (2009), 285–96.

Ahmed, Rehana, 'Networks of resistance: Krishna Menon and working-class South Asians in Britain', in Rehana Ahmed and Sumita Mukherjee (eds), *South Asian Resistances in Britain, 1858–1947* (London: Continuum, 2011), pp. 70–87.

Ahmed, Rehana, 'Equality of citizenship', in Ruvani Ranasinha, with Rehana Ahmed, Sumita Mukherjee and Florian Stadtler (eds), *South Asians and the Shaping of Britain, 1870–1950: A Sourcebook* (Manchester: Manchester University Press, 2012), pp. 21–79.

Ahmed, Rehana, 'South Asians writing resistance in wartime London: *Indian Writing* (1940–1942)', *Wasafiri*, 27:2 (2012), 17–24.

Ahmed, Rehana, Peter Morey and Amina Yaqin, 'Introduction', in Rehana Ahmed, Peter Morey and Amina Yaqin (eds), *Culture, Diaspora, and Modernity in Muslim Writing* (Abingdon and New York: Routledge, 2012), pp. 1–17.

Ahmed, Rehana and Sumita Mukherjee, 'Introduction', in Rehana Ahmed and Sumita Mukherjee (eds), *South Asian Resistances in Britain, 1858–1947* (London: Continuum, 2011), pp. xi–xxxi.

Ahmed, Rehana and Florian Stadtler, 'East Enders go west: the Jamiat-ul-Muslimin's protest against H. G. Wells' *A Short History of the World*', unpublished paper presented at the 'Muslims Making Britain' workshop, School of Oriental and African Studies, University of London, July 2009.

Ahmed, Rehana and Florian Stadtler, 'Muslims protest against H. G. Wells book in 1930s Britain', *Huffington Post* (19 September 2012), www.huffingtonpost.co.uk/rehana-ahmed/muslims-protest-against-h_b_1895942.html (last accessed 6 November 2014).

Ahmed, Saira, *Disgraced* (London: Headline Review, 2009).

Ahmed, Sara, *Strange Encounters: Embodied Others in Post-Coloniality* (London: Routledge, 2000).

Akbar, Arifa, 'Brick Lane rises up against filming of Ali's novel', *Independent* (22 July 2006), www.independent.co.uk/news/uk/this-britain/brick-lane-rises-up-against-filming-of-alis-novel-408885.html (last accessed 6 November 2014).

Alam, Fareena, 'The burden of representation', *Guardian* (17 January 2005), www.theguardian.com/books/2003/jul/13/fiction.features (last accessed 6 November 2014).

Alexander, Claire E., *The Asian Gang: Ethnicity, Identity, Masculinity* (Oxford: Berg, 2000).

Alexander, Claire, 'Imagining the Asian gang: ethnicity, masculinity and youth after "the riots"', *Critical Social Policy*, 24:4 (2004), 526–49.

Ali, Ahmed, 'The Progressive Writers' Movement and creative writers in Urdu', in Carlo Coppola (ed.), *Marxist Influences and South Asian Literature*, vol. 1 (East Lansing: Asian Studies Center, Michigan State University, 1974), pp. 35–41.

Ali, Monica, 'Where I'm coming from', *Guardian* (17 June 2003), pp. 4–5.

Ali, Monica, 'Do we need laws on hatred?', in Lisa Appignanesi (ed.), *Free Expression is No Offence* (London: Penguin, 2005), pp. 47–58.

Ali, Monica, 'The outrage economy', *Guardian* (13 October 2007), www.guardian. co.uk/books/2007/oct/13/fiction.film/ (last accessed 6 November 2014).

Ali, Monica, Laura Jones and Abi Morgan (writers) and Sarah Gavron (director), *Brick Lane* (2006).

Ali, Sameem, *Belonging* (London: John Murray, 2008).

Ali, Suki, *Mixed-Race, Post-Race: Gender, New Ethnicities and Cultural Practices* (Oxford: Berg, 2003).

Ali, Tariq, *The Clash of Fundamentalisms: Crusades, Jihads and Modernity* (London: Verso, 2002).

Alibhai-Brown, Yasmin, *Mixed Feelings: The Complex Lives of Mixed-Race Britons* (London: Women's Press, 2001).

Amis, Martin, *The Second Plane: September 11, 2001–2007* (London: Jonathan Cape, 2008).

Ansari, Humayun, *'The Infidel Within': Muslims in Britain since 1800* (London: Hurst, 2004).

Ansari, Humayun (ed. and intro.), *The Making of the East London Mosque, 1910–1951: Minutes of the London Mosque Fund and East London Mosque Trust Ltd* (Cambridge: Cambridge University Press, 2011).

Appignanesi, Lisa, 'PEN is concerned about protests over the filming of Monica Ali's Brick Lane', English PEN (19 July 2006), www.englishpen.org/pen-is-concerned-about-protests-over-the-filming-of-monica-alis-brick-lane/ (last accessed 6 November 2014).

Appignanesi, Lisa and Sara Maitland (eds), *The Rushdie File* (London: Fourth Estate, 1989).

Asad, Talal, 'Ethnography, literature, and politics: some readings and uses of Salman Rushdie's *The Satanic Verses*', *Cultural Anthropology*, 5:3 (August 1990), 239–69.

Asad, Talal, 'Free speech, blasphemy, and secular criticism', in Talal Asad, Wendy Brown, Judith Butler and Saba Mahmood, *Is Critique Secular? Blasphemy, Injury and Free Speech* (Berkeley, CA: Townsend Center for the Humanities, 2009), pp. 20–63.

Aslam, Nadeem, *Season of the Rainbirds* (London: Bloomsbury, 1993).

Aslam, Nadeem, *The Wasted Vigil* (London: Faber, 2008).

Back, Les, Michael Keith, Azra Khan, Kalbir Shukra and John Solomos, 'The return to assimilation: race, multiculturalism and New Labour', *Sociological Research Online*, 7:2 (2002), www.socresonline.org.uk/7/2/back.html (last accessed 6 November 2014).

Bagguley, Paul and Yasmin Hussain, 'Flying the flag for England? Citizenship, religion and cultural identity among British Pakistani Muslims', in Tahir Abbas (ed.), *Muslim Britain: Communities under Pressure* (London and New York: Zed Books, 2005), pp. 208–21.

Baker, Christopher and Justin Beaumont, 'Postcolonialism and religion: new spaces of "belonging and becoming" in the postsecular city', in Justin Beaumont and Christopher Baker (eds), *Postsecular Cities: Space, Theory and Practice* (London: Continuum, 2011), pp. 33–49.

Ball, John Clement, *Imagining London: Postcolonial Fiction and the Transnational Metropolis* (Toronto: University of Toronto Press, 2004).

Barton, Laura, 'Hot dates and headscarves', *Guardian* (18 February 2009), www.theguardian.com/lifeandstyle/2009/feb/18/shelina-zahra-janmohamed-arranged-marriage (last accessed 6 November 2014).

Beaufoy, Simon (writer) and Kenny Glenaan (director), *Yasmin* (2004).

Bedell, Geraldine, 'Full of East End promise', *Observer* (15 June 2003), www.theguardian.com/books/2003/jun/15/fiction.features1 (last accessed 6 November 2014).

Begg, Moazzam with Victoria Brittain, *Enemy Combatant: A British Muslim's Journey to Guantánamo and Back* (London: Free Press, 2006).

Begum, Halima and John Eade, 'All quiet on the eastern front? Bangladeshi reactions in Tower Hamlets', in Tahir Abbas (ed.), *Muslim Britain: Communities under Pressure* (London and New York: Zed Books, 2005), pp. 179–93.

Benwell, Bethan, James Procter and Gemma Robinson, 'Not reading *Brick Lane*', *New Formations*, 73 (2011), 90–116.

Bhabha, Homi, 'Unpacking my library ... again', in Iain Chambers and Lidia Curti (eds), *The Post-Colonial Question: Common Skies, Divided Horizons* (Abingdon and New York: Routledge, 1996), pp. 109–11.

Blair, Sara, 'Local modernity, global modernism', *English Literary History*, 71:3 (Autumn 2004), 813–38.

Bourdieu, Pierre, *Distinction: A Social Critique of the Judgement of Taste*, trans. Richard Nice (London: Routledge, 1984).

Brace, Marianne, 'Nadeem Aslam: a question of honour', *Independent* (11 June 2004), www.independent.co.uk/arts-entertainment/books/features/nadeem-aslam-a-question-of-honour-731732.html (last accessed 6 November 2014).

Bradley, Arthur and Andrew Tate, *The New Atheist Novel: Fiction, Philosophy and Polemic after 9/11* (London: Continuum, 2010).

Brice, M. A. Kevin, 'Sleepwalking to segregation or wide-awake separation: investigation of distribution of white English Muslims and the factors influencing their choices of location', *Global Built Environment Review*, 6:2 (2007), 18–27.

Brouillette, Sarah, 'Literature and gentrification on *Brick Lane*', *Criticism*, 51:3 (2009), 425–49.

Brown, Colin, 'If we want social cohesion we need a sense of identity' (David Blunkett interviewed by Colin Brown), *Independent on Sunday* (9 December 2001), p. 4.

Brown, Mick, 'Voice of experience', *Telegraph* (27 May 2006), www.telegraph. co.uk/culture/books/3652679/Voice-ofexperience.html (last accessed 6 November 2014).

Bunting, Madeleine, 'This is about real victims', *Guardian* (11 December 2004), www.theguardian.com/world/2004/dec/11/race.religion (last accessed 6 November 2014).

Bunting, Madeleine, 'The muscular liberals are marching into a dead end', *Guardian* (12 September 2005), www.guardian.co.uk/politics/2005/sep/12/ politicalcolumnists.comment/ (last accessed 6 November 2014).

Bunting, Madeleine, 'We were the brothers' (Interview: Ed Husain), *Guardian* (12 May 2007), www.guardian.co.uk/books/2007/may/12/religion.news (last accessed 6 November 2014).

Bunting, Madeleine, 'Religions have the power to bring a passion for social justice to politics', *Guardian* (12 January 2009), www.theguardian.com/ commentisfree/2009/jan/12/madeleine-bunting-religion-social-justice (last accessed 6 November 2014).

Bunting, Madeleine, 'Blame consumer capitalism, not multiculturalism', *Guardian* (6 February 2011), www.theguardian.com/commentisfree/2011/feb/06/capitalism -multiculturalism-cameron-flawed-analysis (last accessed 6 November 2014).

Burgess, Anthony, 'Islam's gangster tactics', *Independent* (16 February 1989).

Butler, Judith, *Precarious Life: The Powers of Mourning and Violence* (London: Verso, 2006 [2004]).

Butler, Judith, 'The sensibility of critique: response to Asad and Mahmood', in Talal Asad, Wendy Brown, Judith Butler and Saba Mahmood, *Is Critique Secular? Blasphemy, Injury and Free Speech* (Berkeley, CA: Townsend Center for the Humanities, 2009), pp. 101–36.

Butler, Judith, 'Is Judaism Zionism?', in Eduardo Mendieta and Jonathan Vanantwerpen (eds), *The Power of Religion in the Public Sphere: Judith Butler, Jürgen Habermas, Charles Taylor, Cornel West* (New York: Columbia University Press, 2011), pp. 70–91.

Cacciottolo, Mario, 'Brick Lane protesters hurt over "lies"', BBC News (31 July 2006), http://newsvote.bbc.co.uk/mpapps/pagetools/print/news.bbc. co.uk/1/hi/uk/5229872.stm (last accessed 6 November 2014).

Cantle, Ted, 'The Cantle report – community cohesion: a report of the Independent Review Team', Home Office (December 2001), http://resources.cohesioninst itute.org.uk/Publications/Documents/Document/DownloadDocumentsFile. aspx?recordId=96&file=PDFversion (last accessed 6 November 2014).

Chakrabarti, M. K., 'Marketplace multiculturalism' (review of US edition of

Monica Ali, *Brick Lane*), *Boston Review: A Political and Literary Forum* (December 2003–January 2004), http://new.bostonreview.net/BR28.6/chakrabarti.html (last accessed 6 November 2014).

Chakrabarty, Dipesh, *Provincializing Europe: Postcolonial Thought and Historical Difference* (Princeton and Oxford: Princeton University Press, 2000).

Chambers, Claire, *British Muslim Fictions: Interviews with Contemporary Writers* (Basingstoke: Palgrave Macmillan, 2012).

Chambers, Claire, 'Countering the "oppressed, kidnapped genre" of Muslim life writing: Yasmin Hai's *The Making of Mr Hai's Daughter* and Shelina Zahra Janmahomed's *Love in a Headscarf*, *Life Writing*, 10:1 (2013), 77–96.

Charles, Ron, 'Holy terrors' (review of Nadeem Aslam, *Maps for Lost Lovers*), *Washington Post* (18 May 2005), www.washingtonpost.com/wp-dyn/articles/A1856-2005May18.html (last accessed 6 November 2014).

Chaudhuri, Amit, 'Qatrina and her books' (review of Nadeem Aslam, *The Wasted Vigil*), *London Review of Books*, 31:16 (27 August 2009), 3 and 5–7.

Chowdhry, Prem, *Colonial India and the Making of Empire Cinema* (Manchester: Manchester University Press, 2000).

Coppola, Carlo, 'The All-India Progressive Writers' Association: the European phase', in Carlo Coppola (ed.), *Marxist Influences and South Asian Literature*, vol. 1 (East Lansing: Asian Studies Center, Michigan State University, 1974), pp. 1–34.

Coppola, Carlo, 'About the author and his work', in Sajjad Zaheer, *A Night in London*, trans. Bilal Hashmi (Noida: HarperCollins India, 2011 [1938]), n.p.

Cowley, Jason, 'London 2012: smaller, greater, braver', *Observer* (10 July 2005), www.theguardian.com/uk/2005/jul/10/olympics2012.olympicgames3 (last accessed 6 November 2014).

de Certeau, Michel, *The Practice of Everyday Life*, trans. Steven Randell (Berkeley and Los Angeles: University of California Press, 1984).

DeHanas, Daniel Nilsson and Zacharias P. Pieri, 'Olympic proportions: the expanding scalar politics of the London "Olympics mega-mosque" controversy', *Sociology*, 45:5 (2011), 798–814.

Djebar, Assia *Fantasia: An Algerian Cavalcade*, trans. Dorothy S. Blair (Portsmouth, NH: Heinemann, 1985).

Döring, Tobias, 'Edward Said and the fiction of autobiography', *Wasafiri*, 21:2 (July 2006), 71–8.

Dougary, Ginny, 'Martin Amis interviewed by Ginny Dougary', *Times Magazine* (9 September 2006).

Doward, Jamie, 'Battle to block massive mosque', *Observer* (24 September 2006), www.guardian.co.uk/society/2006/sep/24/communities.religion (last accessed 6 November 2014).

'"Down with Wells!" Moslem protest against his book', *Guardian* (19 August 1938), p. 7.

Duberman, Martin, 'Foreword', in Noam Chomsky, *Objectivity and Liberal Scholarship* (New York: New Press, 2003 [1969]), pp. v–ix.

Eaglestone, Robert, '"The age of reason is over … an age of fury was dawning": contemporary Anglo-American fiction and terror', *Wasafiri*, 22:2 (2007), 19–22.

Eagleton, Terry, *Ideology: An Introduction* (London: Verso, 1991).

Eagleton, Terry, *Reason, Faith, and Revolution: Reflections on the God Debate* (New Haven and London: Yale University Press, 2009).

Edgar, David, 'In the new revolution, progressives fight against, not with, the poor', *Guardian* (24 August 2009), www.theguardian.com/commentisfree/2009/aug/24/revolution-1989-1979 (last accessed 6 November 2014).

Elden, Stuart, *Understanding Henri Lefebvre: Theory and the Possible* (London and New York: Continuum, 2004).

English PEN, 'The Brick Lane affair: English PEN warns of dangers of community censorship' (press release), English PEN (31 July 2006), www.englishpen. org/legacy/images/brick_lane/Brick%20Lane%20Press%20Release-30%20 July%2006.pdf (last accessed 6 November 2014).

Fanon, Frantz, *Black Skin, White Masks*, trans. Charles Lam Markmann (New York: Grove, 1967).

Faulks, Sebastian, *A Week in December* (London: Hutchinson, 2009).

Fish, Stanley, 'Boutique multiculturalism, or why liberals are incapable of thinking about hate speech', *Critical Inquiry*, 23 (Winter 1997), 378–95.

Fitzgerald, Timothy, *Religion and Politics in International Relations: The Modern Myth* (London and New York: Continuum, 2011).

Friedman, Jonathan, 'Global crises, the struggle for cultural identity and intellectual porkbarrelling: cosmopolitans versus locals, ethnics and nationals in an era of dehegemonisation', in Pnina Werbner and Tariq Modood (eds), *Debating Cultural Hybridity: Multi-Cultural Identities and the Politics of Anti-Racism* (London: Zed Books, 1997), pp. 70–89.

Fuss, Diana, 'Interior colonies: Frantz Fanon and the politics of identification', in Nigel C. Gibson (ed.), *Rethinking Fanon: The Continuing Dialogue* (New York: Humanity Books, 1999), pp. 294–328.

Gallagher, Paul, 'Deprived Newham watches bemused as council ponders move from £110m building after just three years', *Independent* (24 September 2013), www.independent.co.uk/news/uk/politics/deprived-newham-watches-bemused-as-council-ponders-move-from-110m-building-after-just-three-years-8836972.html (last accessed 6 November 2014).

Gandhi, M. K., *An Autobiography: The Story of my Experiments with Truth* (London: Penguin, 2001 [1927, 1929]).

Garrels, Anne, *Naked in Baghdad* (New York: Farrar, Straus & Giroux, 2003).

Genette, Gerard, *Paratexts: Thresholds of Interpretation* (Cambridge: Cambridge University Press, 1997).

Gilroy, Paul, *After Empire: Melancholia or Convivial Culture?* (Abingdon: Routledge, 2004).

Glynn, Sarah, 'Liberalizing Islam: creating Brits of the Islamic persuasion', in Richard Phillips (ed.), *Muslim Spaces of Hope: Geographies of Possibility in Britain and the West* (London: Zed Books, 2009), pp. 179–97.

Goodhardt, David, 'Too diverse?', *Prospect* (20 February 2004), www.prospect-magazine.co.uk/magazine/too-diverse-david-goodhart-multicultur-alism-britain-immigration-globalisation/#.Une9XotFDcs (last accessed 6 November 2014).

Goodhardt, David, 'Discomfort of strangers', *Guardian* (24 February 2004), www.theguardian.com/politics/2004/feb/24/race.eu (last accessed 6 November 2014).

Gopal, Priyamvada, *Literary Radicalism in India: Gender, Nation and the Transition to Independence* (Abingdon and New York: Routledge, 2005).

Gorra, Michael, *After Empire: Scott, Naipaul, Rushdie* (Chicago and London: University of Chicago Press, 1997).

Greater Sylhet Development and Welfare Council in UK, www.gscuk.org (last accessed 6 November 2014).

Greer, Germaine, 'Reality can bite back', *Guardian* (5 August 2006), www.theguardian.com/commentisfree/2006/aug/05/bookscomment (last accessed 6 November 2014).

Gregory, Derek, *The Colonial Present* (Oxford: Blackwell, 2004).

Grillo, Ralph, 'Artistic licence, free speech and religious sensibilities in a multi-cultural society', in Prakash Shah (ed.), *Law and Ethnic Plurality: Socio-Legal Perspectives* (Leiden: Koninklijke Brill, 2004), pp. 107–26.

Gunning, Dave, *Race and Antiracism in Black British and British Asian Literature* (Liverpool: Liverpool University Press, 2010).

Gurnah, Abdulrazak, *By the Sea* (London: Bloomsbury, 2001).

Habermas, Jürgen, 'Equal treatment of cultures and the limits of postmodern liberalism', *Journal of Political Philosophy*, 13:1 (2005), 1–28.

Habermas, Jürgen, 'Religion in the public sphere', *European Journal of Philosophy*, 14:1 (2006), 1–25.

Habermas, Jürgen, 'Notes on a post-secular society', Signandsight.com (18 June 2008), 1–23, www.signandsight.com/features/1714.html (last accessed 6 November 2014).

Harriss, Kaveri, 'Muslims in the London borough of Newham', background paper for COMPAS (University of Oxford, n.d.), www.compas.ox.ac.uk/fileadmin/files/Publications/Research_Resources/Urban/Newham_Back-ground_Paper_0506b.pdf (last accessed 6 November 2014).

Harvey, David, *The Condition of Postmodernity* (Oxford: Blackwell, 1990).

Heawood, Jonathan, 'The battle for Brick Lane', *Guardian* (27 July 2006), www.theguardian.com/commentisfree/2006/jul/27/noskatinginsaris (last accessed 6 November 2014).

Hirsi Ali, Ayaan, *Infidel: My Life* (London: Free Press, 2007).

Huggan, Graham, *The Postcolonial Exotic: Marketing the Margins* (London: Rout-ledge, 2001).

Huggan, Graham and Tobias Wachinger, 'Can newness enter the world? *The Satanic Verses* and the question of multicultural aesthetics', in Liselotte Glage and Ruediger Kunow (eds), *'The Decolonizing Pen': Cultural Diversity and the Transnational Imaginary in Rushdie's Fiction* (Trier: Wissenschaftlicher Verlag Trier, 2001), pp. 25–38.

Hussein, Abdullah, *Émigré Journeys* (London: Serpent's Tail, 2000).

Jack, Ian, 'It's only a novel …', *Guardian* (20 December 2003), www.theguardian. com/books/2003/dec/20/featuresreviews.guardianreview3 (last accessed 6 November 2014).

Jaggi, Maya, 'Colour bind', *Guardian* (7 February), www.theguardian.com/ books/2003/feb/07/fiction.race (last accessed 6 November 2014).

Jameson, Fredric, *The Political Unconscious: Narrative as a Socially Symbolic Act* (London: Routledge, 1981).

Jeffries, Stuart, '"Everybody needs to get thicker skins"', *Guardian* (11 July 2008), www.theguardian.com/books/2008/jul/11/salmanrushdie.bookerprize (last accessed 6 November 2014).

Jenkinson, Jacqueline, *Black 1919: Riots, Racism and Resistance in Imperial Britain* (Liverpool: Liverpool University Press, 2009).

John, Gus, '"Trojan horses" and policing "extremism" in schools' (7 June 2014), www.gusjohn.com/2014/06/trojan-horses-and-policing-extremism-in-schools (last accessed 6 November 2014).

Johnston, Philip, 'The shadow cast by a mega-mosque', *Telegraph* (25 September 2006), www.telegraph.co.uk/comment/personal-view/3632591/The-shadow-cast-by-a-mega-mosque.html (last accessed 6 November 2014).

Kabeer, Naila, *The Power to Choose: Bangladeshi Women and Labour Market Decisions in London and Dhaka* (London and New York: Verso, 2000).

Kalliney, Peter, 'Globalization, postcoloniality, and the problem of literary studies in *The Satanic Verses*', *Modern Fiction Studies*, 48:1 (2002), 50–82.

Kelly, Danny, 'There's just one boss in this family', *Observer* (27 May 2007), www.guardian.co.uk/books/2007/may/27/biography.features (last accessed 6 November 2014).

Khan-Din, Ayub (writer) and Damien O'Donnell (director), *East is East* (1999).

Khan-Din, Ayub (writer) and Andy DeEmmony (director), *West is West* (2010).

Khouri, Norma, *Honor Lost: Love and Death in Modern-Day Jordan* (New York: Atria Books, 2003).

Kosminsky, Peter (writer and director), *Britz* (2007).

Kundnani, Arun, *The End of Tolerance: Racism in 21st Century Britain* (London: Pluto, 2007).

Kureishi, Hanif, *The Buddha of Suburbia* (London: Faber, 1990).

Kureishi, Hanif, *Dreaming and Scheming: Reflections on Writing and Politics* (London: Faber, 2002).

Kureishi, Hanif, *The Word and the Bomb* (London: Faber, 2005).

Kureishi, Hanif, *Collected Stories* (London: Faber, 2010).

Lanchester, John, *Capital* (London: Faber, 2012).

Lea, Richard and Paul Lewis, '"Insulted" residents and traders threaten to halt filming of bestselling novel *Brick Lane*', *Guardian* (18 July 2006), www.theguardian.com/uk/2006/jul/18/film.media (last accessed 6 November 2014).

Leech, Kenneth, *Brick Lane 1978: The Events and their Significance* (London: Stepney Books, 1994 [1980]).

Lefebvre, Henri, *The Production of Space*, trans. Donald Nicholson-Smith (Oxford: Blackwell, 1991).

Lefebvre, Henri, *Writings on Cities*, trans. and ed. Eleonore Kofman and Elizabeth Lebas (Oxford: Blackwell, 1996).

Lefebvre, Henri, *Key Writings*, ed. Stuart Elden, Elizabeth Lebas and Eleonore Kofman (London and New York: Continuum, 2003).

Lefebvre, Henri, *The Urban Revolution*, trans. Robert Bononno (Minneapolis and London: University of Minnesota Press, 2003).

Lentin, Alana and Gavan Titley, *The Crises of Multiculturalism: Racism in a Neoliberal Age* (London: Zed Books, 2011).

Levey, Geoffrey Brahm and Tariq Modood, 'Liberal democracy, multicultural citizenship and the Danish cartoon affair', in Levey and Modood (eds), *Secularism, Religion and Multicultural Citizenship* (Cambridge: Cambridge University Press, 2009), pp. 216–42.

Lewis, Philip, *Islamic Britain: Religion, Politics and Identity among British Muslims* (London and New York: I. B. Tauris, 2002 [1994]).

Lewis, Philip, 'Arenas of ethnic negotiation: cooperation and conflict in Bradford', in Tariq Modood and Pnina Werbner (eds), *The Politics of Multiculturalism in the New Europe: Racism, Identity and Community* (London: Zed Books, 1997), pp. 126–46.

Lewis, Reina, 'Veils and sales: Muslims and the spaces of post-colonial fashion retail', in Richard Phillips (ed.), *Muslim Spaces of Hope: Geographies of Possibility in Britain and the West* (London: Zed Books, 2009), pp. 69–84.

Little, Kenneth, *Negroes in Britain: A Study of Racial Relations in English Society* (London: Routledge & Kegan Paul, 2nd edn, 1972).

'Looking back at Salman Rushdie's *The Satanic Verses*', *Guardian* (14 September 2012), www.theguardian.com/books/2012/sep/14/looking-at-salman-rushdies-satanic-verses (last accessed 6 November 2014).

Mac an Ghaill, Mairtin and Chris Haywood, *Gender, Culture and Society: Contemporary Femininities and Masculinities* (Basingstoke: Palgrave Macmillan, 2007).

McCabe, Colin, 'Interview: Hanif Kureishi on London', *Critical Quarterly*, 41:3 (1999), 37–56.

McEwan, Ian, *Saturday* (London: Vintage, 2006).

McEwan, Ian, 'Martin Amis is not a racist', *Guardian* (21 November 2007), www.theguardian.com/world/2007/nov/21/religion.race (last accessed 6 November 2014).

Macherey, Pierre, *A Theory of Literary Production*, trans. Geoffrey Wall (New York and London: Routledge, 1996 [1978; French original 1966]).

McLeod, John, *Postcolonial London: Rewriting the Metropolis* (London and New York: Routledge, 2004).

McRobbie, Angela, 'Post-feminism and popular culture', *Feminist Media Studies*, 4:3 (2004), 255–64.

Mahmood, Saba, 'Religious reason and secular affect: an incommensurable divide?', in Talal Asad, Wendy Brown, Judith Butler and Saba Mahmood, *Is Critique Secular? Blasphemy, Injury and Free Speech* (Berkeley, CA: The Townsend Center for the Humanities, 2009), pp. 64–100.

Mahmud, Shabana, '*Angare* and the founding of the Progressive Writers' Association', *Modern Asian Studies*, 30:2 (1996), 447–67.

'Making Britain: discover how South Asians shaped the nation, 1870–1950', www.open.ac.uk/researchprojects/makingbritain/ (last accessed 6 November 2014).

Malik, Kenan, *From Fatwa to Jihad: The Rushdie Affair and its Legacy* (London: Atlantic Books, 2009).

Malik, Maleiha, '*Angare*, the "burning embers" of Muslim political resistance: colonial and post-colonial regulation of Islam in Britain', in Marcel Maussen, Veit Bader and Annelies Moors (eds), *Colonial and Post-Colonial Governance of Islam: Continuities and Ruptures* (Amsterdam: IMISCOE Research, Amsterdam University Press, 2011), pp. 199–210.

Malik, Sarita, 'Censorship – life after Behzti', *Arts Professional*, 101 (4 July 2005), www.artsprofessional.co.uk/magazine/article/censorship-life-after-behzti (last accessed 6 November 2014).

Mamdani, Mahmood, 'Good Muslim, bad Muslim – an African perspective', 10 Years after September 11 (October 2001), http://essays.ssrc.org/10years after911/good-muslim-bad-muslim-an-african-perspective/ (last accessed 6 November 2014); reprinted with revisions as 'Good Muslim, bad Muslim: a political perspective on culture and terrorism', in Eric Hershberg and Kevin Moore (eds), *Critical Views of September 11: Analyses from Around the World* (New York: New Press, 2002), pp. 44–60.

Mamdani, Mahmood, *Good Muslim, Bad Muslim: America, the Cold War, and the Roots of Terror* (New York: Three Leaves/Doubleday, 2005 [2004]).

'Manifesto of the Indian Progressive Writers' Association, London', *Left Review*, 2:5 (February 1936), 240.

Manzoor, Sarfraz, *Don't Call Me Asian*, BBC Radio 4 (broadcast 11 January 2005).

Manzoor, Sarfraz, 'We've ditched race for religion', *Guardian* (11 January 2005), www.theguardian.com/world/2005/jan/11/race.religion (last accessed 6 November 2014).

Manzoor, Sarfraz, *Luton, Actually*, BBC2 (broadcast 5 March 2005).

Manzoor, Sarfraz, 'White girls', *Granta*, 112 (2010), 243–54.

Massey, Doreen, *Docklands: A Microcosm of Broader Social and Economic Trends* (London: Docklands Forum, 1991).

Massey, Doreen, *Space, Place and Gender* (Cambridge: Polity, 1994).

Massey, Doreen, *For Space* (London: Sage, 2005).

Meetoo, Veena and Heidi Safia Mirza, '"There is nothing 'honourable' about honour killings": gender, violence and the limits of multiculturalism', in Mohammad Mazher Idriss and Tahir Abbas (eds), *'Honour', Violence, Women and Islam* (Abingdon: Routledge, 2011), pp. 42–66.

Mehmood, Tariq, *While There is Light* (Manchester: Comma, 2003).

Mercer, Kobena, 'Black art and the burden of representation', *Third Text*, 10 (Spring 1994), 61–78.

Milne, Seamus, 'It is an insult to the dead to deny the link with Iraq', *Guardian* (14 July 2005), www.theguardian.com/politics/2005/jul/14/july7.uk (last accessed 6 November 2014).

Milne, Seamus, 'Michael Gove's toxic assault is based on naked discrimination', *Guardian* (11 June 2014), www.theguardian.com/commentisfree/2014/jun/11/michael-gove-assault-on-schools-naked-discrimination (last accessed 6 November 2014).

'Mr Wells and Mohammed', *Guardian* (13 August 1938), p. 10.

Modood, Tariq, 'Political blackness and British Asians', *Sociology*, 28:4 (1994), 859–76.

Modood, Tariq, *Multicultural Politics: Racism, Ethnicity and Muslims in Britain* (Edinburgh: Edinburgh University Press, 2005).

Modood, Tariq, *Multiculturalism: A Civic Idea* (Cambridge: Polity, 2007).

Modood, Tariq, 'Muslims, religious equality and secularism', in Geoffrey Brahm Levey and Tariq Modood (eds), *Secularism, Religion and Multicultural Citizenship* (Cambridge: Cambridge University Press, 2009), pp. 164–85.

Mondal, Anshuman A., *Young British Muslim Voices* (Oxford and Westport, CT: Greenwood, 2008).

Mondal, Anshuman A., 'Bad faith: the construction of Muslim extremism in Ed Husain's *The Islamist*', in Rehana Ahmed, Peter Morey and Amina Yaqin (eds), *Culture, Diaspora, and Modernity in Muslim Writing* (Abingdon and New York: Routledge, 2012), pp. 37–51.

Mondal, Anshuman A., 'Revisiting *The Satanic Verses*: the *fatwa* and its legacies', in Robert Eaglestone and Martin McQuillan (eds), *Salman Rushdie* (London: Bloomsbury, 2013), pp. 59–71.

Mondal, Anshuman A., *Islam and Controversy: The Politics of Free Speech after Rushdie* (Basingstoke: Palgrave Macmillan, 2014).

Moore, Lindsey, 'British Muslim identities and spectres of terror in Nadeem Aslam's *Maps for Lost Lovers*', *Postcolonial Text*, 5:2 (2009), 1–19.

Moore-Gilbert, Bart, *Hanif Kureishi* (Manchester: Manchester University Press, 2001).

Moore-Gilbert, Bart, *Postcolonial Life-Writing: Culture, Politics and Self-Representation* (London and New York: Routledge, 2009).

Moore-Gilbert, Bart, 'From "the politics of recognition" to "the policing of recognition"', in Rehana Ahmed, Peter Morey and Amina Yaqin (eds), *Culture, Diaspora, and Modernity in Muslim Writing* (Abingdon and New York:

Routledge, 2012), pp. 183–99.

Morey, Peter, 'Mourning becomes Kashmira: Islam, melancholia, and the evacuation of politics in Salman Rushdie's *Shalimar the Clown*', in Rehana Ahmed, Peter Morey and Amina Yaqin (eds), *Culture, Diaspora, and Modernity in Muslim Writing* (Abingdon and New York: Routledge, 2012), pp. 215–30.

Morey, Peter and Amina Yaqin, *Framing Muslims: Stereotyping and Representation after 9/11* (Cambridge, MA: Harvard University Press, 2011).

Morris, Chris, Jesse Armstrong and Sam Bains (writers) and Chris Morris (director), *Four Lions* (2010).

Morton, Stephen, 'Writing Muslims and the global state of exception', in Rehana Ahmed, Peter Morey and Amina Yaqin (eds), *Culture, Diaspora, and Modernity in Muslim Writing* (Abingdon and New York: Routledge, 2012), pp. 18–33.

Mukherjee, Neel, '*Maps for Lost Lovers* by Nadeem Aslam' (review) (26 June 2004), www.neelmukherjee.com/articles/maps-for-lost-lovers-by-nadeem-aslam/ (last accessed 6 November 2014).

Nafisi, Azar, *Reading Lolita in Tehran: A Memoir in Books* (New York: Random House, 2003).

Nash, Geoffrey, *Writing Muslim Identity: The Construction of Identity* (London and New York: Continuum, 2010).

Nasta, Susheila, *Home Truths: Fictions of the South Asian Diaspora in Britain* (Basingstoke: Palgrave Macmillan, 2002).

Nasta, Susheila, 'Writing a life: Hanif Kureishi and Blake Morrison in conversation', *Wasafiri*, 21:2 (2006), 19–26.

Nasta, Susheila, 'Negotiating a "new world order": Mulk Raj Anand as public intellectual at the heart of empire (1924–1945)', in Rehana Ahmed and Sumita Mukherjee (eds), *South Asian Resistances in Britain, 1858–1947* (London: Continuum, 2011), pp. 140–60.

Needham, Anuradha Dingwaney, *Using the Master's Tools: Resistance and the Literature of the African and South Asian Diasporas* (Basingstoke: Palgrave Macmillan, 2000).

Nehru, Jawaharlal, *An Autobiography: Jawaharlal Nehru* (Delhi: Penguin India, 2004 [1936]).

Nye, Catrin, *Naturalising Newham*, BBC Radio Asian Network (broadcast 19 September 2013).

O'Malley, Kate, *Ireland, India and Empire: Indo-Irish Radical Connections, 1919–64* (Manchester: Manchester University Press, 2008).

O'Neill, Sean, 'Asian leaders warn of violence against Brick Lane film', *The Times* (22 July 2006), www.thetimes.co.uk/tto/news/uk/article1945823.ece (last accessed 6 November 2014).

Parekh, Bhikhu, *The Future of Multi-Ethnic Britain: The Parekh Report* (London: Profile, 2000).

Parekh, Bhikhu, *Rethinking Multiculturalism: Cultural Diversity and Political Theory* (Basingstoke: Palgrave Macmillan, 2nd edn, 2006 [2000]).

Payton, Joanne, 'Collective crimes, collective victims: a case study of the murder of Banaz Mahod', in Mohammad Mazher Idriss and Tahir Abbas (eds), *'Honour', Violence, Women and Islam* (Abingdon: Routledge, 2011), pp. 66–79.

Phillips, Trevor, 'Let's show the world its future', *Observer* (10 July 2005), www. theguardian.com/uk/2005/jul/10/olympics2012.olympicgames (last accessed 6 November 2014).

Phillips, Trevor, 'After 7/7: sleepwalking to segregation', speech given at the Manchester Council for Community Relations (22 September 2005).

Pilkington, Andrew, 'From institutional racism to community cohesion: the changing nature of racial discourse in Britain', *Sociological Research Online*, 13:3 (2008), www.socresonline.org.uk/13/3/6.html (last accessed 6 November 2014).

Poole, Elizabeth, *Reporting Islam: Media Representations of British Muslims* (London and New York: I. B. Tauris, 2002).

Poole, Elizabeth and John E. Richardson (eds), *Muslims and the News Media* (London: I. B. Tauris, 2010).

Power, Anne, 'The Olympic investment in East London has barely scratched the surface of the area's needs', London School of Economics and Political Science, British Politics and Policy blog entry (15 August 2012), http://blogs. lse.ac.uk/politicsandpolicy/olympics-newham-investment-power/ (last accessed 6 November 2014).

Pratt, Mary Louise, *Imperial Eyes: Travel Writing and Transculturation* (London and New York: Routledge, 1996).

Procter, James, *Dwelling Places: Postwar Black British Writing* (Manchester: Manchester University Press, 2003).

Puwar, Nirmal, 'Multicultural fashion … stirrings of another sense of aesthetics and memory', *Feminist Review*, 71 (2002), 63–87.

'Racial and Religious Hatred Act 2006', *Guardian* (19 January 2009), www. theguardian.com/commentisfree/libertycentral/2008/dec/16/racial-religious-hatred-act (last accessed 6 November 2014).

Ranasinha, Ruvani, *Hanif Kureishi* (Tavistock: Northcote House, 2002).

Ranasinha, Ruvani, 'The *fatwa* and its aftermath', in Abdulrazak Gurnah (ed.), *The Cambridge Companion to Salman Rushdie* (Cambridge: Cambridge University Press, 2007), pp. 45–60.

Ranasinha, Ruvani, *South Asians in Britain: Culture in Translation* (Oxford: Oxford University Press, 2007).

Ranasinha, Ruvani, with Rehana Ahmed, Sumita Mukherjee and Florian Stadtler (eds), *South Asians and the Shaping of Britain, 1870–1950* (Manchester: Manchester University Press, 2012).

Ray, Adil (writer) and Chris Wood (director), *Citizen Khan* (2013–).

Riley, Ferzanna, *Unbroken Spirit* (London: Hodder, 2008).

Rushdie, Salman, *Haroun and the Sea of Stories* (London: Granta, 1990).

Rushdie, Salman, *Imaginary Homelands: Essays and Criticism 1981–1991* (London: Granta, 1992 [1991]).

Rushdie, Salman, *Step across This Line: Collected Non-Fiction 1992–2002* (London: Random House, 2002).

Rushdie, Salman, 'How to fight and lose the moral high ground', *Guardian* (23 March 2002), www.theguardian.com/books/2002/mar/23/salmanrushdie (last accessed 6 November 2014).

Rushdie, Salman, 'The altered states of anti-Americanism', *Guardian* (31 August 2002), www.theguardian.com/books/2002/aug/31/iraq.politics (last accessed 6 November 2014).

Rushdie, Salman, 'Fight the good fight', *Guardian* (2 November 2002), www.theguardian.com/books/2002/nov/02/iraq.salmanrushdie (last accessed 6 November 2014).

Rushdie, Salman, *Shalimar the Clown* (London: Jonathan Cape, 2005).

Rushdie, Salman, 'In bad faith', *Guardian* (14 March 2005), www.theguardian.com/politics/2005/mar/14/labour.religion (last accessed 6 November 2014).

Rushdie, Salman, *Joseph Anton* (London: Jonathan Cape, 2012).

Ruthven, Malise, *Islam: A Very Short Introduction* (Oxford: Oxford University Press, 1997).

Sahota, Sunjeev, *Ours are the Streets* (London: Picador, 2011).

Said, Edward W., *The World, the Text, and the Critic* (Cambridge, MA: Harvard University Press, 1983).

Said, Edward W., *Out of Place* (London: Granta, 1999).

Salem, Shahed, 'A history of mosques in Britain', *Architects Journal* (19 April 2012), www.architectsjournal.co.uk/a-history-of-mosques-in-britain/8629263.article (last accessed 6 November 2014).

Samad, Yunus, 'Book burning and race relations: political mobilisation of Bradford Muslims', *New Community*, 18:4 (1992), 507–19.

Samad, Yunus, 'The plural guises of multiculturalism: conceptualising a fragmented paradigm', in Tariq Modood and Pnina Werbner (eds), *The Politics of Multiculturalism in the New Europe: Racism, Identity and Community* (London: Zed Books, 1997), pp. 240–60.

Sandhu, Sukhdev, 'Come hungry, leave edgy' (review of Monica Ali, *Brick Lane*), *London Review of Books*, 25:19 (9 October 2003), 10–13.

Sandhu, Sukhdev, *London Calling: How Black and Asian Writers Imagined a City* (London: HarperCollins, 2003).

Sanghera, Gurchathen and Suruchi Thapar-Bjorkert, '"Because I am Pakistani … and I am Muslim … I am political" – gendering political radicalism: young femininities in Bradford', in Tahir Abbas (ed.), *Islamic Political Radicalism: A European Perspective* (Edinburgh: Edinburgh University Press, 2007), pp. 173–91.

Sanghera, Jasvinder, *Shame* (London: Hodder, 2006)

Sanghera, Jasvinder, *Daughters of Shame* (London: Hodder, 2009).

Sanghera, Jasvinder, *Shame Travels: A Family Lost, A Family Found* (London: Hodder, 2012).

Sardar, Ziauddin, 'Spaces of hope: interventions', in Richard Phillips (ed.), *Muslim Spaces of Hope: Geographies of Possibility in Britain and the West* (London: Zed, 2009), pp. 13–36.

Sayyid, Salman, 'Contemporary politics of secularism', in Geoffrey Brahm Levey and Tariq Modood (eds), *Secularism, Religion and Multicultural Citizenship* (Cambridge: Cambridge University Press, 2009), pp. 186–99.

Schaffer, Kay and Sidonie Smith, *Human Rights and Narrated Lives: The Ethics of Recognition* (Basingstoke: Palgrave Macmillan, 2004).

Shah, Saeed, 'As their country descends into chaos, Pakistani writers are winning acclaim', *Guardian* (17 February 2009), www.theguardian.com/books/2009/feb/17/fiction-pakistan-hanif (last accessed 6 November 2014).

Shamsie, Kamila, 'Martin Amis's views demand a response', *Guardian* (19 November 2007), www.theguardian.com/books/booksblog/2007/nov/19/martinamissviewsdemandare (last accessed 6 November 2014).

Sharma, Madhav, 'A view from inside', in Lisa Appignanesi (ed.), *Free Expression is No Offence* (London: Penguin, 2005), pp. 32–8.

Siddiqui, Hannana, '"There is no 'honour' in domestic violence, only shame!": women's struggles against "honour" crimes in the UK', in Lynn Welchman and Sara Hossain (eds), *'Honour': Crimes, Paradigms, and Violence against Women* (London: Zed Books, 2005), pp. 263–81.

Singh Rai, Jasdev, 'Behind Behzti', *Guardian* (17 January 2005), www.theguardian.com/stage/2005/jan/17/theatre.religion (last accessed 6 November 2014).

Sivanandan, A., *A Different Hunger: Writings on Black Resistance* (London: Pluto, 1982).

Smith, Zadie, *White Teeth* (London: Penguin, 2000).

Solomos, John, *Race and Racism in Contemporary Britain* (Basingstoke: Palgrave Macmillan, 1999).

Stone, Richard (chair), *Islamophobia: Issues, Challenges and Actions. A Report by the Commission on British Muslims and Islamophobia* (Stoke-on-Trent: Trentham Books, 2004).

Stourton, Edward, interview with Salman Rushdie, *Today*, BBC Radio 4 (broadcast 29 August 2005).

Straw, Jack, '"I felt uneasy talking to someone I couldn't see"', *Guardian* (6 October 2006), www.theguardian.com/commentisfree/2006/oct/06/politics.uk (last accessed 6 November 2014).

Tarlo, Emma, *Visibly Muslim: Fashion, Politics, Faith* (Oxford: Berg, 2010).

Taylor, Charles, 'Why we need a radical redefinition of secularism', in Judith Butler, Jürgen Habermas, Charles Taylor and Cornel West, *The Power of Religion in the Public Sphere*, ed. Eduardo Mendieta and Jonathan Vanantwerpen (New York: Columbia University Press, 2011), pp. 34–59.

Taylor, Matthew, 'Brickbats fly as community brands novel "despicable"', *Guardian* (3 December 2003), www.theguardian.com/uk/2003/dec/03/books.arts (last accessed 6 November 2014).

Thapar-Bjorkert, Suruchi, 'Conversations across borders: men and honour-related violence in the UK and Sweden', in Mohammad Mazher Idriss and Tahir Abbas (eds), *'Honour', Violence, Women and Islam* (Abingdon: Routledge, 2011), pp. 182–200.

Toynbee, Polly, 'My right to offend a fool', *Guardian* (10 June 2005), p. 27.

'A travesty of honour' (review of Nadeem Aslam, *Maps for Lost Lovers*), *Economist* (1 July 2004), www.economist.com/node/2876737/ (last accessed 6 November 2014).

'The trouble with Brick Lane' (leader), *Guardian* (27 October 2007), www.theguardian.com/commentisfree/2007/oct/27/books.immigration (last accessed 6 November 2014).

Tripathi, Salil, 'No offence', Special to the *Wall Street Journal* (11 August 2006), www.englishpen.org/legacy/images/brick_lane/No%20Offence%20by%20Salil%20Tripathi.pdf (last accessed 6 November 2014).

Upstone, Sara, *British Asian Fiction: Twenty-First Century Voices* (Manchester: Manchester University Press, 2010).

Upstone, Sara, 'Representation and realism: Monica Ali's *Brick Lane*', in Rehana Ahmed, Peter Morey and Amina Yaqin (eds), *Culture, Diaspora, and Modernity in Muslim Writing* (Abingdon and New York: Routledge, 2012), pp. 164–79.

Visram, Rozina, *Asians in Britain: 400 Years of History* (London: Pluto, 2002).

Walter, Natasha, 'Citrus scent of inexorable desire', *Guardian* (14 June 2003), p. 26.

Walter, Natasha, 'The book burners do not speak for all of Brick Lane', *Guardian* (1 August 2006), www.theguardian.com/commentisfree/2006/aug/01/comment.bookscomment (last accessed 6 November 2014).

Waring, Wendy, 'Is this your book? Wrapping postcolonial fiction for the global market', *Canadian Review of Comparative Literature*, 22:3/4 (1995), 455–65.

Wells, H. G., *A Short History of the World* (London: Penguin, 1936).

Werbner, Pnina, 'Allegories of sacred imperfection: magic, hermeneutics and passion in *The Satanic Verses*', *Current Anthropology*, 37, Supplement: special issue on 'Anthropology in public' (1996), 55–86.

Werbner, Pnina, 'Essentialising essentialism, essentialising silence: ambivalence and multiplicity in the construction of racism and ethnicity', in Werbner and Tariq Modood (eds), *Debating Cultural Hybridity: Multi-Cultural Identities and the Politics of Anti-Racism* (London: Zed Books, 1997), pp. 226–56.

Werbner, Pnina, *Imagined Diasporas among Manchester Muslims: The Public Performance of Pakistani Transnational Identity Politics* (Oxford: James Currey, 2002).

Whitlock, Gillian, *Soft Weapons: Autobiography in Transit* (Chicago: University of Chicago Press, 2007).

Williams, Raymond, *Culture and Materialism* (London: Verso, 2005 [1980]).

Yaqin, Amina, 'Inside the harem, outside the nation: framing Muslims in radio journalism', *Interventions*, 12:2 (2010), 226–38.

Yaqin, Amina, 'Muslims as multicultural misfits in Nadeem Aslam's *Maps for Lost*

Lovers', in Rehana Ahmed, Peter Morey and Amina Yaqin (eds), *Culture, Diaspora, and Modernity in Muslim Writing* (Abingdon and New York: Routledge, 2012), pp. 101–16.

Yassin-Kassab, Robin, *The Road from Damascus* (London: Hamish Hamilton, 2008).

Yousaf, Nahem, *Hanif Kureishi's* The Buddha of Suburbia: *A Reader's Guide* (New York and London: Continuum, 2002).

Zaheer, Sajjad, *A Night in London*, trans. Bilal Hashmi (Noida: HarperCollins India, 2011 [1938]).

Zaheer, Sajjad, 'Reminiscences', in Sudhi Pradhan (ed.), *Marxist Cultural Movement in India: Chronicles and Documents (1936–47)* (Calcutta: National Book Agency, 1979), pp. 33–47.

Žižek, Slavoj, *The Universal Exception: Selected Writings*, vol. 2 (London and New York: Continuum, 2006).

Žižek, Slavoj, 'Liberal multiculturalism masks an old barbarism with a human face', *Guardian* (3 October 2010), www.theguardian.com/commentisfree/2010/oct/03/immigration-policy-roma-rightwing-europe (last accessed 6 November 2014).

Index

'n.' after a page reference indicates the number of a note on that page. Literary works can be found under authors' names.